Such A Life On Such A Planet

Carole Jett

"...this book ultimately succeeds in explaining the human side of what may seem to many to be a strange, obscure belief system."

- Kirkus Reviews -

To all those who've guided me along the way.

You know who you are.

Contents

Prologue

A most unusual life... At the age of nineteen, she set her sights on finding out if there was a God and who or what, He or She might be. When she sets her sights, she means to never give up! She was raised Catholic, school and all. But upon a closer look, there were just too many inconsistencies in Catholicism. While at this time, the New Age had just begun. Woodstock, candles and crystals, tarot cards, Ouija boards, meditation, psychedelics, and swamis.

A psychic who wrote many books, Edgar Cayce, predicted a great earthquake was coming to California, and the state was going to break off at the San Andreas fault and slip into the Pacific Ocean. He convinced many twenty-thirty somethings of this impending doom. By now, she was working at the CBS Television Studios, and the Smothers Brothers actually flew out of the state on that day in 1969. Having read all of Cayce's books, she remained unconvinced regarding this particular prediction.

In addition, she was reading everything in the spiritual/religious/occult section of the library, and there were many, many books. It was fun for her to check all these out, while for two years, she and her close party buddies explored. (They were three married couples and one funny single guy.) Although entertaining at their parties, the occult was not quite enough and answered not her burning questions. So, she turned to reading the histories and teachings of the religions of the world: Christian, Buddhist, Daoist, Hindu,

Confucius, Zoroaster, Mohammed, Ancient Egyptian, Tibetan Book of the Dead, I Ching, and more.

It was the time of The Beatles' Maharishi and many other Hindu Yogi masters leading the parade. She finally hit on one curious book, "The Autobiography of a Yogi" by Paramahansa Yogananda, and became one of its adherents. Not long after, she discovered she was pregnant again, her husband was fired from his job, and as in the case with all young, aggressive business types, he found a better one in Honolulu, Hawaii, no less. So goodbye, L.A. ♥

And that is where the real story begins!

MAP OF OAHU

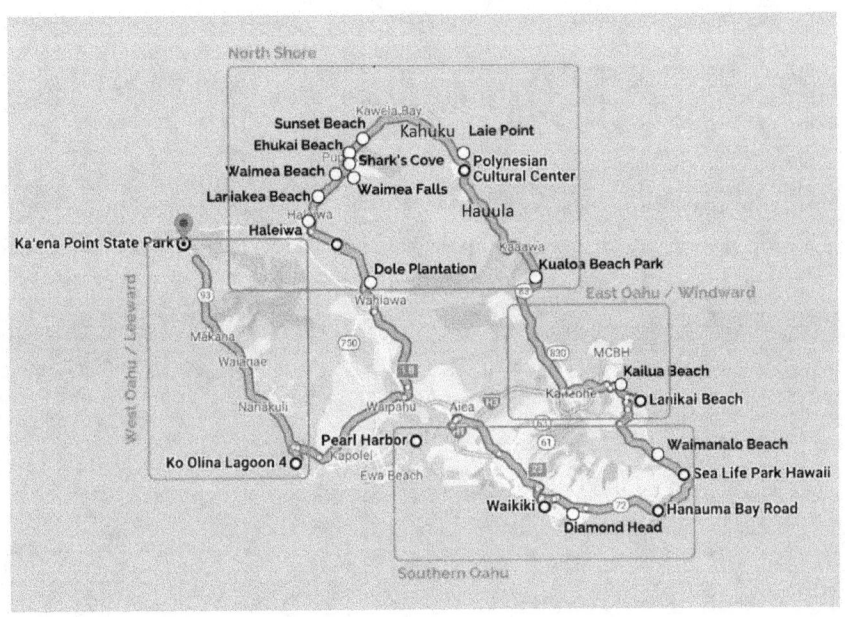

Chapter 1

Little ghouls and ghosts, witches, and mummies were running around trick-or-treating for goodies. It was a Happy Halloween night in Kaimuki, Hawaii, a suburb of Honolulu just east of Diamond Head. My husband had taken our two youngsters, an angel, and a little red devil, around to fill their pumpkins; while I, seven months pregnant, was doing door duty handing out treats to other costumed bell ringers and door knockers.

I was sitting on the sofa reading a new book on the mysterious, ancient Egyptian religion of the Pharaohs and just finishing a chapter explaining the Ka and the Ba when I heard light knocks on the door. I raised my rather bulky body off the bamboo sofa and answered it. There stood two little hula dancers in plastic grass skirts, modest Hawaiian tops, and real Plumeria leis. Their mother was at their side.

"Trick-or-Treat," I heard sweet voices say.

I reached into my candy bowl for small, Halloween-themed cellophane bags of candy that my children and I had assembled together earlier in the day. Included in each was a packet of candy corn, Hershey's Kisses, a tiny Tootsie roll, and Smarties. I dropped one bag into each of the girl's plastic pumpkins. The pleasant, smiling woman held out a large, substantial book. The glossy white dust jacket had an unusual title, *The Urantia Book*. Under the title were three large blue concentric circles.

"I've heard you might be interested in reading this."

Without thinking, I took the book in my hand and, feeling its considerable weight, I grasped it in both hands.

"My name and phone number are inside. Call me after you've taken a look."

Never shy about investigating a new book, I agreed. Then she turned as her hula girls skipped toward the next townhouse condominium door. I closed mine and returned to my spot on the Hawaiian print sofa. Sitting down, I placed the tome on my lap; actually, I had no lap. The book rested on my thighs. The stark white cover with the three azure blue concentric circles was pleasing to the eye.

I studied the cover more closely. Below the circles was a listing of the four parts of the book: Part I, *The Central and Superuniverse*; Part II, *The Local Universe*; Part III, *The History of Urantia;* and Part IV, *The Life and Teachings of Jesus.*

Curious, I opened it and began to skim through its many pages. About midway through, I happened upon a page that described the ancient Egyptian religion: *The inhabitants of the Nile valley believed that each favored individual had bestowed upon him at birth, or soon thereafter, a protecting spirit which they called the Ka. On the walls of a temple at Luxor, where is depicted the birth of Amenhotep III, the little prince is pictured on the arm of the Nile god, and near him is another child, in appearance identical to the prince, which is a symbol of that entity which the Egyptians call the Ka.*

Further, the page noted that the *Ba* represented the soul.

My first thought was, "Wow, that's similar to what I just read. Only my book did not mention the hieroglyphics on the wall of the temple at Luxor. This author is certainly knowledgeable."

The chapter was titled Paper 111. Upon closer inspection of the book, there were no chapters, only different Papers—196 of them. To find out who this expert Egyptologist was, I skipped to the last page of Paper 111 and found: *Presented by a Solitary Messenger of Orvonton.* "Hmmmm… curiouser and curiouser!"

Little did I realize how that Halloween night in 1970 would impact my life, taking me on a voyage sailing away from the sheltered bays of certainty into an ever-expanding sea of inner security and around the world in the process.

Our family had recently moved to Hawaii from Los Angeles, California. It was a career move for my husband, and I certainly had no regrets, even though we left grandparents behind. Hawaii was so beautiful and a wonderful place to raise children, not to mention a great place for relatives to visit.

My life was typically busy with my daughter entering first grade, my four-year-old son at home, our soon-to-be-born baby girl, and performing the duties of the social wife of a young entrepreneur.

On the first day of school, my daughter wore a new dress and sandals. The school was just across the street from the condominium complex, and her new friends came by to walk with her. The playground was all grass, not concrete as it had been back in California. When she returned after the school day, she was shoeless.

"Where are your sandals?"

"Oh, I took them off. No one wears shoes at school... Mom, I need some flip-flops."

"Flip-flops? What are flip-flops?"

She put her hands on her six-year-old hips and said, "What you are wearing, silly."

Okay, this 'haole' family was beginning to learn the new ways. What I was wearing were known to me as thong sandals. (A haole is a Caucasian resident or visitor. It is not a pejorative.)

We went shopping for flip-flops, but she still went barefoot to school. I never did find out what happened to those sandals.

Whenever I could find the time, I read this new, extraordinary book in my life. It was usually in the evening when the children were in bed, and my husband and I were watching television. The information on the Egyptian religion was in Part III, *The History of Urantia*. I had turned to the beginning of that part and begun reading. It was not long before I learned that "Urantia" was the name of our planet Earth in universe terms.

After a couple of weeks, I called the woman who had given me the book. We had a fascinating conversation, and I asked her where I could get my own book. She told me to call the publisher whose name was printed on the first page of the book: The Urantia Foundation, Chicago, Illinois. I called the long-distance operator to get the area code and then called Chicago information. Receiving the number, I phoned and inquired about obtaining a book. They told me how much it cost plus shipping. All I had to do was send a check, and they would send me a book. The check was in the mail the next day.

Just before Christmas, the book arrived. I took it out of its thick cardboard box, and voila, a brand new book untouched by human hands, well almost. When I opened the cover, inside was an insert about the Urantia Foundation and another organization, the Urantia Brotherhood. The Brotherhood's mission statement read: The activities of Urantia Brotherhood Association are intended to spread the teachings of *The Urantia Book* "By word of mouth, a quiet person-to-person approach that proceeds without fanfare, focusing as Jesus did upon each individual's spiritual progress."
"Interesting. No media." I thought.

A week later, my new friend came over to retrieve the book she had loaned me. We talked while her girls played outside with my son. She had a study group and invited me to join. I was not interested but thanked her and looked forward to our phone conversations whenever possible.

The new year brought a new baby. She was a little doll and lovingly welcomed into the home. But all was not well with her. During her first-month pediatrician visit, the doctor discovered she had not gained any weight. He told me it must be my breast milk. I began watching my diet more carefully. I rocked her for hours in our cane rocking chair since she would nurse so slowly. The next monthly visit to the doctor showed a weight gain of only three ounces. He was puzzled and told me to stop breastfeeding and put her on formula.

At her three-month visit, she had gained only a few more ounces. The doctor ordered tests; they all came back negative. He figuratively threw up his hands, telling me, "I have no idea what is wrong with your child."

Unfortunately, I remembered my grandmother telling me that in her day, women wanted at least three children for insurance. One was sure to die before early childhood, so I rocked my infant and believed she might die.

During my time living at the townhouse condominium, I made friends with other mothers who had children around my own's ages. Jane and her husband, Jim, became close friends. They had a son my son's age and a baby girl about two months older than mine. Jane came to the rescue. Jim was a local haole, and his family had been on the island for three generations. She knew her way around and gave me the name of the best pediatrician on the island.

I was in the office of Dr. Tenby within a day. He examined my daughter and gave me his diagnosis. However, he warned me that he could not be certain since this condition was very rare in female infants. It was considered a male infant problem. He sent me to a pediatric surgeon. The surgeon, too, agreed it was not a definite diagnosis, but he would be willing to operate. My husband and I were desperate to try anything, and the surgeon seemed competent, except he was a tall man with big hands. How in the world could he operate on the tiny pyloric muscle of the stomach of a seven-pound baby? Of course, then, I had no idea it was done by instruments. We said, "Yes, please try!"

I will never forget seeing my baby in a hospital crib with an IV needle in a vein on the side of her little forehead.

The operation was a success. Not only did she live, but she also thrived. I could not help but think of all the other parents who had to deal with life and death issues for their infants and were not so fortunate.

After her recovery, I decided to join the Urantia study group. There I met five other women studying one Urantia Paper at a time. I was the novice in the group. The meetings began to open up the meaning of many of the new concepts printed on practically every page. One friend that became influential in my life was Marian. She had been reading a while and was an interesting character. Marian's children were of similar ages to mine.

I cannot begin to say how grateful I was for those meetings. But at one of the meetings, the conversation veered off course from studying the Papers and into the realm of how they came to be. To me, it did not matter. The majestic, startlingly beautiful, seemingly so complex yet logical piece of work spoke for itself. How it got here was not of interest to me. There was no human author attached to any of the Papers. All I knew in my small, mortal brain was that if a human being had been able to write this work, their name would have been prominently displayed.

Two names were discussed, Dr. William Sadler and his wife, Dr. Lena Sadler, and how they had devoted their lives to seeing the Urantia Papers printed into *The Urantia Book* just like the one I held in my hands. I felt gratitude to this man and woman, who were now both deceased. But as to my accepting the book as valid truth, their lives were not relevant. I was going to read every word of its 2,097 pages and make up my own mind.

After going through this terrible time with our infant, my husband began drinking again. He had a problem with alcohol when we lived in California but had seemingly conquered it. When we moved to Hawaii, he would occasionally have a drink socially. I little realized he had begun to have drinks with business associates before coming home. It did not affect his work in the least. He was an ambitious, intelligent entrepreneur, and our financial situation was only improving. Our marriage had been far from perfect, but I thought Hawaii and a new child would make a difference. As it was, it started unraveling, but not before my eyes. My eyes were not ready to see.

During our time together in the evening, if I was reading *The Urantia Book* instead of watching the television program, he would make resentful comments. I would let him have his say and often put the book down, though not always. He complained when I would get a sitter for the children and go to a weekly afternoon study group. He complained if it was a family affair, and I took the children. One meeting was held in the evening, and I wanted to get a sitter so he could come along. He was not interested.

Marian was hosting the evening meeting at her house. My husband was late getting home from work, but I was ready to go when he arrived and was in our bedroom, where the baby was asleep in her crib. He came into the room in a fury, shouting, "You are not leaving!"

I lowered my voice not to wake our child, "I most certainly am. It does not seem unreasonable to me that you should take care of your own children if you don't want to come with me."

The next thing I knew, he had thrown me onto the bed and was straddling my body. He had his hands around my neck and started squeezing. How to describe what goes through a mind in times of peril. Shock? Fear! He had never been physically abusive before, only verbally. Yet he was strangling me as my four-month-old lay quietly in her crib. My first instinct was to fight for my life, but he was by far physically stronger. The animal instinct, 'fight or flight,' is so strong. But in those split seconds, words blared out in my mind, "Go slack! Go slack!" And I did. With no fight and purposely holding my breath, he stopped.

Taking his hands away from my throat, I could feel his eyes looking down upon me. I did not move. Then slowly, I pretended to revive. Relief spread across his face as he got off the bed. I got up, saw that my baby, by some miracle, was still asleep, and walked out of the room. My other two children were sitting in the living room watching television. I grabbed my purse and Urantia Book and kissed them goodbye. The evening went on as normal for them.

Little did I know that while my husband attempted to assert his power over me, power struggles were just beginning within the Urantia movement over the direction it should take and ensuing legal battles over the copyright of the book's text. Unlike the failed attempt of my husband, the powers and money of the people so determined to destroy the copyright of the book and change its course would eventually win, plunging the book into obscurity.

13

Chapter 2

Our Kaimuki townhouse was a three-bedroom condo, but one of the bedrooms had sliding Japanese-style doors just off the living room, and we reserved it for guests. My sister made good use of that room when she came to stay with us on a college summer break. She got a job as a waitress at the Don Ho Show and had a great summer. I cried when she left.

The master bedroom still contained the crib, and the second bedroom my older daughter and son shared. My husband's business was doing well, so he decided we could afford a more suitable home for our growing family needs. We went searching before the start of the school year and found a lovely home in the special enclave of Lanikai.

Lanikai is a small beach community just south of Kailua on the windward side of Oahu. What makes this community so unique is that there is only a one-lane road leading into and out of a mile-long cul-de-sac. The lane into the community meanders below a low cliff that overlooks the sea toward the cul-de-sac end. After making the turn at the curve of the road, the one-way drive out is along a reef-protected, white sand beach interspersed with beach homes. Between the low cliff and the beach road is a ten-block radius of residential homes.

The cliffside is dotted with many houses, which is where we found ours. It was built into the cliff at the end of the cul-de-sac.

The garage was on the street level, then up twenty gently rising flagstone steps to the home. Entering the front door into the spacious living room, on the right was a large picture window that looked out over the center of the enclave onto a panoramic view of the sparkling, aqua sea and the tiny twin islands of Na Mokulua. The home was a five-bedroom dwelling with plenty of room for our family and visitors.

We could not believe our good luck and moved in before the first day of the school year at Lanikai Elementary. Our eldest daughter started second grade, and our son was in kindergarten. At first, my son was not enthusiastic about attending school. The school bus stop was just two houses down, and when children gathered to get on the bus, he somehow often missed it. The little rascal would return home, and I would have to gather the baby and drive him to school. This was frequently happening. I could not figure out why until my neighbor told on him. She related how he would hide behind a large Oleander bush just before the bus arrived and stay hidden until it was out of sight. So that put an end to that trick.

To the outside world, our family life was idyllic, and for a while, it was. My husband was happy with his home, his business, and his family.

I would rise early in the morning before sunrise, make herb tea, and spend time reading a Paper of the book. My goal was to have it read within two years. I was still attending the study group with no more complaints from my husband. I would often host it. Those nights he was sure to work late.

.Along the beachside around the cul-de-sac was a sandy cove cut off from the main beach by a rocky protrusion. The local residents would frequent this section of the beach. On the sea, small catamarans sailed in the soft trade winds just outside the reef. The cove was our 'backyard,' and the baby loved to crawl and later toddle through the sand to the warm waters of the shallow shore. The older children made friends quickly and were often off playing in the neighborhood. On the weekends, my husband was a regular on the beach volleyball court.

The baby's first Christmas was a joyful event for the whole family. Santa Claus came to the children of Hawaii even though no one had a chimney. But the New Year did not bring peace. My husband had been traveling to the mainland for his business, and no matter where he traveled, he always stopped in San Francisco for a one-night layover. I began to wonder why. When I asked him, he had no answer.

By late spring, he was drinking every night and often arrived home after the children were in bed. It was amazing to me how he could get up the next morning, shave, shower, put on his expensive suit, look sharp, go off to work, and work successfully.

One morning I asked him, "Don't you ever have a hangover?"

He looked at me and bragged, "I don't get hangovers."

And it seemed to be true. (To his credit, much later, he went through the Alcoholics Anonymous program and stuck with it.)

In the past, our married life had its ups and downs. His temper was explosive but rare. He could be a loving husband and father, yet those times were fading, fading into oblivion as his drinking and successful business enterprise took center stage.

My mother came for a visit. During that time, one evening, my husband called to say he had a business dinner and would be home later. Around 10:00 p.m. Mom and I were sitting in the living room talking. We heard a fumbling at the front door. I expected my husband to come walking through, but the noise just kept up as if someone was trying to unlock the door with no success. I got up and opened the door. The man of the house practically fell in with the key in his hand. He was so drunk he had not been able to find the keyhole. I had never seen him so impaired. Staggering, he put his arm around my shoulders for support. I automatically put my arm around his waist and walked him to the stairs, up one step at a time. I did not want to make a scene in front of my mother.

When we made it to the bedroom, he began to undress. First, his suit coat, his tie was in the pocket. Next came his dress shirt. I noticed the shirt was so wrinkled it looked like he had slept in it. I asked, "What happened to you? You look like you slept in your shirt?"

He talked back immediately; he could always talk, drunk or sober, and sound relatively sober.

"Oh, that. I got into a fight with the bartender."

"Really? You? A fight? At the expensive places you and your business friends frequent?"

"Yeah. It was the bartender's fault."

Then he proceeded to go into a detailed description of some fictitious fight.

17

I was not buying it. I took his wrinkled shirt and, surprise, surprise. He *had* slept in it! There was fuchsia lipstick on the collar. I could not help thinking, 'lipstick on your collar' is an old clichè, but I realized that the clichè had its origin in truth. I showed him. He waved me and the shirt away and lay down, passing out. I did nothing. There was no use arguing. There never was anymore.

I returned to the living room, where my mother still sat on the sofa. She only looked at me wryly but made no comment. She was rarely one to interfere.

This incident was not the last straw. It was only the second to last. As soon as my mother left, I refused to sleep with him in the same bed. He moved into the fifth bedroom. The last straw was the effect our broken marriage was having on the children.

My daughter, who had just turned eight years old, had become rebellious. My son was a sad little five-year-old. His father, when home, would pay little attention to him. He would not even read him a story before bedtime. The little guy would pick out a book from his bookcase and take it into the TV room, trying to climb up into his father's lap. But he would be rebuffed and would drop down on the floor crying. My husband never looked away from the television. I would have to pick up a crying child and carry him to his room, then distract him by opening the book and pointing to the first colorful picture. His small body would begin to unwind as we read together until he closed his eyes in sleep. It broke my heart.

My marriage was over. I was raising the children by myself. It was time to put an end to the sham. But how? For four long months, I wrestled with this depressing dilemma. Anyone who has gone

18

through a divorce knows it is hell. I prayed for an answer. I knew my husband's character well enough that to just go through the normal process (if there is such a thing) of moving my children and myself into a rented home and filing for divorce would be a nightmare. We were his, his family, his property, and most importantly, his bulwark from being alone. He could also be dangerous, as I had seen in the past. And he would fight me tooth and nail over money. It had always been his way of control.

I was accustomed to rising early before the household to read the Urantia Papers. Now instead, I walked the block to the beach cove and sat on the sand, waiting for the sun to rise. It gave me a time of peace and prayer, asking for guidance. I held close to my heart the words stated in one of the Papers: *"Let not your heart be troubled, neither let it be afraid." The peace of Jesus is, then, the peace and assurance of his child who fully believes that their career for time and eternity is safely and wholly in the care and keeping of an all-wise, all-loving, and all-powerful spirit Father.*

I gathered great strength from these words, although the future seemed so fraught with uncertainty. I had no idea what to do but vowed with His help, I was going to do something. Things could no longer remain the way they were. At the end of this miserable four-month period, I had lost so much weight I looked like a twelve-year-old.

One morning as the sun began to show itself over the distant island of Maui and its highest peak, I heard a rustling on the rocks that separated the cove from the main strand of the beach. I looked over and saw a somewhat familiar face. It was a blonde-haired guy

I had seen around earlier in the week. He was staying at a neighbor's vacation rental behind her house. He jumped down from a rock and, landing on the sand, noticed me.

Tentatively walking toward me, he said, "I'm sorry…I hope I'm not disturbing you."

"No, not really. Aren't you staying at Melonie's place?"

"Yes."

Then smiling at me, he asked, "May I sit?"

"Sure."

He sat down next to me, and we began to talk. He told me his name was Paul, and he was from Canada. He was a commercial artist back in Calgary but had saved up money to spend a year traveling around the world. He mentioned the states he had already visited and talked about the countries he was headed to.

Listening to Paul's story, it occurred to me to tell him about the Urantia Papers; he listened with rapt attention. He asked if he could come by later in the afternoon and take a look at the book that these Papers were compiled. I said sure and told him where I lived.

The sun had risen in all its glory. Realizing my household would be stirring, I stood up, brushed the sand from my shorts, and said goodbye. As I walked home, little did I realize that this brief encounter would dramatically alter the direction of my life and save my children from untold misery.

Chapter 3

Of course, my husband knew our marriage was in trouble. He was no fool. He was sleeping in the extra bedroom, after all. But he always felt he had the upper hand, for he controlled the money. Besides, his friends told him, "What's a woman with three young kids going to do?" He trusted that things would pass, and he would get his way.

Paul became a quick study of the book, asking questions that I could not always answer and initiating interesting discussions. One day, looking carefully at the book's dust jacket, he asked, "You know, with my commercial artist background, I was wondering why this particular design on the jacket was chosen. It's quite simple."

Finally, I could answer easily. "Do you remember the part in the Bible where it says that there was a war in heaven and Archangel Michael fought against Lucifer?"

"Yeah, kinda."

"Well, there really was a war in heaven, only not like here on earth with weapons, but it was just as fatal, even more so."

"What do you mean?"

"Let me show you."

I searched the Table of Contents, then flipped through the pages. "Here I found it: *This war in heaven was very terrible and very real. While displaying none of the barbarities so characteristic of physical warfare on the immature worlds, this conflict was far more deadly; material life is in jeopardy in material combat, but the war in heaven was fought in terms of life eternal.*"

Paul's eyebrows went up, and his forehead creased as he contemplated what I had just read. "So, you're saying the Bible is right in its way."

"Yes."

"Okay…But what does that have to do with the cover?"

"I'm getting to that part. First of all, it was Gabriel representing Michael, who actually fought against Lucifer: *Gabriel proceeded to Jerusem, and establishing himself on the sphere dedicated to the Father—the same Universal Father whose personality Lucifer and Satan had questioned—in the presence of the forgathered hosts of loyal personalities, he displayed the banner of Michael, the material emblem of the Trinity government of all creation, the three azure blue concentric circles on a white background.*

The Lucifer emblem was a banner of white with one red circle, in the center of which a black solid circle appeared."

Paul thoughtfully asked: "This banner of Michael is three blue concentric circles on a white background, which is where they got the book jacket?"

"Yes," I agreed.

"And Lucifer's banner was a solid black circle inside a larger red one on white?"

"Yes."

"You know…if you invert these colors, put Hitler's Swastika inside the solid circle, you'd have the symbol of the Nazis."

"I've thought that too."

"Man, oh man, this is crazy!"

"Is it?"

Our study together went on for another couple of weeks, during which I must have been wearing my unhappiness with my marriage on my sleeve. For one day he shocked me and said, "I'm going to be leaving soon. Why don't you come with me? My next stop is Tahiti."

At first, I had no response. Was he asking me to travel with him? I cautiously answered, "I could never leave my children."

He shrugged his shoulders and said, "Bring them along."

Before I could object, he went on, "I'm the second oldest in a family of twelve children. I've got plenty of experience. Besides, I like your kids."

This was a startling turn of events. Up to this time, our friendship had been purely platonic.

I had been putting money away for the last few months and had somehow accumulated over $5,000. The more I thought about Paul's proposal, the more it seemed the right course. Still, I would attempt to settle things with my husband over and over again. Each time he would become furious.

Looking back on the situation, it seems I was on automatic pilot, not knowing for sure if I would actually carry out the act of taking my children out of the country. I talked it over with my Urantia study friend, Marian, who thought it was a bold idea. I confided in Jane, whose husband, Jim, was an attorney. Both women kept my deliberations a secret. But Jane tried to talk me out of leaving. She thought I should stay and fight for my rightful half of our money. She also warned that if I abandoned my husband and went off with the children, I could lose custody. That did not make sense to me since I was taking them with me, but it precipitated my move to make the separation legal.

I went ahead and applied for a passport. In 1972 a passport included the children and a parent in one book. The picture we took is quite amusing. I am sitting with a seventeen-month-old on my lap, flanked by a laughing kindergartner and a serious-looking, freckle face, beach-urchin on my left. Of course, they had no idea why we were taking the picture and miraculously never mentioned it.

I bought appropriate backpacks for my daughter and son and packed them. They would carry their own clothes. I purchased a yellow duffle-type bag with carrying handles and packed my things and the baby's, plus cloth diapers and some disposable ones. She still took a bottle, so three went in, only to be lost one by one along the way. I put our 'luggage' in a large closet downstairs and waited and wondered if I was really going to do this. My stress level was terribly high, but so was an inner determination to do what was right. I had come to believe that God had my back.

The next Sunday afternoon, I decided to bring up the subject once again of our dissolving marriage. My husband and I were standing in the living room alone, my back a short distance from the eight-foot picture window, looking out to the calm blue sea. The discussion grew heated on his part. By this time, I had no heat left, but I was not going to give up trying to get him to see reality. Maybe

24

things could be worked out amicably, and I would not have to resort to extreme measures.

Within minutes he became incensed. He grabbed my upper arms and held me so tightly that I could not move. I did not know if I was going to be picked up and thrown through that window, landing three stories below. It was just a sheet of window glass, no safety glass here. As quickly as I could think, I said to him, "Okay, okay, I'm sorry. This beautiful day is not the time for us to get so serious. Why don't you go play your volleyball game, and we'll talk about it later?" And just as quickly, he let go of me, satisfied he had won again. He left the house to go to the cove.

I knew this was it. My youngest was taking a nap in her crib. I called the neighbors looking for the other two and had them sent home. Nervously I wrote a note to my husband that we had left, he would not be able to find me, and I would call him at work tomorrow morning.

When my daughter and son got home, I had them change into travel clothes as I cheerfully told them we were going on an adventure. The baby and I were ready. We all went to the downstairs closet and got out the backpacks. I helped them put their packs on while repeating the adventure bit. These were not unusual words for my children to hear. They had heard them throughout their lives under different situations, even looking for a path out of the Los Angeles traffic to find an alternate route.

We flew down the stairs to the garage, got into the 1967 Mustang, left the new racing-green Camaro in the garage, and off we went. I stopped at the place where Paul was staying and, miraculously, caught him to say I was leaving and driving into Honolulu to stay at the Ala Moana Hotel.

He smiled at me, "Brave girl, I'll meet you there tomorrow."

My children innocently waved goodbye while I told them we would be going on a trip with Paul.

Upon checking into the hotel, I was on the phone setting things up. First, I called my parents in the states. I spoke to my mother and told her my situation. She was not happy but offered no alternative. Not that I was looking for one. Then I called Marian, who now lived on the North Shore, to tell her that I had left. I asked if she would go to my house the next day at 11:00 a.m. and take the children's clothes and their multitude of toys. I told her an extra key was under the orchid planter by the door. She was more than willing to do so. The North Shore of Oahu, the Sunset Beach area, had many young families, some on welfare, and it could all be put to good use. I had made up my mind; there was no turning back. I did not want my husband to be surrounded by mine and the children's things which would only bring on greater sadness. I wanted him to realize the marriage was over. He should move on.

I called Jane and Jim and told them what had happened. I asked her if she would go to the house around 1:00 p.m. and take all my clothing and jewelry and anything that reminded my husband of me. Jane agreed. With Jim, I explained that I wanted a legal separation agreement drawn up. We spoke at length. I wanted no alimony, only child support, and complete custody. (Jim added medical and schooling through college.) He tried to talk me out of going but, getting nowhere with his arguments, gave up and said it would take a couple of days. No one knew where I was staying.

That evening my husband returned to an empty house and my note. I am fully aware it must have been terrible for him. He went looking for us, driving out to Marian's. She did not mention our arrangement for the next day but honestly told him she did not know where I was.

At the hotel, we all went to bed just after dark, my toddler in a hotel crib with her bottle and the three of us in a king-size bed. I talked with them and said we would be away for a while. When they asked how long, I admitted I did not know for sure. I told them we would be flying to a different island called Tahiti. In the quiet of the night, all I could hear was my little one sucking on her bottle. Then I said, "We will be camping along the way."

"Camping?" Came the excited voice of my daughter. "We've never been camping before."

"Yep, it will be our first time," I replied.

After a few moments of thought, I added, "We will be the four Musketeers...camping."

My son, in the middle of us girls, spoke up, "The four Musketeers and Paul."

"That's right." I smiled to myself in the dark.

Soon thereafter, the children were all asleep.

I knew my husband would be at work on Monday. What else would he do? I called at 10:00 a.m. We arranged to meet for lunch, and I set the restaurant. I told him Jim was working on a separation agreement. Jim had already called him first thing in the morning, so he knew.

That lunch meeting is indelible in my mind. The restaurant was a prominent Honolulu establishment with booths and tables. When I arrived, my husband was sitting in a booth; he was calm and wearing his business persona. Maybe it all did not seem real to him, and this was just another business lunch. Or maybe Jim had convinced him that I had only temporarily lost my mind. I informed him I was going to take the children to Tahiti to think things through. It was the truth from my perspective. I was not sure what would happen from there. All I knew for sure was that my children and I were heading toward certain change, just what it was I could not foresee. I was running on faith and a bit of young dumb courage. I was twenty-six years old.

We talked about the separation agreement, and after finishing lunch, he walked me to the airline ticket office a block away on Prince Kuhio Avenue. We bought the round-trip tickets for the children and myself, which I had reserved. He also purchased $1000 in a traveler's check at the bank. Then I mentioned I was traveling with a Canadian friend.

"Canadian! Is it that guy Paul who is supposedly traveling around the world?"

"Yes."

His face quickly reddened, but he had no further comment. We agreed to meet at Jim and Jane's home the next evening to sign the separation papers.

Before I had lunch with my husband, Paul had checked into the hotel and taken a room on the same floor. He also booked the same flight to Tahiti. We were scheduled to leave early Wednesday morning. While I met my husband for lunch, Paul took the children to the hotel pool.

When I returned, we all went shopping at the Ala Moana Shopping Center for camping equipment. Paul's backpack was quite elaborate, with a tent and all. He had a Canadian flag sewn on the backpack flap. His hands were free to carry his classical guitar in its case. We purchased light sleeping bags for each child and myself and a tent that would sleep, my family. All was set, except I had yet to pick up my passport.

The week before, I had called the Honolulu Passport office and was told my passport would be ready for pick up the following Tuesday. The two days before departure were hectic, to say the least. Late Tuesday afternoon, we drove downtown to the passport office. It took forever to find a parking space. We did not walk through the government door until two minutes before closing, only to find out my passport was not ready. I calmly and politely asked why not and started getting the runaround. The worker turned to look at the large clock on the wall behind him, by now 4:05 pm and told me to come back tomorrow. The office was closed. We pleaded that our plane left the next morning at 6:00 a.m. The clerk just said, "Sorry."

My heart sank, but I was not leaving! We stood there in a sort of Custer's Last Stand. Then a supervisor appeared from a nearby office and asked the clerk to find my papers. The supervisor glared at the clerk, who hurriedly found the paperwork and passport and had me sign. I thanked the supervisor profusely.

Paul wanted to go with me to Jane and Jim's home, but I wasn't sure it was a good idea. Reluctantly I acquiesced. When we arrived, the children went off to play with their friends, and the adults sat in the living room. The mood was tense but calm. It *was* good Paul was there. There was no melodrama. The documents were looked over and signed. Upon leaving, the youngsters said their goodbyes to their father. Only my oldest sensed something, gently patting him on the back during their hug.

Chapter 4

It was pouring rain when we landed in Tahiti. Sheets of warm tropical water greeted us at the small airport of the capital Papeete. Humidity rushed into the plane once the door was opened. We hurried down the clanging metal stairs, crossed the puddled tarmac, and sought shelter in the open-air terminal. There were two passport control officers on duty stamping passports and one customs agent who waved us and our retrieved luggage through. We passed into a small reception area.

Our plan was to rent a car and drive around the island looking for a camping site. A man came up to Paul, asking in heavily accented English if we wanted to rent a car. He had only one car, for which he was charging an exorbitant rate. Paul haggled in French to no avail. He paid the man for one day and asked where there were camping sites. The guy just shrugged, not seeming to understand the question. So into the car, we piled, and off we went in the driving rain.

There was one main road that wound between the steep lush-green mountainside and the sea. Most of the interior is uninhabitable. After a while, we came upon a Tahitian bus pulling over for a stop. The bus was a large vehicle filled with local people getting wet. There was a roof, but the sides were open with bench seats and a single pipe railing around. Of course, the weather was warm, and as we passed it, my two oldest children thought it would be fun to be passengers. They would get their chance but not today.

Not finding anything resembling a campsite along the main road, after an hour, we spotted a small market and stopped. It was the first time I had seen unrefrigerated milk in a carton. We bought two cartons and some American peanut butter, French berry preserves, and a Tahitian loaf of bread. Our first meal in Tahiti was not going to be a feast, but I knew the children would eat it.

A short distance from the market was a one-lane asphalt road on the right. Paul decided to see where it led. We drove slowly through the continuous rain and, after ten minutes, saw a grass clearing between a grove of spindly trees on the ocean side of the road. Paul pointed out a water spigot and pronounced this was the place.

The children stayed in the car while Paul and I set up the bigger tent. After we were all inside out of the rain, he informed me that he was going to take the car back.

"Really?"

"Yes, we won't need it, and it's way too expensive."

I stressed, "I have no idea where we are in this rain. Do you?"

"Don't worry. I'll get back to the airport and hitchhike or take one of those buses. It'll be fine."

"But those buses don't come down this road, and how will you recognize it?"

He only smiled and said, "I'll be back."

Then he left.

There I was, sitting in the tent with my children around me. I began to feel very insecure. On the plane when we had first taken off from Honolulu, I was sort of numb and thought to myself, "You did it."

Now sitting in the middle of nowhere with the sound of the rain hitting the tent, I began to think, "What have you done?" I looked into the sweet faces of my young responsibilities. So far my children had been angels with no problems, and few complaints or questions. Jesus Christ's words came into my mind, "Be you as little children." For the first time, I realized what he meant. Trust your heavenly Father, as little ones trust their parents. Here were my children fully trusting in me, and I prayed I would never give them pause to do otherwise. I put my apprehensions aside, and we made peanut butter and jelly sandwiches. While passing the time, we sang songs, told stories, and played word games. (B-I-N-G-O still pops up in my head from time to time.)

Did I mention that before eating, we said grace? This was not an everyday practice of our family, but it seemed like a good idea.

Two hours later, as dark approached, so did Paul. It was still raining. When he unzipped the tent, and I saw his smiling face framed in wet blonde hair, I was very relieved, to say the least.

The children slept in the large tent while Paul and I retired in his pup tent.

The next morning, we heard numerous young voices outside the tent. We unzipped the flap to a beautiful sunny morning, and my children were playing with a couple of local Tahitian children. There was a home across the street setback from the road, and we came to find out that we were camped on their property. Oops!

Just beyond the wooded area, not far down the road, were other local homes. We were in a village and welcomed with open arms. The owner of the property and the neighbors offered their detached bathrooms and showers for our use. Nothing like this had happened in their little community before. We became celebrities from America and Canada. Paul communicated adequately with his French, and the children played happily despite the language difference.

We spent eight days camping there and were fêted at barbecues, even getting to know the local revolutionary. We had meals at his home while he would regale Paul in French about his exploits. He showed us a scrapbook of newspaper clippings of himself protesting for independence from France, including pictures of him being arrested. He talked proudly about his incarcerations. The family had a motor scooter and would lend it to us to go to the little market at the top of the road while they watched my children. Looking back, it all seems surreal, but at the time, we just accepted it and were grateful.

Before we left the island, we took the owner of the property, a widowed lady with six children, to a very nice French-Tahitian restaurant on the water. All the diners were white Frenchmen and women. Here we sat eating huge lobsters that the neighborly widow had ordered for the three of us. She was the only native Tahitian in the place, except the busboys. English-speaking diners with a local woman in an expensive, delightful restaurant presented an unusual picture.

The day we packed up and left, the villagers came and honored us with leis of small shells. In Hawaii, leis were made of flowers; here, they were using shells. These people would be considered poor in the states, and I did not want to accept their gifts, but Paul pointed out that it would be an insult not to. One of the families owned an old pick-up, and the oldest son drove us and our gear to the main road, where we caught a bus. Finally, my children got to ride on one of the open-air buses to town. They loved it; I was petrified they would fall out.

We checked into a hotel in Papeete and had a few days before my return tickets expired. Paul and I seriously discussed the future. He wanted me to continue on with him. He and the children were getting along so well that it seemed natural. Before I agreed, we went to the airline office to see what we could exchange the tickets for.

Well…I could exchange them for tickets that would first take us to Pago, Pago capital of American Samoa, then on to Western Samoa, next to the island of Fiji, and the last stop was Auckland International Airport in the capital of New Zealand. It did not take long to decide. We were bound for New Zealand!

Chapter 5

Arriving at the small airport of Pago Pago, we learned there were no camping sites in American Samoa. For that matter, there would be no camping sites in Fiji either. (We were not in Kansas anymore.) There was only one hotel, a large international concern. We registered, found our room, and then went to the pool. Paul and I joined a couple of businessmen who were having drinks in the shade of the bar while the children splashed in the pool, the little one on the broad pool steps with her floaties. The hotel was a way station for business travelers who sold their goods throughout the Pacific Islands.

The next morning we rented a car to drive around the island. The only problem was the road ended about halfway. It was a two-lane black asphalt road with villages on one side and the beach on the other. The Samoans wore the traditional wrap-around skirt or lavalava, the women tied it around the chest, the men around the waist. It was certainly suitable for the climate. The homes were mostly round huts built with strong round wooden posts holding up thatched palm frond roofs that spread down from a point at the center. The walls were woven grass mats hung from support beams. At night the mats would come down for shelter, and in the morning, they were rolled back up. We started our drive early enough to view some of the late risers rolling up their walls. Inside these symmetrical huts were only the bare minimum, hammocks and a few other pieces of furniture. A large round man still lay in his hammock. Some would say the island was a sleepy little place. I would say it was asleep.

After two days, we flew to Upolo, the main island of Western Samoa. What a startling difference! As soon as we got off the plane, we saw people bustling about.

I remarked to Paul, "Such a difference in the two Samoan Islands."

He informed me: "In American Samoa, your government gives the tribal chiefs money to dispense. Western Samoa is a territory of New Zealand, and the people get nothing from the government. They are on their own."

On Upolu, we ended up in the only viable hotel in town. It was right out of a Graham Greene novel with skinny British gentlemen sitting in shabby stuffed chairs in the lobby, reading newspapers while smoking cigarettes. Lazy ceiling fans wafted the smoke around. The desk clerk was an ancient expat. The hotel was three stories, with the rooms built around a courtyard and large communal bathrooms down the open latticed hallways. We checked into a room on the second floor. This place had seen better days, but it certainly had ambiance.

Traveling with three young children had many challenges and going to countries where the majority of the population still lived in very rural dwellings made it more so. There were no laundromats or disposable diapers. Before we left Hawaii, Paul had stuffed as many Pampers into his large backpack as would possibly fit. By the time we made it to Western Samoa, there were only dirty cloth diapers I had packed.

The hotel bathroom was clean enough, except the curtainless shower was a clawfoot tub with the recent renovation of a shower head. I don't believe that tub had been cleaned in the last ten years. It was the color of gray fog. The diapers needed to be washed along with our clothes. Therefore, the tub had to be cleaned and sanitized. Paul went downstairs and asked the desk clerk, who just shook his head at this request.

The hotel was on the main street of the town with small local restaurants and a market. We ate dinner at one of the restaurants and shopped at the market for bananas for the morning and what few cleaning supplies they sold: Ajax, scrub brush, bleach, and a box of Ivory Snow detergent.

While I was the busy, grumbling hotel maid, Paul took the children to the courtyard and played guitar with the youngsters dancing around like giggling gypsies. He had only been playing a short time when a door on the first floor opened and a young girl, about six years old, came out. She sauntered up to Paul to watch him play and then joined in the revelry with our dancers.

Her twenty-something parents followed shortly thereafter and, sitting on a squeaky, French rod-iron bench, began a friendly conversation with Paul. They were from New Zealand and were on their way to Hawaii.

Coincidently, the last couple of nights, Paul and I had been discussing our trip. Our plans were to stop in New Zealand, do the tourist thing, and then go on to Australia with the intention of looking for a place to rent for a while. The New Zealanders and Paul talked while I joined in between wash loads. They told us we should not bother with Australia except, maybe, to visit the Gold Coast. If we were truly thinking of staying somewhere, New Zealand was the place. They were from a town called Whangarei and convinced us we would love it there. They gave us something to consider. After all, our plans were not set in stone.

The next day we rented a car to tour the island. Along the way, we chanced upon a village ceremony where six young men, all in mid-calf wheat-colored grass skirts with shell bracelets, were chanting and dancing in a Polynesian masculine manner. We stopped and got out of the car a short distance away from the villagers watching the men. No one seemed to mind our presence. My children were enthralled with this impressive sight, and so were we. How lucky we were to come upon this event, as these muscular men performed for their people on some festive occasion.

Our next destination was Fiji, where I managed to cut my foot rather deeply on some coral at the beach. It became a painful travel nuisance.

All the inter-island planes we flew on were small commercial aircraft but, fortunately, large enough not to disturb my claustrophobia.

In Fiji, we landed on the East side of the main island of Viti Levu. Fiji had recently been granted its independence from Britain, and the citizens were very proud of that fact.

When we arrived at the city of Suva airport, a refined-looking Indian gentleman came up to us and asked if we were looking for somewhere to stay. Obviously, we were tourists. He told us of his cousin's guesthouse with eight comfortable and spacious rooms. The price was fair, plus they had a small dining room where two meals a day were served. We accepted his offer. He drove us in a VW van to the guesthouse. The place was far cheerier and cleaner than the hotel in Western Samoa, and we had our own bathroom.

We enjoyed a few days of sun and surf, where I stepped on that jagged piece of coral the first day. The town boasted a small pharmacy. The pharmacist/owner sold me iodine, cotton, and gauze. There was no tape for sale. And, low-and-behold, there was one package of disposable diapers, a brand that was not sold in the states, but who cared? I snatched them off the shelf, not even checking the price.

When we booked our flight to New Zealand, we discovered the plane took off from the Nadi airport on the opposite side of the island. The next morning after finishing a delicious breakfast of banana pancakes in the guesthouse dining room, we checked out, paying for our room and meals, or so we thought.

The rental car was delivered, and we packed up and drove on. The beaches were beautiful, but the climate was not as tropical. The closer we got to New Zealand, the less tropical the islands became, although they were still warm.

Upon reaching Nadi, we got out of the car and walked around a busy local marketplace buying fruit for later. We ate lunch at an Indian restaurant, then drove to the airport and turned in our car.

Our flight was not leaving for another five hours, so we decided to walk to a nearby hotel and take a room for the night even though we would not be staying. With three young children, hanging out at the Nadi airport was not ideal. Not having any reservations, we were glad they were not fully booked. The added bonus was the pool.

In the late afternoon, while my two oldest were in the pool and my toddler was taking a nap, Paul and I were sitting at an umbrella'd table just off our room when an Indian gentleman approached us and asked if we had come from Suva. We told him yes. He stunned us when he told us that we had left his cousin's guesthouse and our breakfast was not on the bill when we paid. He asked politely if we would pay him for the meal, and he would see that his cousin received the money.

Of course, we paid, and when the man left, Paul commented, "How in the world did he find us? Either the guesthouse owner has a whole lot of cousins, or we certainly stand out."

I added, "Probably both."

In the hours it took to fly to Auckland, New Zealand, we went from warm to winter. The cut on my foot disappeared within two days, no more tropics. Everything seemed upside down, and it was, considering its location on the globe compared to North America. We were suddenly thrust back into civilization at the modern international airport; passport control and customs were no longer together in an open-air building. Having flown across the International Date Line, we lost a full calendar day. Did I mention it was winter?

We stood in the passport control line at the busy airport. When we got to the officer, the white-haired older gentleman looked at Paul's Canadian passport and stamped it. Canada as well as New

Zealand, and many other countries were part of the British Commonwealth. He took mine, flipped through the pages, and asked, "Where is your visa?"

VISA? It had never occurred to us that I needed one. No other country so far had asked. Paul spoke up, "We didn't know she needed one."

"Well, she does. They do."

Paul added rather too brusquely, "But they are with me. And I'm a member of the Commonwealth!"

"They are American."

Once again, regarding a passport, we were not sure what to do. Were we supposed to go back to Fiji? We held our ground. The place was crowded and busy; our line was not moving.

Quickly, Paul argued, "She is my fiancé."

The older gentleman looked at Paul, then at me, then my children, including the toddler who was in Paul's arms. He looked back at Paul with a look like, Are you crazy, young man?

Yet miraculously, he stamped my passport and said, "If you are staying, get them a visa!"

We let out our breath.

We caught a taxi into the city. The taxi driver was a jovial fellow talking non-stop, asking us where we were from and where we were going.

Paul said, "We're thinking of settling here for a while."

The taxi driver's eyes got bigger in the rearview mirror, and he said, "You being from North America and all, you've probably been to Disneyland."

My children, almost in unison, said, "Yes, we have. It's the best."

My daughter added for emphasis, "I was there for my fifth birthday party."

The taxi driver went on, "Then you want to stay in Napier. It's tops. It's where I'm from…Yes, Napier, they have a park just like Disneyland."

Hmmm, I thought, "Really?"

The driver took us to a nice, mid-size hotel close to shops and restaurants. The main branch of the Auckland library was also within walking distance. It was late at night, so we went to sleep before heading out the next day to buy warm clothing.

Chapter 6

New Zealand consists of two long, large islands: the North Island and the South Island. Auckland is on the North Island. The South Island, closer to the South Pole, is considerably colder. Compared to where we had just traveled from, the fact that the North Island was warmer escaped us. After visiting a nearby department store, we walked comfortably in our new winter clothes, heading for Auckland's main library. I had discussed with Paul the program whereby the Urantia Brotherhood sent books to all the main libraries in English-speaking cities. We decided to see if Auckland had received one.

The library was a modern-style building. We walked through broad glass doors and looked for the children's book section to keep my two oldest happy. My daughter loved libraries. When she was two years old, and we were getting ready to go to the library, she could not resist playing with the stereo knobs again. I told her we were not going and plopped her in her crib. She cried like her heart was broken. I looked at her and thought, "How can I use the library as a punishment?" So, I lifted her out and off to the library we went.

At the Auckland library with its large room of children's books, she was in heaven and quickly took charge of her brother, picking out books for him and for her to read at the children's table.

Paul, carrying my toddler, and I went on to the information desk. We asked if they had *The Urantia Book*. The librarian asked for the spelling of the book before searching the records. We stood there waiting.

Finally, she said, "Yes, I think we do have the book, but I don't see a catalog number for it. Let me look further. Can you wait, please?"

We gladly agreed. We stood there for some time. When she returned, she had a new book in her hand. "This was in the basement. I don't know why it hasn't been brought up and cataloged. It's a handsome book."

Looking at it closer, she asked, "What section should it be in?"

"Religions of the World."

"Thank you, I'll take care of it. Can you come back later? It will be ready to be checked out."

We told her we would, although Paul had carried my book throughout our travels in his backpack. We did not return. Our aim was to get it on the shelf. We also visited two bookstores to ask about the book and suggested they order it.

It was time to figure out where we wanted to live, and we needed transportation. Paul decided to buy a car instead of renting one. He bought the Auckland Star newspaper and returned to our hotel room. He began studying the classifieds. All of a sudden, he got very excited, "Look, there's a used Daimler for sale. I've always wanted to own one."

I had no idea what a Daimler was. From the desk, he got a pen and hotel stationery to figure out how much it was in US dollars.

Then he grew even more excited, "It's only $500 US. Let's go see it."

We all bundled up and left the hotel, taking a taxi to the address in the classifieds.

Well, was I in for a surprise! Here was this marvelous four-door, silver automobile that looked like a cross between a Bentley and a Rolls Royce, except the steering wheel was on the wrong side; actually, the road was too.

The interior of the car was leather with a highly polished mahogany dashboard and side panels; it was in mint condition. Our family took it for a spin, and the engine purred. When we returned, the owner gladly accepted five US $100 dollar bills. I realized then how far our money would stretch living in this charming country.

The next morning with our Daimler all packed, we headed north to Whangarei. Cruising along in our new automobile behind a big truck, Paul was just about to go around it when a ping could be heard throughout the car. Within seconds, the windshield began to crack like a spider web. He pulled over to the side of the road. By the time the car stopped, the spider web had spawned many webs. The truck had thrown off a pebble from its tire that hit the windshield. There was no way we could drive that way. Paul got out of the car, went to the trunk, brought out a tool, and from the inside began chipping out part of the glass in front of the driver's side. Small shards of glass were all over the dash. What a mess!

This happened about halfway to Whangarei, with more than an hour left to drive. We were quite a sight, pulling into a Whangarei motel. The owner was very helpful, and the next morning the

Daimler was at a shop. The windshield had to be ordered and shipped from Auckland. It took three days before we had the car back. The shop owner loaned us a funky car which was better than nothing. Having a look around, it was a nice town, but it did not feel like home to us.

Late one evening, with the children asleep, Paul and I were poring over the map of the North Island when we spotted Napier, the place where New Zealand's Disneyland was. We decided to slowly head there and stop at towns along the way, traveling south over a period of three days.

Napier was right on the coast. That was a plus. Entering the town along the shoreline, we drove by a simple amusement park set on a pebble beach. Could this be the place the taxi driver was talking about? It was. Turning onto the main road into town, we were struck by the sight of the architecture. It was 1930's Hollywood art deco style. This was the place for us. It felt like home.

On August 15, 1972, we rented an unfurnished house one block from the pebble beach amusement park, close to the elementary school, and within walking distance to town. We shopped at a used furniture store. New Zealand had only two television channels; both were government-run. We had watched them at the hotel and decided a TV was not necessary. We bought a large dining room table, and Paul brought home a huge roll of unprinted newspaper plus lots of crayons. He decided he was going to put his artistic skills to work and teach my children how to draw. They spent hours working on their collective murals. My son showed talent. Paul also presented my eldest with a used upright piano. He bought a book and began to teach her. She was a willing student, practicing an hour every day.

I worried about how the children would react to school in a new country. I need not have. The first day they both came home happy as clams. When the teachers learned they were from Hawaii, they were treated like little stars and asked to tell the other students what life was like there. They made friends both in school and in the neighborhood. A Maori family lived on the corner, and being accustomed to playing with local Hawaiians, the children became playmates within a day.

Our house had a white picket fence in front. The baby, now nineteen months, had the yard for her playground. She was not allowed to go out of the gate, but she liked to hang around inside when the other kids played on the sidewalk. She never cried about it; it was just the way it was. There was a detached studio behind the house, so Paul set it up for painting. My family became his models. We watched our pennies but lived comfortably. I became adept at different ways of cooking mutton; it was very inexpensive and fresh. Together Paul and I spent at least two hours a day studying and discussing the Urantia Papers. Life was good.

I wrote to my parents and gave them our address. I asked them to notify the children's father.

It took a month for the telephone company to deliver a phone and hook us up. It was time for my children to speak with their father. So we called; I talked to him first. He was polite on the phone. My two oldest took turns talking to him. They innocently spoke to their father as if nothing had changed. And in reality, between them, nothing had. If anything, he was probably listening more carefully to their childish conversation. I did ask them not to share too much of our adventures since he had not been with us. I explained that I did not want him to feel left out. Their young minds could understand that logic.

Before hanging up, my son handed me back the phone, "Daddy wants to talk to you again."

The father of my children said, "What about your child support?"

It was a good thing I was sitting down. If not, you could have knocked me over with a feather.

"You could start paying it."

"I'll send an American Express check. Should I use the address your dad gave me?"

"Yes. Thank you."

"When are you coming back?"

"I don't know."

We said our goodbyes, and life went on until December. It was going to be a warm Christmas like in Hawaii since it was the beginning of summer in New Zealand. One day Paul and I were discussing future plans. Paul's Canadian citizenship enabled him to get a job with no problems. Our conversation provoked serious thoughts regarding the future. I sat there thinking about what exactly was best for my children. Before I could even articulate the thought in my mind, my lips moved to say, "I think it's time to reunite the children with their father. We should probably return to Hawaii."

Paul was startled and questioned, "Why?"

"Hmmm…I'm not sure, but I think it's what we're supposed to do."

After a long pause, "You're probably right."

Within a couple of days, I called the children's father and told him. He could not have been happier or more accommodating, even arranging our return flight.

Paul and I started planning. Since New Zealand is so close to Australia, it seemed obvious that we should travel back by way of that country. We contacted the landlord and asked if he wanted our furniture. He did. We drove back to Auckland, where Paul had a buyer for the Daimler.

First, we flew to Christchurch on the South Island and toured for a few days. Then we flew to Sydney, Australia. What a charming modern city on a bustling harbor. After spending a day taking in the sights, we rented a car to drive north along the coastline up the Gold Coast, then to the city of Brisbane where we had arranged to fly back to Honolulu.

The journey took us along coral sea-beds right off the highway. Here and there, freshwater streams flowed into the light blue-green ocean, where my children demanded to stop to see if there were any crocodiles in the brackish water. We saw white sand beaches and intermittent trailer parks perched on small cliffs with a view of the Pacific.

Near Surfers Paradise Beach, we stopped and rented a spacious hotel room. That particular day there were no surfers out nor any beachgoers. Along with the employees of a beach food stand, we were the only ones at the biggest beach we had seen throughout our travels. And we were not there long. It was 120 degrees Fahrenheit with no palm trees for shade.

My toddler had lost her last bottle at the Auckland airport, and I was remiss and did not keep her hydrated. She had such a sweet disposition and never complained about anything. That night she became ill with a high fever. Paul raced to the nearest drugstore. The pharmacist brought up the possibility of dehydration. He came back to the hotel, and, along with baby aspirin, I made her drink water every half hour. After a nearly sleepless night, she was fine in the morning.

On December 24th, Christmas Eve, we were at Brisbane International Airport for a twelve-hour direct flight to Honolulu. That hours-long trip was a trial in family endurance, but we weathered it well. My children were seasoned travelers by this time. Crossing back over the International Date Line, when we landed, it was still December 24.

My husband was now living in a condominium in Waikiki. He had previously made plans to take his new girlfriend on a trip for the holiday week and had offered us his place to stay. Taking a taxi to the high-rise condo, the concierge gave me the key. We rode the elevator up to the seventh floor and found the apartment. The key let us into a very nice place, but not one decorated for the holidays. We unpacked our backpacks, and when I opened a closet door to put them away, I found the large box that held our family Christmas decorations. I had collected special baubles during the years, and of the few family things he saved, these were among them.

On to Ala Moana by taxi, we went shopping for a tree and presents. Paul took the children to a different area of a store while I quickly bought toys, a few Hawaiian print clothes, flip-flops, and stocking stuffers. It turned out to be a great Christmas, with decorations, presents, turkey, and all.

That night I called my parents, and they were very happy to talk to their grandchildren, knowing they were back in Hawaii. I called Jane and Jim and wished them Merry Christmas. They already knew I was coming back. But I got a big surprise when I called Marian, she knew too.

I asked her, "How did you know?"

Marian laughed, "Your ex is on vacation with my girlfriend."

"Really? How in the world…."

She told me that after I left, my husband would drive out to the North Shore on the weekends. Marian introduced him to a close friend of hers, and they started dating. And there was more… Her friend was a teacher, and she and another teacher started a school on the North Shore. My husband helped them get the school licensed through his attorneys, and now there was an innovative school for children ranging from preschool through fourth grade in the sleepy little town of Kahuku, just at the point where the North Shore begins.

That sounded good to me. In fact, it sounded wonderful. I was worried about starting my daughter and son in another school in the middle of the year, so this type of atmosphere seemed right. I asked Marian what she thought of the school. She had high praise.

While cleaning up after Christmas dinner, I found in a kitchen drawer two sets of car keys: one for a Mercedes and the other were the keys to the Camaro. Could it be true that he had not sold that car? Paul and I went to the parking lot on the roof of the building, and there under the night sky was a white Mercedes coupe parked next to the racing green Camaro. We had a car!

Two days later, after making good use of the condo's washing machine and dryer, we took down the tree and packed up the Camaro. The children would start school at the new school in Kahuku, and we wanted to look for a house somewhere close by. There are numerous official camping sites in Hawaii, so we drove along the windward coast road towards the North Shore. Finding Hauula Beach Park, only five miles from Kahuku Point, we set up our tents on a large grassy area that advanced onto a narrow sandy beach. It had all the proper facilities, including a small playground. We were back in the USA. Our tents had not been used since Tahiti, and this time, we were not in someone's front yard.

Purchasing the Honolulu Advertiser, we searched the classifieds for places to rent in the area. After two days, we found a furnished three-bedroom house on a cul-de-sac not far from our campsite. The furnishings were typical Hawaiian-style with colorful print cushions. The backyard was like our campsite, a grass area with the narrow beach at the sea. Although the beach was not sand and made up of large boulders, the price was right. Who needs sand in your backyard when there are white sandy beaches everywhere? We rented it.

The following weekend, the children's father drove out to pick them up. They were so happy to see him, though the youngest furrowed her brow, trying to remember exactly where she had seen him. But with her brother and sister by her side, she was fine. I had reminded the two of them that I did not think Daddy would be interested in our life in New Zealand since he probably missed them unless, of course, he asked.

During the two weeks back in Hawaii, Paul and I began to realize something had changed. Our life together no longer seemed to fit. Our destiny together wasn't the same. That weekend we spent alone, the future became prominent in our conversation. He had brought up the subject I wanted to avoid. Paul was a commercial artist who had spent the last year living out his dream. He never traveled the whole world, there was much more to see, but that paled in comparison to what we had experienced together. But now, he knew it was time for him to go back to work, and that meant to his country where he would easily find employment in his field. Sunday morning, we woke up very early. We wanted to watch the sunrise. This was how we first met, and it was to be the last sunrise we would enjoy together. We sat on a large flat rock at the edge of the grass where the rocks met the sea. As the sun crested the horizon, we sat silently side by side as a new day dawned for us in our Father's universe.

When the children returned that afternoon, Paul and I had a party set up. We did not want them to be sad about his leaving, so we decided to make it a celebration with balloons, cake, and ice cream. After telling them that the party was for Paul because he was going back to Canada, they became downcast, but we did not let them dwell on it. I cut the cake, which we ate with ice cream, and then gathered our towels and toys and went to the beach. For them, the timing could not have been better. They had just spent their days being spoiled by their father.

The next day we all drove Paul to the airport with hugs goodbye. Comings and goings on airplanes were nothing unusual for the family.

Chapter 7

In mid-January, my children and I drove the short distance from home to the school at Kahuku. We were looking for a graded dirt road on the right, one block past a local hamburger stand. My son, the pathfinder, spotted it first, directing me to turn.

A short distance further, we saw a large, old wooden church. The weathered white paint was peeling off the walls, but the children running around on the grass in the yard did not seem to care. There were a few cars parked on a small lot next to the yard. I pulled my car in, and we got out. From the parking lot, we could see on the side of the church four newly repaired stairs to a landing that led to an office door.

My children and I walked up the stairs and along the landing, passing an open window where a young woman was sitting at a desk on the inside of the office. She greeted us through the window before we even entered. When we were in the office, Judy introduced herself. We were expected, and she was delighted that my two oldest would be attending the school. Her four-year-old daughter was a student. With the addition of my children, there would now be twenty-five children at the accredited school, all haoles. I was surprised at the small number of students.

Judy gave me some papers to fill out while my children ran ahead into the main body of the church. After filling out the registration, she gave me the new-parent tour. We walked from the office through an anteroom called the Sesame Street room; Ernie, Miss Piggy, and Kermit adorned the walls. There were little chairs in neat semi-circle rows like a miniature theater and a television up on a specially built ledge. Each day the children had the choice of watching Sesame Street at 11:30 a.m. or playing outside before lunch. On the left were two child-size bathrooms with painted signs for boys and girls.

Just as we entered the spacious main body of the old church, we heard children arguing in the far corner. I looked, and there in that corner were the toys I had asked Marian to gather from our Lanikai house, including the entire play kitchen setup with matching table and chairs. In addition, our large toy box was against the wall. There stood my son clasping some of the toys to his chest, demanding that they were his, and they were. Oh, boy!

The ruckus drew the attention of Judy, myself, and also Steve, the teaching partner of my husband's girlfriend. I hurried to the corner and had the duty of explaining that the toys now belonged to the school. I told my son that when we left, we had given the toys away, so now all the children could play with them. He lowered his six-year-old head, saying nothing, still clutching the toys. After a few moments, he handed them back to the little girl who had been 'cooking dinner.' I gave my son a hug; he hung onto me tightly for almost a full minute. Steve observed the whole scenario before introducing himself.

The North Shore of Oahu in 1973 was an undiscovered jewel. From the Filipino community of Kahuku, west along Kamehameha 'Kam' Highway (a two-lane road) to the town of Haleiwa resided a small cosmopolitan group. There were friendly locals with harmless barking dogs and an occasional rooster, dedicated surfers (some world-famous), welfare recipients, and well-to-do second residences. The sea was also a haven for divers and net and spear fishermen. Young haole, twenty-something couples with children lived inexpensively as did single mothers. Of course, there were hippies. It was the 70s.

Kahuku boasted a cattle ranch with managerial staff and cowboys. There were also prominent Polo pony stables. Further along, Kam Highway was the Mokuleia Polo Field, located on the beach side about midway between Kahuku and Haleiwa. It was big news when the Prince of Wales visited to ride in a match.

The area hospital was in Kahuku with a small competent staff of doctors and nurses. During the next year, my eldest would break her arm and become an overnight patient

The North Shore is most famous for its surf spots Rocky Point, Sunset Beach, Waimea Bay, Pupukea, Banzai Pipeline, and more. All along the road, except for the parks, private neighborhoods nestled between the coastline and Kam Highway. It was a surfer's paradise.

Steve lived just south of Sunset Beach Park. The front porch of his rented two-bedroom, wood-frame home hung over the beach, the front stairs ending on the sand.

The school was a community unto itself. I became close friends with one of the mothers whose oldest was in kindergarten, and the youngest was my toddler's age. Sheila started dropping by in the morning after her husband left for work. We drank coffee together while the toddlers played. Sheila knew something about everyone and attempted to become my matchmaker. I was not interested. For the first time, I was living alone with my children. And it was nice. The children's father had agreed to pay our rent, and the child support frugally covered our other expenses.

But then...one morning in March, Sheila and I were in my kitchen chitchatting when she told me the latest. Steve's Australian girlfriend had gone back to her country. My! What a coincidence, both Steve and I had lost mates to return to a British Commonwealth country.

I had to admit that piqued my interest, but I was sure many of the other ladies, and single mothers on the North Shore were piqued too. So I took a week to think about it. The following Friday, I dressed in a lime green halter top that matched nicely with my newly acquired tan and went to pick up my children.

I talked with Judy and some other mothers in the office while waiting for the bell to ring. It was a handbell, reminding me of my Catholic school days when the nuns rang similar bells.

Steve came into the office wearing one of his trademark Aloha shirts and a trail of children behind him. He was a dark-haired, attractive guy with a surfer's body, a twinkle in his eye, and a great laugh.

He smiled at us and said, "Well hello, ladies."

We all acknowledged his greeting just as pandemonium broke out, with the children matching up with their mothers. I could not have planned it better as my children came sauntering in dead last.

Steve put his hand on the heads of my two and said, "These are quite a pair you have here."

I said, "I hope that means something positive."

My son wiggled away and went out the office door. But my daughter lingered.

Steve continued, "You know your daughter is a math whiz."

She beamed, and I smiled; I knew.

Saying goodbye, we left for the car. Just as I put the key in the ignition, Steve came up to my open window and said, "Listen, my roommate and I are having a barbecue tomorrow. Why don't you come by with the kids?"

"They will be with their father this weekend."

Not missing a beat, he said, "Why don't you come over anyway?"

"All right, what time?"

"Come around three. My place is easy to find."

He gave directions, of which I made a mental note.

Saturday afternoon, I was nervously driving along Kam Highway, trying to follow the directions Steve had given me. He told me to pass Kami's Market, the local convenience store, and turn right. That was all I had clearly remembered. I have always been directionally handicapped and proceeded to get lost. I eventually remembered he had said it was at a dead end. Retracing my route, I found a dead end and recognized his older, tangerine VW bus in an open garage.

Climbing the few stairs of the home's covered porch, I knocked on the wood frame of an unlocked screen door. To the right of the porch was a small patch of banana trees; green bananas hung from one of the stalks. Steve soon appeared in an unbuttoned Aloha shirt and khaki cargo shorts and swung the screen door open for me.

"Hey, you made it."

"Yeah, I got a little lost."

Leaving my sandals at the door, we passed through the living room. Immediately, I sighted a view of the ocean through wood-framed windows across a sunroom three steps below the front room. I could hear the glorious sound of the waves. To the right of the sunroom, an open door led us outside to a landing and stairs. Steve's roommate, Jack, was putting charcoal in a large round grill just beyond the landing on a sandy knoll by the side of the house. He put down the bag, wiped his right hand on his surf trunks, shook my hand, and introduced himself, "Hi, welcome to our little piece of Paradise. I'm Jack."

"Hello, I'm Carole."

I noticed that although I was late, I seemed to be early. I was the first partygoer.

Steve said, "How do you like the front yard?"

I stood there, taking in the long sweep of white sand and deep blue sea. It was not a tranquil turquoise. There was no protective reef. It was just a wide-open ocean with waves cresting further out and continuously rolling and slowing until reaching the shallow water of the shore. It was breathtaking. I loved it.

Before I answered, Steve said, "Do you want to go for a walk?"

"Sure."

Little did I realize, as I descended the weather-beaten wooden stairs I was about to go on an audition.

The sand on the North Shore beach is not hard-packed. It is more like soft snow freshly fallen. For the first few minutes, we walked by the sand-packed shoreline, the ocean's waves gently splashing our feet, then receding. We talked about general matters getting to know one another. After the next five minutes, still enjoying Steve's company, I began to notice with each step a slight, sinking feeling beneath my feet. We came to a coral formation protruding onto the shore with puddles of salt water collected in its tide pools. Skirting it, we walked in deeper dry sand. Now my mind began to recognize that my legs were getting tired. We kept walking.

There was no question that I was going to soldier on with a smile on my face. Yet, in the next ten minutes, I was in a world of hurt. I did not know if all the other available single women would have walked a mile in my shoes—bare feet rather, but I knew they would have loved the chance to try. Unfortunately, my legs were coming to the end of their endurance. I could not even contemplate walking back to the house. Did he notice? I never knew.

Finally, he said, "Let's walk up to the road and hitch back."

"Oh yes. Thank you, God!" I thought.

Walking up to the road through even deeper sand was a herculean task, but I was not going to fail now. Reaching Kam Highway and crossing the wonderful asphalt, Steve stuck out his thumb, and a surfing buddy in an old pickup stopped. I squeezed in the middle of the bench seat, trying not to be too obvious in catching my breath. Back at the house, the barbecue was just getting started.

I guess I passed the test. We began dating, and it quickly blossomed into romance. My friend Sheila was delighted. The roommate Jack moved back to the states in June. I made my last rent payment that month, and Steve and I would live together after I returned from the mainland in July. We were both twenty-seven years old.

Chapter 8

The Urantia Brotherhood sponsored their First Western Urantia Conference in Los Angeles, California, on June 29 to July 1, 1973. Marian had told me about it the month before. Since I was planning to take my children to visit their grandparents in Hollywood, I decided to attend. I was interested in meeting others who were studying the book besides the five women in our study group. Marian made arrangements to stay with a friend in Beverly Hills and traveled the week before. The conference was held at a private school in Brentwood, a charming community that borders Beverly Hills and West Los Angeles.

My mother met the family at LAX (Los Angeles International Airport) and could not have had a bigger smile on her face, or her arms opened wider. The two oldest children ran to her while my toddler hung back. She did not recognize her. Mom understood and handled the situation so beautifully that by the time we reached the car in the parking lot, she and my youngest were holding hands.

Two days later, I picked up Marian in Beverly Hills, and we drove the short distance to the school. After we parked the car across the street and were walking toward the building, a flurry of activity arose. An entourage appeared, led by a redheaded guy about my age. People standing on the front lawn went to greet him. Marian, too, seemed to get caught up in the spell. I asked her, "What's going on?"

Pointing to the redhead, "That's Mo Siegel."

"Who's Mo Siegel?"

"You know, he's the one that started that health food company that puts Urantia quotes on the boxes."

I thought, "Right, I've read those; what a smart marketing idea."

Marian went on glowingly, "Mo's building a terrific business. He's a sharp entrepreneur."

Hmmm…a sharp entrepreneur! I had been married to one, and the automatic respect that infects the uninitiated had no effect on me. Marian apparently knew him and left me in her wake to meet up with his group. I went on into the school.

Entering the cool of the building, I saw people milling around in the foyer and some heading through wide-open double doors of the school auditorium. I soon learned that readers of the book had traveled from all over the United States. I began introducing myself to many friendly faces. There were a few hundred people attending the conference, and it got started that afternoon.

Over three days, the leaders of the Urantia Foundation and the Urantia Brotherhood gave interesting talks in the auditorium. They spoke from a podium next to the stage; the audience sat in folding chairs.

The most memorable speakers were Emma Christensen, President of the Urantia Brotherhood; Thomas Kendall, a Trustee and President of the Urantia Foundation; Clyde Bedell, author of the *Concordex of The Urantia Book*; and Martin Myers, a young Foundation trustee.

Ms. Emma Christensen was a tall, poised, white-haired elderly woman. She was the first president of the Urantia Brotherhood and the last person living, directly involved from the early 1920s until the delivery of the Revelation in 1934-1935 and thereafter. In many eyes, she was irreplaceable for its printing and copyright in 1955. Exhibiting a total lack of pretension. Ms. Christensen read many quotes from *The Urantia Book* centering on love and the teachings of Jesus. She impressed me with the idea that the duty of a reader of the Urantia Papers was to lead others to the love of God first. Then, by how we lead our lives, they will become interested in the Revelation. For illustration, she read one particular quote: *Jesus endeavored to make clear that he desired his disciples, having tasted of the good spirit realities of the kingdom, so to live in the world that men, by seeing their lives, would become kingdom conscious and hence be led to inquire of believers concerning the ways of the kingdom.*

The Urantia Foundation president, Thomas Kendall, was a sincere and cordial man. He welcomed all of us, representing many different regions of the country.

Clyde Bedell was an older white-haired gentleman whom I listened to with interest. He had single-handedly created the *Concordex of The Urantia Book*, which I had recently purchased. His book was a combination of an index and a reference guide that I found invaluable in my study. I felt gratitude toward this man. I was told he put the Concordex together using 3"x 5" index cards. He must have had cards all over his house. For example, under Dark Islands of Space: *These are the dead suns and other large aggregations of matter devoid of light and heat. The dark islands are sometimes enormous in mass and exert a powerful influence in universe equilibrium and energy manipulation. The density of some of these large masses is well-nigh unbelievable.*

Martin Myers, a new Trustee and the youngest speaker, gave a discourse almost exclusively regarding the problems of keeping the text of the book and trademarks, the three azure blue concentric circles, and the word Urantia from being misused. The talk was long and mentioned many problems that had arisen between members. I had not been aware that there were any problems, nor did I find it relative to me at the time.

The evening entertainment was lively. The auditorium was cleared of folding chairs. On stage, entertaining silly skits were performed, and musicians jammed. There was a banjo player whose name, Richard Keeler, I would not learn for many years. He did a duet with a talented guitar player, Vern Grimsley. I had heard of Vern from Marian. She told me he had a popular radio program broadcast from San Francisco, teaching the spiritual message of the book without mentioning its name. He was a tall, good-looking fellow with sandy blonde hair and plenty of charisma. He was a popular leader in the Urantia movement with an interesting story.

Vern Bennom Grimsley began reading *The Urantia Book* in 1956 while still in high school. He was the only reader in his town in Kansas until he introduced it to his sweetheart, and they studied it together. In 1958 he contacted the Foundation. He was seventeen years old and wanted to purchase four books that he could loan out to friends. At that age, he was already a part-time radio announcer, but his life's goal was to become a minister in his protestant church.

During his college years, he belonged to a fraternity where he introduced the book to his fraternity brothers. Three of them would participate in the next generation of leaders in the Urantia movement. After he graduated Phi Beta Kappa with majors in philosophy and psychology, he and his wife (a graduate in the humanities) decided to unite their efforts in the service of God. Instead of pursuing a career in the protestant church, he went to work in a different kind of ministry; she went to work to support them.

The newly married Grimsleys lived in Berkeley, California, and Vern began a ministry at the UC Berkeley campus, calling it "On Campus." His discussions/debates with students regarding the existence and love of God were recorded and broadcast on the American Forces Radio Network. Concurrently, he was given primetime airtime at 5:45 p.m. on KFAX in San Francisco. The young husband and wife team named the broadcast the "Spiritual Renaissance Broadcast". Fortunately, the station manager waived the fifteen-minute broadcast fee because he liked the message. Its substance was that we are all brothers and sisters in the family of God, and each individual has a spark, a spirit of God the Father within. He taught the gospel of Jesus' teachings rather than the gospel about Jesus' life.

Vern's broadcasts were not only inspiring but enlightening and humorous. He liberally used references from poets and statesmen

68

sprinkled within his message. He was a naturally gifted broadcast personality and public speaker.

By 1976 his broadcast coverage would reach over one hundred million people and extend throughout the U.S., Europe, Asia, and as far as the Middle East over Radio Jordan. He never asked for donations believing it would take away from his message. Public speaking engagements were one source of income.

Perhaps to his detriment, he was very much in agreement with the ideals of the Urantia Foundation regarding advertising. (The mandate of no advertising through media, only person-to-person contact.) When an Arizona Urantia Book study group began commercials for the book before and after his broadcast, he warned them that if they continued, he would discontinue broadcasting in their area. His conservative position caused animosity among some Urantia Brotherhood members who believed that things were not moving fast enough and the Urantia Foundation mandates must be loosened.

By the end of 1984, twenty years after Mr. and Mrs. Grimsley began their successful ministry, the association they had built, "The Family of God," would begin a quick decline. It would be a great loss of leadership in the movement and for the outreach of the teachings of love and brotherhood. The reason for this unfortunate demise would become 'a cause célèbre' within the movement. Most of those that had supported him would disavow him. But at my first conference in July of 1973 in Brentwood, California, his popularity was well established.

Chapter 9

As prearranged, my children stayed with their grandparents for the next couple of weeks while I flew back to Hawaii. In the last week of July, their father took them on a cruise to Alaska.

Steve picked me up at the airport, and while we drove to the North Shore, we made plans to turn his house from a surfer's pad into a family home.

Two bamboo sofas sat forlornly in the living room; the cushions had seen better days. I bought new blocks of foam and bright Hawaiian fabric and took them to Marian's to use her sewing machine. While I was sewing, Steve was building bunk beds. Two bedrooms were on the left side of the house, the master headboard was a window to a view of the ocean.

We fell asleep every night by the sound of the waves and woke up in the morning to a scenic sight, enabling Steve to immediately check out surf conditions.

The second bedroom became my eldest daughter's, and into the sunroom went the bunk beds for the other two, plus their slowly accumulating toys. That room was open to the living room, but we usually all retired about the same time; there was no television reception in the area. To the right of the living room was an archway leading into an adequate kitchen with a breakfast nook against a wall where a wood frame window looked out on the view. The house was not fancy but living directly on beautiful Sunset Beach made up for everything. Our rent was an unbelievable $69.00 a month.

Steve had two surfboards: one longboard and one regular. He kept them on the side of the house with his diving spear and lay net. A lay net is a fishnet about a hundred feet long and seven feet deep with buoys on the top and weights at the bottom. The net is arranged fan-like in an inner tube attached to a flat wooden bottom. On moonless nights, Steve and a friend would snorkel out in front of our house with the net in the tube and drop the weighted side along a stretch of sea. During the night, the fish swam into the net and were caught. Early in the morning, the guys dove to the bottom of the net, detached the weights, then pulled the net to shore. He and his fishing partner would divide the catch. My children became adept at eating pan-roasted, small whole fish, avoiding any little bones. Adding a Manoa lettuce salad and rice made for a healthy dinner.

By the end of August, the children were fully enjoying the beach house. Life was rolling along nicely when Judy told Steve she was quitting her office job at the school. And a few days later, his teaching partner broke the news that she was getting married (not to my ex) and leaving Hawaii.

Steve and I began a serious debate that would last a few days. I told him I could take Judy's place. He was not so sure. I had clerical experience since I had worked for an attorney at the CBS Television Studios before moving to Hawaii. Steve was resistant, but I was persistent. I felt it was the right path. Besides, I did not expect to get paid. The only compensation would be free tuition for my three children. Any amount left over would go for the survival and flourishing of the little school. I would worry about pay later when and if the school succeeded. He reluctantly agreed. Yes, it was a risk to our relationship, but if things got stressful, Steve had the ocean, and I had my lunch dates in Honolulu with Jane at the Yacht Club, where she and Jim were members.

The school year began the first week of September with thirty students. One licensed teacher was no problem since we had a strong mother volunteer program. The mothers on welfare, in exchange for lesser tuition, brought their skills to school: painting, pottery, nature projects, and all-around help in reading, math, and supervision.

This was an idyllic time; I treasured every moment of it. I was with my children, living with a man I loved, working at a rewarding job, and living in an inexpensive, undiscovered paradise. Of course, there are always surprising incidents to temporarily burst bubbles.

My husband was filing for divorce. It was overdue. One day when we were speaking on the phone arranging for me to drive the children to Honolulu for the weekend, he said, "It's not fair that another man is raising my kids."

I found that a rather bizarre statement. It was not an easy responsibility for Steve to take on. "You had over eight years to do it during our marriage and ignored them."

He was not happy with that answer. "I am going to fight you for custody."

My blood began to boil. I held the receiver of the phone so tightly I was surprised it did not snap. "If you do, this time I will be gone, and you will never find us!"

Silence.

"Then, I'm lowering your child support."

"That's big of you. You don't pay me much anyway."

"You want to turn this into a fight?"

"Not over money."

And that was the end of the conversation. I was not happy about it, but most importantly, I had won on the custody issue.

A few weeks later, Jim called to give me the date of the court hearing. I asked him if I needed to be there since the legal separation document was to be the divorce settlement, except for the change in child support. "No, you are not the plaintiff." I did not attend.

Chapter 10

By the new year, the school's enrollment was up to forty-five students between the ages of four and ten years old. One of the mothers, Robyn, who had two of her children in the school, started volunteering twice a week even though she paid full tuition. She was a natural teacher. We asked her to work for us as a teacher's aide. She happily accepted. We became good friends. After school, we often went to Del Webb's Kuilima Hotel at Kahuku Point and played tennis on the courts. We were always the only ones there, and nothing was ever said to us. Her husband was a working artist and North Shore surfer.

In February, some local children enrolled, and our numbers increased. We were no longer known as a haole school. With expert advice and some blood, sweat, and tears, Steve and I applied for a government Title IV grant.

The term 'local' does not mean Hawaiian, although some have Hawaiian heritage. There was actually a broad range of heritages. One of our young students had eight ethnicities: Portuguese, Chinese, Japanese, Samoan, Filipino, German, Korean, and Hawaiian. He was a handsome little boy.

We waited and hoped the grant would be awarded on the fact that, in addition to children whose mothers were on welfare, we now had local children, and the school had room for growth. On the 1st of May, our hard work paid off, the grant was a go, and if our enrollment increased, there would be more money forthcoming. Steve and I were ecstatic. We went to the island of Kauai for the weekend to celebrate.

Unfortunately, our celebration was premature.

The Kahuku Community Association owned the church that the school leased. The following Friday, after our Kauai trip, the Filipino man that collected the rent came into the office and wanted to talk to Steve. Steve was teaching. Bennie said he would wait. I went and told Steve. He soon came into the office.

"What's up, Bennie?"

He nervously came right to the point, "The community wants to take the church back. They are going to use it for karate classes and other things."

Steve gave me a worried look, then asked, "Is that just for the summer?"

"No, for good. I'm sorry for you, but it's been voted on. It's done."

He turned around and left, forgetting to take the rent. Steve and I stood there alone in the office. Talk about the wind being taken out of our sails just when we thought we had it at our backs.

After school on Fridays was our designated cleaning day. While Steve, Robyn, and I attended to our chores, we were a silent crew. We knew that finding another facility was going to be difficult.

Reaching home, Steve immediately grabbed his board and paddled out, even though the waves were mediocre. I fixed dinner for the children. When they went next door to play, I took a walk on the beach to talk to God, that spark of the Father—my own personal spirit gift—one like every individual in our world is gifted. I often hold quiet conversations with that indwelling spiritual presence. It usually brings me peace, courage, or at least the ability to press on.

Sunset Beach is named Sunset Beach for a reason. While I walked along the shore, the sun put on a wondrous display as it slid below the horizon. Overhead a canopy of clouds caught its rays. An umbrella of oranges, pinks, fuchsias, and purples covered the entire sky. It was a canvas worthy of celestial artisans. In the azure sea, I could see Steve straddling his board, watching the spectacular show from his favorite spot. He lifted his arm and gave me a sign before lying on his board to catch a wave.

Steve and I searched from Hauula to Haleiwa. And we were not alone; parents got involved. No one wanted to see the school close. We looked at everything available and places that were not, but they were either not large enough or safe enough to house the school. Our hopes were fading. There was one facility in Kahuku, an annex to the Methodist church, but it was already leased. We never gave it a second thought.

One morning when I was in the office alone, a Korean gentleman came to the open door. I invited him in. Perhaps he was a parent inquiring about the school.

"Aloha, I am Reverend Kim, the Pastor of the Methodist church."

I introduced myself and, gesturing to the chair next to my desk, said, "Please have a seat."

The Reverend obliged, "I hear the community association has taken back this building, and you are looking for a place for your school."

"Yes, that's true. We haven't had much luck so far."

"Have you ever seen our facility next to the church?"

"Only from the road."

Just then, Steve came into the office, and introductions were made. But not by me. I was sitting there very still. The Reverend spoke similar words to Steve as he had to me. Then he said to both of us, "Why don't you come by this evening around 7:00 p.m. and let me show you around? My home is behind the church."

Steve and I must have had puzzled looks on our faces. Reverend Kim continued, "The lease on the church's facility is up next month, and I don't like the people or the use they make of the space. We use it on Sundays, of course. I think from what I've heard, your school might work out quite well."

"We'll be there, thank you," answered Steve, grinning from ear to ear.

That evening at seven sharp, Steve and I arrived at Reverend Kim's home. His wife answered the door, and shortly thereafter, we walked with the Pastor over to view the Sunday school building.

The building was designed in an open-air Hawaiian style. It was every bit as spacious as our old church, just a different configuration. The tall roof extended to the back with an overhang sheltering a large patio from rain. Its wide-screen sliding door led to a long table with benches for snacks and lunch. The lengthwise walls were whitewashed cement blocks. The center of the interior was large enough for the congregation to enjoy a social after service and was flanked on both sides by four open classrooms for Sunday school, eight in all. At the entrance of the building flowed a covered walkway that led by a kitchen and then to boy and girl bathrooms with three stalls each. Beyond those was an office with large louvered glass windows on three sides. We could not have designed anything more perfect. We signed the lease that night.

In August, we were preparing the building to open in September. The father of a kindergarten youngster was a mural painter. We provided the paint, and he painted the cement block walls of the classrooms with rainbows, castles, unicorns, and other enchanting scenes.

Word gets around in a close-knit community, and the acceptance by the church further legitimized the school. Our enrollment exploded. With the additional Title IV money, we hired four teachers and bought furniture and many more learning tools. Robyn stayed on.

Our educational philosophy was a combination of Montessori and Piaget. If a four-year-old desired to learn to read and had the cognitive skill, he or she was allowed into the class at that skill level, the same with math. If a child of seven or eight was slower, they would be in the appropriate lower class. At 9:00 a.m., reading was taught at all levels, and math followed after a break. Because the school was so open, there was no embarrassment in whichever class you attended.

During the second month, a local woman came with her three sons. The boys were aged eight, nine, and eleven. They hung around outside the office while the mother talked to Steve and me. Reverend Kim had set up the meeting, and he was in the office also. The woman wanted to enroll her sons. I was more than surprised. Most of our local children were either preschool age or in kindergarten. We were licensed for all primary grades, but other than my own daughter, there were only four others in upper grades. Reverend Kim had encouraged her to enroll the boys. She was not happy with the rate her sons were learning in the local school, and she admitted there were discipline problems at school. The eleven-year-old could barely read. The boys were not happy about being brought to our 'hippie' school. But Steve and I agreed, with the encouragement of the Reverend, that we would give them a try.

By the second week, these boys were a delight. Besides Steve, we had two other male teachers, and the boys quickly adapted, much quicker than we expected. Since the oldest boy's reading ability was so low, he sat at the first-grade reading level during its time. That teacher was a great guy and bonded with the boy, who soon did not care that he was in the beginner reading class. Since his mind was far more developed, he moved right along from class to class and, before the end of the year, was reading at grade level. He was one of our many success stories, along with his brothers.

That winter, the North Shore experienced one of its record sea storms. Every winter, there was stormy weather producing huge waves. The wave action in front of our house was always far from shore, but you could see its majesty, and the sound was louder. The winter conditions would have a deleterious effect on the sandy beaches, with the tide bringing the whitewater onto shore and then taking the sand when it retreated, leaving the coral beds exposed in many places. In the spring, the sand would begin to reappear, and by early summer, the ocean had redeposited it as if it had never left. But the winter of '73 was different.

One night as Steve and I were asleep, there was a knocking on our bedroom door. It was loud enough to wake us up over the sound of the winter waves. Of course, I knew it was one of my children, "Come in."

My son opened the door partially, sticking his head in, "The stairs are gone. The waves took them away."

It was nearing dawn, so his small face was visible, and his eyes were big as saucers. I thought he'd had a nightmare, so I said, "Honey, go back to bed. You're just having a bad dream."

He closed the door. Steve and I drifted back to sleep when there was, once again, a knock. "What is it?"

He opened the door again, "No, it's not a dream. The stairs are gone."

I got up and followed him to the patio door to show him everything was all right. When I opened it, splash! A wave banged up against the wall of the kitchen and then receded. I looked down at the swirling whitewater. The stairs were, indeed, gone.

That morning Steve and I took the children to Robyn's house, who lived up Pupukea Road. We returned to our house only to watch as the waves slowly but surely undermined the foundation of the beach side of the house. It swirled in an odd pattern and worked a deep U-shape under the sunroom where the two children slept, eventually causing the cement floor to cave in and be carried away. It did not undermine the east side under our master bedroom or the west side under the kitchen.

At one point, Steve and I were sitting on the wide kitchen windowsill in awe at the strength of this action. The crashing waves were out at sea, but their tidal action came in to do tremendous damage up and down the coast. An Ironwood Tree just to the right of the house that had been there for many years was uprooted and washed down the beach like a rolling log.

The sun was shining; it was so incongruous. It seemed as if it should have been raining or at least cloudy. As we sat there, a helicopter flew directly over our house. Then another joined it. They hovered fifty or so yards in front of us over the rough sea. After what seemed a search, a basket was lowered with a diver inside. Soon we saw a body being lifted into the basket and raised with the diver into the helicopter. Then both helicopters continued to search the sea. It was a sad sight.

We knew that many tourists had come out to watch the awesome power of the storm. A county vehicle drove up and down Kam Highway with a loud PA system warning people to stay off the beach. The ocean is deceiving; in a set, five or six waves sweep in at a certain distance, then the last one comes in almost twice the distance. Two young, tourist couples had been sitting on the wall by the road at Waimea Beach Park when the end of a set had come in and towed them back out to sea. The men survived; the women, one pregnant, did not.

When the storm was over, the front sunroom wall of the house remained hanging over a very large hole in the floor. When the hole had begun to open, Steve and Robyn's husband managed to rescue the bunk beds. They moved them into my eldest daughter's bedroom, so all three children shared the cramped space for a while.

We put a plywood wall between the sunroom and the living room. During high tide, you could look down under a gap in the barrier and see the water gently lapping the coral under the house. My children were fine with the strange view, but when their friends came inside to see the house whose wall hung over the water, it frightened one little girl.

Once the water receded, Steve decided to fix the house himself. He, along with surf buddies, secured thick telephone poles to the bedrock coral, rebuilt the floor, and added a new front porch, plus stairs, of course. The landlord paid for the materials, and the finished product was better than before. By summer, our beach was back to normal.

My friend Sheila came over to view the finished construction project. She had just gone through a divorce. We were sitting on the beach in front of the house when she told me she had decided to move to the island of Maui with her two children. I found it ironic that when she and I first met, she was seventy-five pounds overweight. She lost all that weight, and now she lost her marriage.

"Why do you want to live on Maui?"

"There is nothing to keep me here. I'm on welfare now, and I can go wherever. Maui is a nicer place than this."

"It's not so bad here."

"For you, not me."

"Where are you going to live?"

"Don't know; I'll camp out first and look for something. I already have the gear. Bobby liked to camp with the family." Her voice turned bitter, "He left it behind. Nice of him, don't you think?"

I remembered something Jane recently told me and said, "My ex has a piece of property on Maui. Some acres bought on spec."

"Do you know where exactly?"

"No."

"Maybe he would let me camp there."

"Not sure it's campable. I guess you could talk to him about it."

She took his phone number. He did let her put up tents. There was a dirt road and a water line to the property, but nothing else except four acres of Eucalyptus Trees. He charged her $50.00 a month for water while she looked for a job and a house. The lot was one of six others that had been subdivided from a large parcel Up Country near Makawao. Sheila had three neighbors who had built nice homes on their acreage. It was a somewhat bohemian lifestyle since there was no electricity or telephone.

Chapter 11

The following school year was a great success. There were six teachers, and enrollment had reached one hundred and twenty students. One afternoon, while I was in Honolulu shopping for supplies, a representative of the Hawaiian Bureau of Child Care Licensing and Title IV program came for a surprise visit. One of our mother volunteers was in the office filing when the woman official asked to see the Administrator. The mother went to fetch Steve, who was teaching a class. Steve introduced himself, and the official asked to see our enrollment documents, the school's books and other papers. He didn't even know where to look. I had been doing all this type of work. When I pulled up, he was pacing the walkway and starting to sweat. With relief, he introduced me, and I proceeded to meet with the official. I was able to answer all her questions and show her the documents she requested. After our meeting, she asked, "Why aren't you the Administrator?"

I did not want to get us into any bureaucratic trouble, although I had no choice but to answer honestly, "Steve has a college degree. I do not."

She nodded and shook my hand, saying, "Thank you for this meeting."

Steve and I could not help but wonder if the school was going to have any governmental problems. Six weeks later, our renewal license came in the mail—the document stated: Administer Carole Jett.

By April, Steve and I were discussing the possibility of opening another school in Haleiwa. Our life had taken on a long-range perspective. So...I brought up the subject of marriage. It had been over two years since that first walk on the beach. I talked; Steve listened. One day he agreed. It was not a particularly romantic moment, but a plan was made. In July, we would have Reverend Kim marry us on the beach in front of our house and rent a party tent for the reception. It was bound to be a North Shore event.

On a Wednesday evening in May, I was at the stove frying homemade tortillas in a cast iron skillet for fish tacos. Steve was sitting at the breakfast nook, the twilight sky in the window behind him. Just as I was pulling a tortilla from the hot oil and chatting about the wedding reception, Steve said, "You know, I'm not sure about all this. I'm not ready to get married."

I stopped and looked at him. He meant what he said.

A heart can shatter into a thousand pieces in one moment. I know because mine did. My mind was a blur. All I remember saying was, "It's a good thing we didn't send out the invitations."

I had no thought of altering our living circumstances. We had a good life. But those pieces of my heart would not quite fit back together.

A couple of weeks later, while driving on the Honolulu freeway, a sharp thought shot through my mind, "It is time to leave Steve."

I was so surprised I pulled over to the right side of the road and stopped in the emergency lane.

Really? Where did that come from?

Continuing my route home, I thought long and hard. The more I relived that odd thought, the more I realized it was the same voice that had blared out, "Go Slack! Go Slack!" the night my husband was strangling me. That voice saved me once. Was it real? Should I heed it? I had been a risk taker in the past, was I going to do so again?

That night I told Steve I was going to leave. I did not know where or how, but the children and I were leaving. I do not think it registered with him at first. How could it? We had an almost perfect life. When the month came to an end, I had not wavered. He began to take it seriously. He said to me one day, "When school is out, why don't we take separate vacations and think about our relationship." I agreed.

My sister had made plans to visit in the summer. She arrived at the time Steve left. The children went to the mainland with their father. After a few days on Oahu, Sis suggested we go to the island of Maui. We booked our flight for the next week. I wrote to Sheila at her P.O. Box that we were coming. She did not have a phone and was still camping on my ex's property. Not thinking she would have time to reply, I wrote her that we would meet her for lunch at the only restaurant in town, the Makawao Steak House.

Makawao is a cowboy-style town on the northwest slope of the dormant volcano Haleakala. It is cattle ranch and agriculture territory. The climate is cooler due to its elevation of 1600 feet. In the late 1800s and early 1900s, Portuguese families immigrated to Maui, settling Up Country and buying small parcels of land. Many found work hiring on as paniolos (cowboys) at the Haleakala Cattle Ranch.

My sister and I stayed in Lahaina at the Pioneer Inn. She rented a car and drove us up to Makawao on the morning we hoped to meet my friend. The Up Country road snaked through fields of sugarcane. Tall stalks of cane, hidden by its razor-sharp, slim leaves of green, swayed in the gentle trade winds. Hawaii is so diverse in its beauty. Higher up, past the fields, the rearview mirror afforded a view of the vertical slope we were traveling. We pulled the car to the side of the road to look down on a panorama of sugarcane fields folding into the surrounding deep blue sea.

Reaching the small town of Makawao, we remarked upon its old west character. There were guys walking around in Levi's and cowboy boots. Happily, Sheila was waiting for us at the restaurant. It was great to see her and her two children again. I introduced them to my sister.

We were enjoying a lunch of local grass-fed steak and fries while country western music played over stereo speakers at a reasonable level when Sheila said, "Sorry, I'll be missing your wedding."

"Unfortunately, you won't be missing it. Steve decided he isn't ready for marriage."

"What! Is he crazy? You're the best thing that ever happened to him."

I smiled at my cheerleader, "Of course, I agree, but it's not going to happen."

"That's too bad. He's a good man anyway."

"He is, but I'm leaving."

"Leaving him?"

"Yes."

"Now you're the crazy one," she said while looking at my sister for agreement. Sis just shrugged her shoulders.

"Are you going to stay with the school?"

"Probably, I'm not sure."

After finishing our lunch, Sheila wanted to show us her campsite, and we were interested to see it. Her car, a white Datsun station wagon, was parked in front of the restaurant. She waited for us to pull out of the small parking lot. We followed her, turning right, off of the main street and ascending up a two-lane asphalt road. It was not the Hawaii I knew. We were in a forest of tall trees, and the smell of damp Eucalyptus leaves permeated through the open car windows. Mailboxes dotted the sides of the road, some in clusters leading down dirt roads. Here and there were grass clearings where homes were visible.

After a couple of miles or so, Sheila turned right onto a dirt road where two cars would have difficulty passing. We followed a short distance, turning right again up a short incline, and parked our rental car behind hers. The deep bark of a large dog startled us. On the left side of the driveway, above a ridge about five feet high, my sister could see looking down upon us a German Shepherd straining at its chain. The Shepherd barked fiercely, but after Shelia petted the animal, letting him loose from the chain tethered around a sturdy tree, he quieted down. Sis and I gave each other inquiring looks and got out of the car cautiously. The dog came up to sniff us. He was a smart animal, obviously sensing that his master approved of us. My sister was less perturbed than I. She and her fiancée owned a big unruly Black Lab.

Sheila had a nice setup if you like camping. There were three 8x10 tents with the front side panels tied back, zipped-up mesh panels for doors, and back windows for ventilation: one for her, one for her two children, and one used as an indoor kitchen and living room. They were positioned on three sides at a safe distance from a dugout fire pit surrounded by stones with a large grill laid on top. She proudly took us to a private area surrounded by greenery where two steel drums were rigged up as a shower. One drum was sawed with an opening where firewood would burn, heating the water in the drum above. She had been there a year and seemed quite comfortable with it all.

Showing us further around the property, we walked down a narrow path through a small forest of Eucalyptus Trees. At the end of the path was a grassy clearing. Just beyond, a wire cattle fence marked the property line. On the other side of the fence was pastureland, where a chestnut horse grazed.

While my sister chatted with my friend, I looked beyond the pasture and could see down the slope of the mountainside all the way to the distant ocean. From the lush green pasture to the dark blue sea, the view was magnificent. Gazing at that scene of serene beauty, it dawned on me that I was looking at the new hand I was being dealt. God holds all the cards if you give Him the deck.

MAP OF MAUI

Chapter 12

Steve's and my separate vacations were over. We had come to different conclusions regarding our relationship. I was moving on; he was ready to marry. It was bittersweet but too late. My ex-husband, who was still on the mainland with the children, and I had already discussed my proposal. He owned the land that I would build a house on for the children. It would be something they would always have, a port in the storm of life. When the house was built, he agreed to put the property in all three children's names.

Before leaving Maui, Sheila and I had discussed my setting up camp in an small clearing halfway down the path between the trees. We would be far enough apart for privacy yet near enough as close neighbors. I was not exactly sure of the date I would be back, but I wanted to have everything set up before the children returned from the mainland. She told me to write with my flight information, and she would pick me up at the airport. It was all set.

At school, I trained one of the teachers who had decided that teaching was not for her. She jumped at the chance to be the Administrator. I would leave the North Shore with enough money to build a small house and live prudently while building it. I planned to add on in the future.

On a Friday evening, Steve drove me to the airport in the new VW van school bus. After unloading my baggage, he looked at me sadly, "You know, I had promised myself never to get involved with one of the mothers at school...." That stopped me up short. I gave him a weak smile. (What could I say?) He got back in the van and drove off.

I arrived on Maui on the last flight. When I walked into the small, open-air Kahului airport, Sheila was not there to greet me. She was late, I thought. As the baggage carousel revolved, my things arrived: three suitcases and two cardboard boxes. Once again, I was down to the bare minimum.

Carrying each piece separately to the curb, which was only a few feet away, I waited and looked through the night for the white Datsun wagon. Air travelers were met and left. The airport cleared out. I was the only traveler remaining. It had been over thirty minutes, and the airport was shutting down. Now what? Luckily, there was one taxi still parked down the curb, and I hailed it. A slightly built local woman drove up and spoke to me in Hawaiian Pidgin through the open passenger window, "You need ride?"

"Yes, I am going Up Country to Makawao."

She got out of the car and opened the back of her Ford station wagon. We began loading it together. She said, "I see you stand long time. You ride no show?"

"No, she didn't, and I am not exactly sure where I am going."

She looked at me quizzically, "You say Makawao?"

I explained to her that my destination was Makawao, only higher up on the road where the Eucalyptus Trees grew. I had not driven the day my sister and I visited and had not paid close attention. The woman said, "No problem."

When we arrived in Makawao, the small town was shut down. There were only a few streetlights. We learned there were two roads up from town. First, we turned right and drove by a mountain road, Olinda Road. There were some trees, and it looked familiar, but not *that* familiar. So we turned around and drove by the other mountain road, Piiholo Road. It was not until I recognized a pineapple field to the right of Piiholo Road that I thought, maybe. "I think it's this one."

The taxi driver was not familiar with Makawao either. We were both driving blind. Fortunately, there was a half-moon, so we had some light. She turned up the road, and we were hopefully headed in the right direction. We drove through the Eucalyptus forest and by some roadside mailboxes where dirt roads turned off. I directed her to turn right on one until we quickly came to a dead end, not the dead end I was looking for. She backed out, and we went further up when I spotted another group of mailboxes and a dirt road. "I think it's that one."

At that point, I could not tell who was more anxious, her or me, as a cloud covered the half-moon. She drove on down the dark, bumpy road slowly, her big station wagon swaying with each rut. Then on the right, I saw an inclined driveway and what could be the tail end of a white car. Tentatively, I said, "I think this is it."

"Okay, lady," she nervously answered.

Just as we pulled up, the German Shepherd started barking loudly. The local woman cowered and was putting the taxi in reverse when I excitedly said, "This is it!"

93

We sat in the car listening to the distinct bark of the Shepherd before Sheila appeared with a flashlight. I shouted out the window, "Sheila, it's me."

She shined the light in my face. I breathed a sigh of relief, and so did the human angel sitting in the driver's seat. She had to be the nicest taxi driver in all of Maui to have stuck with me and not turned around and dropped me at a hotel in the city of Kahului.

Sheila and I unpacked my things while the driver remained behind the wheel. The dog, chained to the tree, continued to bark. I paid the fare and gave the woman as big a tip as I could afford.

Once inside my friend's tent, while laying out my sleeping bag, Sheila told me she had not received my letter. Her two children never stirred throughout the whole ordeal and woke up in the morning to find their 'kama'aina' auntie there.

The next morning, we all drove down to Kahului, and I bought two large tents plus camping equipment for my family. Together we assembled the tents and had some good laughs. Tent poles can be a mystery to put together. We also assembled bunk-bed cots for my two youngest and a cot for my eldest. My tent housed a waterbed (it was easiest for Sheila and me to transport and assemble), two metal trunks for clothes, two small tables, one for a camp stove and the other for a fluted kerosene lamp by my bed, plus a large ice chest. Later, I acquired a wooden picnic table with attached benches.

When I met my children at the Maui airport, they were ready for their next adventure and piled into the station wagon, happy for us to be together again. As I walked them along the path through the trees to our campsite, my eleven-year-old daughter smiled, "The four Musketeers again, eh Mom?"

I was surprised she remembered my words from that night at the Ala Moana Hotel before taking off to Tahiti.

They were enrolled at the Makawao Elementary School and, together with Sheila's daughter, walked down our dirt road to Piiholo Road, where the school bus picked them up. It wasn't all that much fun when it rained, but they were little troopers. My four-year-old daughter was not yet ready for school. Sheila's young son and my daughter became great playmates. They raced Big Wheels up and down the path.

One Saturday late morning, Sheila came down to our campsite and asked if we wanted to go to a basketball game. Her boyfriend was playing a pick-up game at the local high school gym. So we got ourselves ready, and off we drove, all seven of us in the Datsun, boys in the way back.

The game had started before we arrived. The bleachers were sparsely filled with friends of the players. We climbed a few rows and sat down. Everyone was about the same age as us, with children running around. Sheila started to tell me who was who when I noticed a muscular guy with longish blonde hair. He was wearing a red T-shirt with the logo of a lumberyard on his chest and walking toward us. Sheila said, "Looks like Mike is coming over."

"Hi, Sheila."

"Mike. Who let you out of your cage?"

He ignored her and said to me with a smile, "Hi, I'm Mike."

My friend withdrew her claws for the moment and introduced me as he sat down on the bleacher below us. She told him that I had moved to Maui to build a house on the property. He knew the place since he had done some brickwork on a neighbor's house two parcels over from ours. I was learning that Up Country was a community like the North Shore; most everyone knew most everyone.

"Have you got anyone in mind…for the house, I mean?"

"She's barely got on the island," scoffed Sheila.

Cheering rang out as a team scored points. Then Mike said to me, "I built my house in Haiku."

Sheila added, "You mean the one your ex is living in."

Mike's face reddened, "Yeah, that one."

Trying to ignore Sheila once again, he turned to me, "You have a great piece of property there. If you'd like, I could come up and maybe give you some ideas. I'm sure I could find the time."

"You mean you're in-between jobs," taunted Sheila.

It seemed she was being awfully rude to this guy, but I said, "Sure, I can use all the advice I can get."

The next afternoon Mike came up to the property. I walked him down the path to where I wanted to build. Gazing at the view, he whistled, "It is a perfect spot."

Telling him my budget, I asked, "What could I build for that money?"

He took some moments thinking, then said, "You could build an A-frame. Probably with a dormer."

"What's a dormer?"

96

Gesturing with his arms like a half A, "It's a windowed extension on the roof of an A-frame. It adds space and height to the loft."

"I was considering an A-frame. The dormer idea sounds even better."

"Can I see the rest of the property?"

"Of course."

I gave him a tour of the entire property, walking through the trees and back to his truck parked behind Sheila's Datsun. He seemed like a knowledgeable guy. With my budget, Frank Lloyd Wright would not be taking the job. I asked him, "What do you think? Could I hire you?"

"Well, I'm finishing up a job right now. I guess I could help you get started in a couple of weeks. I'll draw up some plans. See what you think."

"Sounds great. Can we meet maybe sometime next week?"

Opening up the door to his truck, he hesitated a moment, then said, "Have you been to Mama's Fish House in Paia? A friend of mine owns it."

"No, I haven't been much of anywhere yet."

"Okay then. How about dinner on Friday?"

I smiled. He was not bad looking, and despite Sheila's obvious disapproval of him, I said, "Sure."

"I'll be up at seven."

As he was backing out of the driveway, Sheila came up, "So he hit on you already."

"What is your problem with him? Do you have some kind of history I should know about?"

She thought a minute, "I know his ex-wife."

"And."

"We got into it once. I don't like her."

"That's it?"

"Pretty much."

I thought about our friendship back on the North Shore and remembered she could hold grudges and sometimes act a little strange. But it never affected me.

Friday evening Mike and I discovered we had a lot in common. Both of us had been raised Catholic, and before I was introduced to *The Urantia Book*, I had practiced meditation through Yoganada's Self-Realization Fellowship. Mike had studied and still practiced that form of meditation. I talked to him about the teachings in the Urantia Papers, and he was interested.

Later that night, he parked the truck and walked me back to the tent. Sheila had made sure the children were in bed fast asleep. He unzipped my tent, and we went in, lighting the glass-fluted kerosene lamp. We sat on the bed, and I showed him the book. He liked what he saw. Within a few weeks, I found myself in another relationship.

Mike had many friends. Some were party people, and others were in construction; some were both. On the weekends, we were always going somewhere, and the children were always welcome.

Building the house had become kind of a community project. Often, Mike would trade work with fellow friends to help out.

It was really a wonderful thing he did for me. Otherwise, the money I had naively planned for the house would not have covered the actual cost.

After the foundation of the house was built, he had my son and daughter helping us too. They hammered nails with their limited skill set. We could truly say that the house was a family project.

It was the end of spring when we were able to move in. Once the propane gas was hooked up and we had a stove, my eldest daughter came up and hugged me; she was beside herself with joy, "Mom, Mom, we can bake chocolate chip cookies!"

During the seven-month process, Sheila and I spent a lot of time together during the week. I never bought a car, so we went to the beach with the little ones, shopped, went to the laundromat, and did general errands. On some evenings, we sat around her campfire while the kids played. She was a good mother. Her boyfriend had moved in shortly after work on my house began. He was a slightly built, quiet, local guy.

One afternoon, when the house was nearly finished and Mike was living with me, Sheila and I had what seemed to me an odd conversation. We were in her tent talking and waiting for the children to walk down the road from the school bus stop when she said, "Why do all the good things happen to you?"

I was not sure what she was getting at. I did not view my life as particularly easy. But everything good that happened to me, I naturally attributed to one being. So, without hesitation, I answered, "I don't know, but I have faith. Faith in my Father, God."

"Oh God, BS!" she declared, "My father is my god."

I knew that her father had bought her car and sent her checks from time to time. I also knew that he offered her greater help if she would find work and get off welfare. Nonetheless, I thought he could help her more. Living a tented existence was arduous, especially through the rainy season, and she had gone through two. Then she said, "Besides, on my thirtieth birthday, I'll receive my inheritance. And you know that inheritance is a million dollars."

No…I did not know that her inheritance was a million dollars. I did know that her mother had died when she was nine years old, and she claimed her mother was an heir to a prominent Canadian company that had set up a trust fund for her. She had never mentioned a dollar figure. It would turn out that the inheritance story was only in her mind, a mind that had been receiving pharmaceutical diet pills legally for three years. Many friends knew the inheritance story, no one but the doctors that prescribed the medication both on Oahu and on Maui knew the amphetamine story.

Chapter 13

By the beginning of summer, the windows were in, and the house was mostly completed. It was wonderful for the family to finally be able to move in and out of the tents. There was still no electricity or telephone service to any of the parcels. Although, the county had recently begun to put up electricity poles at the bottom of Piiholo Road.

In July, my parents came to Maui, staying at a hotel in Kahului. They rented a car and came Up Country, finding us easily thanks to the map in my father's head. They were expected, and the children were waiting for them at the top of our new grated driveway on the opposite side of where Shelia parked. The children could not wait to show off the house that they helped build and the garden of vegetables we were tending.

My parents drove down to the A-frame with all three youngsters in the back seat. When they were out of the car and looked at the house, I could see disappointment in their eyes. This was a bit rustic from their L.A. point of view. I was not surprised, and I gave them a lot of credit because they smiled and said it was very nice. Upon entering, my mother made a point to appreciate the view out of the sliding glass picture window in the living room.

After a short visit, my father suggested they take us to lunch in Kahului. Once there, he insisted that we stay at the hotel in a room they paid for. It was fun for the children, they got to watch Willy

Wonka and the Chocolate Factory on television, and I enjoyed visiting with my parents. My mother, a consummate shopper, took us to the Kahului Mall because we had not packed anything. The department store Liberty House became an instant favorite of hers. We enjoyed my parents' short stay, and while dropping us back at the A-frame, my father pressed five $100 dollar bills in my hand and gave me a hug.

In August, my ex-husband came over to see the children. He arrived in the late evening in a rental Cadillac. It was so out of place in the setting, but it was also so him. He met Mike, and they got along fine. When the children went to sleep, we talked about the future. He was moving back to the mainland to expand his business and wanted to know if I would be willing to send the children to him for periods of time in the summer. I was.

There was another matter I discussed with him. Our daughter had completed the sixth grade, and I did not want to send her to the local junior high. There was a private school on Olinda Road (the other tree-lined road in Makawao) for grades seven through twelve. It was a day school and a boarding school. She had already taken the entrance exam and was eligible to enroll. He agreed to pay her tuition. With that settled, the next morning, he took the children for a week to stay at a condo in Kaanapali, a ritzy area north of Lahaina.

Come September, all the children were in school, the youngest now in kindergarten. I had some free time. An older hippie entrepreneur had started a tie-dye factory, and a friend of mine was sewing for him. She got me a job. I worked three days a week in a gaggle of girlfriends and made extra money. On the weekends,

Mike and I and the children would usually be at the beach with friends or at a party. One friend, a trust-fund guy, had a large house on twenty grassy acres in Haiku with a great indoor-outdoor stereo system, a Ping-Pong table, the first video game Pong, and two Honda dirt bikes. Often, we would stop by; there was always something going on.

By December, Sheila was acting more strangely. She had turned thirty and was waiting for her inheritance. She began going to the bank once a week, dragging her hapless boyfriend along and asking the manager if there had been a money transfer from her father. There had not. Once, she accused the manager of holding out on her.

On New Year's Day, Mike, the children, and I were returning from the beach. We turned into our driveway to the house. Driving just a short distance, parallel to Sheila's campsite, Mike braked abruptly; there was something stuck in the middle of the road. He got out of the truck and pulled a long metal carpenter's file from the ground. He brought it to the truck to show me, "This is the file Sheila lent me. I thought it was down at the house."

"Then what is it doing in the middle of the road?"

Mike opened my door, "Let's go ask her."

We left the truck where it was and walked through the trees. Sheila was chopping wood; axe raised high. She saw us, and WHACK, she split a log. Her boyfriend was standing around. Mike said to her, "Do you know what this was doing in the middle of the road?"

"I put it there. Mike, when you borrow something, you should return it."

Her answer gave me a creepy feeling. She had to have been at the house going through his tools. But things were about to get a whole lot creepier.

"Actually, I put it there so you guys would stop, and I could tell you what I did today."

"Okay, Sheila," Mike crossed his arms, goading her, "What did you do today?"

"I bashed in the glass doors to the medical building and the welfare office in Kahului."

"You did what?"

She repeated her astonishing claim and added, "With a lead pipe."

Mike looked at her boyfriend and asked him, "Is she kidding?"

The guy shook his head, "No, I was in the car and saw it."

What could we say in response to this frightening piece of news? After a few stunned moments, we just turned around and left. Discussing if we should notify the police, Mike decided against it. There was no proof. I was not too sure.

The next weekend she pulled the same stunt; it was the glass doors of her bank. Mike and I had no idea this had happened.

On Tuesday, I decided to go talk to her and tell her she had to move. She could call her father or something, but she had to go. When I got to the top of the property, her car was parked in the usual spot, but all was eerily quiet. I called out her name. No answer. I called again. Her boyfriend came out of a tent.

"Where is Sheila?"

"The police took her away yesterday."

He told me what had happened on Sunday, and someone had taken down her license. It did not take long to find out who and where she was.

"Where are the kids?"

"The cops took them too. Social Services has them."

"What about school? My kids must have come to walk with them to the bus stop."

"Yeah, I said they had already left."

Events moved quickly. She was in jail, and Social Services contacted the children's father on Oahu. He came and got them.

I felt safer, and I was not alone. How word travels quickly in a community is a mystery, but it does. The next day Mike and I were shopping in the local convenience store when one of our neighbors came up to us and said, "You must be happy Shelia is off your property. I had a disturbing incident with her myself recently."

Three days later, Mike and I were at the home of married friends. It was noon. Their phone rang.

Tom answered. After a few moments, I heard him say, "Are you sure?"

He hung up, turning to me, "James just saw Sheila hitching up Piiholo Road."

"No way. She doesn't have bail money, and nobody is going to let her out."

"He said he's pretty sure it was her."

I went to the phone and called the police. It had to be a mistake. It was not. The sergeant at the desk told me that after she was in jail the first night, they knew she was not mentally right. They transferred her to the psych ward at the hospital. The doctor evaluated and agreed.

Now I was livid. "Then why was she released?"

"We cannot hold anyone judged mentally ill for longer than forty-eight hours unless they sign a consent to commit themselves."

I could not believe what I was hearing, "What about her crimes?"

"Doesn't matter."

"That's crazy!"

"Tell that to the ACLU," he groused.

Mike and I raced home. We parked the truck behind the station wagon. As we entered, all was quiet. I was not. The boyfriend was alone, sitting on a milk crate, tinkering with something.

I said to him, "Shelia is out of jail. You have to go."

At that moment, the tent flap was pulled open, and there she stood, looking at me with a defiant smirk on her lips. A cold chill went through my body. I quickly settled down and calmly said, "You need to go back to the hospital. You are not well."

"I'm fine. The doctors released me."

"Well, then you need to go to your car and get off this property now."

"You can't do that. I pay rent."

"I'll have my ex-husband send you the $50. Please leave."

The next thing I knew, she had me by my long hair and wrestled me to the ground. This made me angry, and I fought back.

Fortunately, Mike pulled her off of me. I would have lost that battle, for sure. He pushed her to her boyfriend, who held her.

Getting up, I said, "I am going for the police."

We left. When we got near the bottom of Piiholo, a cop car was driving up. Mike flagged it, and the cop pulled over, parking in the wrong direction behind us. We got out of the truck, and I told him what had happened. He smiled at me like I was some silly woman who had gotten into a catfight. At that moment, the white Datsun came careening down the road, passed us by, and was gone.

"That was her!"

"Then your problem is solved."

He did not understand. I gave up. We returned to the property. The boyfriend was still there.

Mike told me to go down to the house. He put the German Shepherd in the cab of the truck while he and the boyfriend pulled down the tents, throwing everything into the back. Mike took the stuff, the boyfriend, and the dog away.

I hardly slept for a week. She was loose. We drove the children to school and picked them up. Mike did not feel the threat like I did, and maybe he was right. All her things were gone; he did not believe she would return. Yet who knew?

At the end of the week, Sheila went berserk again. Her boyfriend was staying with his brother and wife; they had a three-year-old son. Friday night, she tried in vain to get the guy to come back to her. He refused and sent her away.

Early the next morning, while all slept except the little boy who was watching cartoons, Sheila took her lead pipe and began bashing

107

in all the glass jalousie windows that ran the entire length of the living room wall. Glass flew everywhere. Miraculously the little boy fled the room and was not physically injured. The brothers subdued her. The police came. Before she was handcuffed, somehow, she was able to get into her backpack, and taking out a wad of money, she threw the bills at the police. "Here, take this instead of me." They took her.

This time she was not released. She was committed to the Kaneohe Mental Hospital on Oahu. I was told her father and stepmother had come from the mainland and, along with a committee of psychiatrists, authorized her commitment.

Chapter 14

The rains came and washed away the vestiges of Sheila's campsite. Spring brought wildflowers in the pasture beyond the living room window. One afternoon, I was mending my son's jeans when I saw two girls riding horses bareback in the field, their long blonde hair flying in the wind. One of them caught my eye in particular; it was my eldest daughter. I watched as she rode the horse with only a pad, no saddle, no stirrups. Soon they were out of sight. I knew she was at her closest friend's home on Olinda Road; I had no idea she could ride a horse.

My son's best friend also lived on Olinda Road. I would pack his lunch so he could hike down a gully not far from the house. His friend would do the same from his home. They would meet in the middle and explore for most of the day. My youngest had lost her favorite playmate but managed to keep herself busy driving her Big Wheel and generally pestering me.

In the summer, the children's father arranged for them to visit him on the mainland. I flew with them to Oahu. The Hawaiian Airlines terminal was not in the main terminal, so I saw to it that they had caught the connecting United Airlines flight. Jane picked me up afterward. I stayed with her and Jim for a few days. Then I visited Robyn and her family on the North Shore before returning to Maui. She had gone back to school to get a teaching credential and was no longer at Steve's school but heard he was doing fine. I left it at that. Marian and her children had moved to the Big Island, the island of Hawaii.

Arriving back on Maui, Mike picked me up at the airport and drove us home. We turned into the driveway, and there before our eyes was Sheila's large metal file stuck in the middle of the road. Mike braked; I sucked in my breath. It could NOT be. Mike pulled the stake out of the road. We sped to the house. The door was unlocked, which was not unusual. We tentatively went inside; all was normal. Everything seemed undisturbed. I climbed the ladder to the loft, still normal until I spotted a silver eagle ring with a turquoise stone. Sheila had given me the ring two years ago for my birthday. It had been in a small jewelry box at the bottom of my metal trunk. Now, it was on my nightstand next to where I laid my head. A chill ran down my spine.

By this time, we had a phone. I called the police. They told me Sheila had been released from the institute. Upon her release, she had been given a one-way ticket back to Maui. I snapped at the cop, "Back to the scene of her crimes, how nice! Couldn't you have at least contacted those of us involved with her?"

"Sorry, that's not procedure."

I was seriously freaked out.

It was Saturday afternoon. Mike searched the grounds and, not finding her, said to me, "Let's get out of here. People have to know."

The trust-fund guy was throwing a party as usual. Our friends would be there. When we arrived and announced that Sheila was back, they were as shocked as we were. But hey, what the hell, it would be all right. She was better now, or the doctors wouldn't have let her go.

"You think?" I asked disbelieving.

"Sure. She was just trying to get your attention."

Before I knew it, someone put a glass of white wine in my hand. I raised it to my lips, my hand visibly shaking. I drank that cold wine down; then, another was in my hand. In a short while, the wine had managed to mask my anxiety, and I was playing Ping-Pong while listening to Fleetwood Mac on the outside speakers singing, "I'm over my head...."

Our party host's two dirt bikes were buzzing around with guys riding through the flat pastured acres. It looked like fun. I had ridden them a couple of times and thought I knew what I was doing. I said to Mike, my turn next. He looked warily at me and my clothing. I had not changed from my traveling clothes: an Indian print cotton sundress and sandals with a one-inch heel. One of the guys stopped a bike, got off, and gestured to me. Now it was my turn.

I straddled the bike, revved the engine, put it in gear, and was off. It was a lovely, warm, sunny Hawaiian day, perfect for a ride. I was circling the area still in sight of the house. Up ahead in the distance, I saw my host's three white German Shepherds galloping through the lovely green pasture. "Hmmm...why are they out?" The dogs were always locked up when the dirt bikes were in use. (How they got loose, no one ever knew.) Unfortunately, the animals turned in my direction and came charging toward me in pack formation. They were far enough ahead for me to reason, "No way are they going to hit me." But they kept coming. As they came closer, my thoughts were, "One for the Father, one for the Son, and one for the Infinite Spirit. Okay, okay, that won't help; these dogs are charging right at you. Will they go left, or will they go right? Surely they will not head straight at me and the bike." (I always thought German Shepherds were smart, Sheila's was. These were not!)

I was in the process of downshifting to slow my speed and decided to go straight. And 'that's all she wrote.' The white-coated beasts ran straight into me. I hit all three of them. My stubby-heeled sandal was caught while shifting gears. The bike took my left leg with it, flying to the right, and the rest of my body went to the left. Inside my head, I heard an unmistakable crack. And then I was face planted in the grass while the bike lay a few feet away. The dogs whimpered off; they were not hurt. I was. I could not get up. So I did what anyone with a broken leg would do; I laid still and felt like retching.

The party was going on in full swing; my ride was entertainment for some. By that, I mean Mike and others had watched me take the bike for a spin. When I crashed and fell off on the soft grass, they waited for me to get up. After what seemed like interminable minutes, Mike figured something must be wrong and ran the distance to me.

"Are you all right?"

"No, I think my leg is broken."

"But you weren't going very fast."

"It's broken. I heard it inside my body. Please take me to the hospital."

Others soon joined Mike. They stayed with me while Mike went for the truck. He backed it up and put the tailgate down. With the help of a friend, they lifted me. They did not have my left leg secure, and it dipped where the break was. Mike was horrified, "You're right. It is broken."

The pain had now set in with a vengeance.

They laid me in the back of the truck; there was no lining, just metal. At least someone had thrown down a blanket. The Kahului Hospital was a thirty-minute ride. I felt every bump, every pebble we drove over. It hurt a lot.

It was dusk when we reached the hospital. Emergency personnel put my leg in a blow-up splint before removing me from the truck. I was hyperventilating from the pain. The personnel were two ambulance drivers, and they were so calming for my tortured mind. I was taken to X-ray and left lying on the hard table, but I had the splint, so the pain had considerably subsided. Just around the corner of the room, I could hear my X-rays flopping around, and I guessed they were being hung in one of those light viewers. I heard the nurse greet a doctor. Then I distinctly heard him say, "This is a mess. I can't operate tonight; I've been in surgery all day. Pack her in ice."

When he came around to talk to me, he looked weary. He introduced himself as an Orthopedic Surgeon and told me the tibia was spiral fractured and would probably need a screw inserted to heal. Also, the knee could be damaged; he wouldn't know for sure until he operated, which would be first thing in the morning. He was a nice man, and his manner gave me *some* confidence that everything would be all right.

Nurses came, lifted me onto a gurney, and transferred me to a room. The ambulance drivers returned for their splint. I did not want to give it up! But they gently convinced me:

1. It belonged to the ambulance, and they had to take it;

2. My leg would be packed in ice and be okay.

I relented just as the nurse came in with pain medication and ice. There was nothing more Mike could do, so he went home.

By 7:00 a.m. I was in surgery. During the operation, the doctor discovered that cartilage, lots of cartilage, in my knee had shattered and had to be removed, and I now had a screw holding my spiral-fractured tibia together. I woke up in a hospital room with a cast up to my hip and Mike looking at me woefully.

I smiled at him, "It's okay. Just a material world mishap."

He shook his head, "Darlin', the anesthesia hasn't worn off."

He was so right.

Mike and friends were good about visiting, but my days and nights were spent staring at the wall clock, making sure that every four hours, the nurses were in with the pain medication.

After a week in the hospital, the doctor came to do his rounds. I told him I wanted to go home. He shook his head no. I started to cry. I had nothing against the place or the nursing staff. I just could not take another day there. The doctor said he was sorry, but I should really stay a few more days. I cried harder. Mike walked in at that moment. The doctor explained to Mike he wanted me to stay, but, "If I let her go, can you take care of her."

Mike looked at my tear-stained face, "Sure I can."

"All right. I'll discharge you."

I was still weeping and said, "Thank you." I meant it from the bottom of my heart.

He wrote out a prescription for heavy pain medication.

Finally at home, I crutched up the few stairs to the back door and on into the house with the lovely view out the glass window. There was no way I was going up a ladder to the loft. Our sofa was a long, well-cushioned, comfortable piece of furniture that became my bed. Mike was working, contracting another job. So he stocked a small ice chest with drinks and food. I only needed to get up to use the bathroom. He bought me books. My sister came to help for a few days and brought me more books. Too many times, I fell into a drugged sleep and dreamed that Sheila was trying to get into the house through the sliding glass window, or worse, she was swinging a lead pipe, shattering it. I woke up alone and in a cold sweat.

In mid-August, my children returned. The cast was off my leg, and I had learned to navigate on crutches. But I did not feel safe in my own home. Not knowing where or what Sheila was up to, my chief concern was not my window. The house was constructed of wood. Like most homes in the area, it was built slightly raised from the ground, and it would be easy to start a fire underneath. I could not get the image of that silver ring on my nightstand out of my head. I wanted to move away from Makawao, maybe back to Oahu. My eldest daughter loved her school. Since it was also a boarding school, the prospect of boarding was fine with her. Mike and I talked it over. He had a friend who was doing some work on a newly built condominium complex in Kihei.

Kihei, a town on the south shore of Maui, was far enough away in distance, topography, and atmosphere from Up Country for me to feel safer. It was a beach community on the coast, and the driest part of the island, sagebrush and Kiawe thorn trees were at home there.

Investors bought individual condominiums to rent out in the new complex, and Mike thought we could find a reasonable lease. A friend of ours was interested in renting my house. He was a heavy equipment operator and did not have the same concerns as I.

By the beginning of the school year, my family was living in a reasonably priced, fully furnished condo on the second floor. The complex consisted of eight two-story buildings, each with eight units having separate outside entrances. Most of the condos were occupied. I felt safety in numbers. It was located along the main road of Kihei, across from a narrow sandy beach. Where many times after dinner, I would walk across the street, sit down on the sand, and watch the sunset.

From our balcony, we had a view of the sea where Humpback whales came to spawn. My son and youngest daughter liked their new school. In Makawao, they had been outnumbered by locals, which sometimes caused problems for haoles. My oldest came home from boarding school on weekends. There were many children of all ages living at the condo, plus a swimming pool and jacuzzi, which was great for the children and my recovering injury.

As soon as I was free of crutches, I found work as the administrator of a preschool. Mike bought me a car, a year-old, four-door Toyota that had been part of a Dollar rental fleet. Things were looking up and calming down.

Chapter 15

New Year's Eve parties to usher in 1978 at the Kihei condominium complex were hosted by many condo residents; doors were thrown open to revelers. Our next-door neighbor, whose front door mirrored mine, welcomed my family. For the first time, I heard the music of a talented piano-playing singer, Billy Joel. Little did I know that I was to enter the world of this musician and many others in the music industry.

Mike went Up Country for a party. He did not come back for three days. On New Year's Day, I was expecting his return; by evening, I hoped to receive a phone call. Yet the next day came, and I heard nothing from him. I worried that something might have happened to him, but I had to admit if that was true, someone would have called me. My heart was heavy. Once the children were asleep, I sat on our balcony long into the night, gazing at the stars of our Father's universe, forcing myself to face the truth. If our relationship was still strong, we would have been together for the New Year celebration.

Ever since we moved to Kihei, Mike's feelings had begun to wane. His friends and business dealings were centered Up Country and the Kahului area. My children and I had settled comfortably into Kihei. Up Country no longer had any draw for me, except to pick up my daughter from school on weekends, so I had to take responsibility for the change even though my feelings for him had not changed.

Once Mike did return, he told me he had met someone else a month ago. He had not wanted to hurt me until he was sure of how he felt. I was angry, "You could have told me. Why in the last three days didn't you even call me? Don't you understand not knowing is far worse!"

He had no answer. But after all he had done for me and my family, I could not stay angry. By the end of January, Mike officially moved out. We had experienced a lot together, and he had moved on; that was reality. I had not, but…we made it an amicable breakup. What was the point to do otherwise?

In April, a good friend of mine from my days working as a secretary at CBS came to visit. Amy had been to Oahu when I lived in Lanikai, and whenever I visited the mainland, we would see each other. She was no longer a secretary but had entered into the field of television production.

Friends of hers were taping the "Kenny Rogers Special," and she thought it would be fun for us to go. The production location was on a sandy cove in Hana. She had no idea that Hana was as far as one could go on the island of Maui; the island road literally ended just beyond the town. It was a two and a half-hour drive, mostly on a two-way twisty road over fifty-four small bridges, just like the song "54 Bridges to Hana Town." The bridges were across the pathways of slim waterfalls trickling down black lava rock running underneath to the sea. It was a scenic drive through a tropical landscape.

I made arrangements for my children, and Amy and I left around noon. We drove through the center of the island, reaching the north shore. We had lunch at Mama's Fish House in Paia. Then, once on the Hana Highway, we stopped at Hookipa Beach Park to watch experienced surfers navigate reefs and drop into perfectly curling waves in the deep waters.

We reached the cove in Hana when the sun was low on the horizon. Parking the car and descending to the beach, I could see the setup of a beach luau surrounded by stage lights, the sound of generators hummed in the background. A volleyball net was strung, and my friend and I ducked under it to walk toward the production area. A very tall, lanky guy began walking toward us and called out, "Amy, you made it."

"I told you I'd be here. It was a long drive."

Then the guy said, "Is this your friend who lives here?"

"Oh, sorry." She turned to me, "This is Doug. He's the editor of the show."

Doug led us over to the set, then left to help the grips (lighting and rigging technicians). There were many cables spread over the sand for lights, cameras, and microphones.

When the sun was down and dark descended, the taping of the show began. My friend and I joined the paid extras sitting with the featured stars around a campfire. Kenny Rogers hosted the show, playing guitar, singing, and joking with the comedian Don Knotts.

It was fun, but I had been around productions before and knew it always took a lot longer than the actual show that would air on television. After the taping was over, Doug came up to me and started a conversation. "So, you are lucky enough to live here on the island."

I wanted to say that I was not sure about being lucky, but instead, I nodded in agreement, "Yeah, I've lived here for a while. I honestly never get tired of its beauty."

"You know, I didn't have to come here with the show. An editor doesn't have anything to do with the taping. I just couldn't resist the opportunity. Hawaii has always been a dream for me."

"It's a dream for a lot of people, I guess."

"Yeah, well, I've surfed a lot of waves in California but never here."

Without enthusiasm, I thought, "Hmmm, a surfer." But he was a pleasant fellow and awfully lean and tall. He wore round wire-rimmed glasses. Then he said, "Do you want to take a walk on the beach? There isn't much for me to do here except wait until the grips clear everything so I can catch a ride back to the hotel."

Looking at him closer, I said, "You do look a lot like John Lennon."

"People tell me that. I can sing like him too."

"You can?"

He could. He sang the chorus of "Imagine." If I had closed my eyes, I would have thought John Lennon was standing by my side.

We walked and talked for almost an hour. Finally, my girlfriend saw us coming back to the nearly empty area. She had been having drinks with the director and others in the production trailer in the parking lot. By now, it was after 11:00 p.m.

On the drive back to Kihei, I asked her about Doug. She told me he was a nice guy and easy to work with. He was also a musician. Then she reclined the seat back in my car and fell asleep.

The long drive gave me a lot of time to think about that 6'4" likable fellow. Yet I never thought I would see him again.

The next day, I dropped Amy at the airport. She was catching the same flight as the production crew traveling back to the mainland. When I returned home, my phone rang. It was Doug. He was at the airport with everyone else and had asked my friend for my number. He said to me, "If you'll have dinner with me tonight, I'll miss the flight and stay over until tomorrow."

"Well, sure, but shouldn't you be leaving with the others?"

"I'd rather see you. What do you say?"

"Okay."

"I'll call you from the Intercontinental Hotel, and we'll set up a time."

"Fine, it's a nice place. Talk to you then."

When I hung up, I wondered how he knew that the Intercontinental was the closest hotel to my condo. I learned two characteristics of Doug's; he was spontaneous and resourceful.

That night at dinner, I learned two other things. He had a son two years older than my youngest daughter, and he had a wife.

We were having a wonderful time, sharing a good bottle of wine, and enjoying an appetizer when he mentioned the wife. My wine glass stopped in mid-flight to my lips.

"A wife? What are you doing here with me?"

"It's all right."

"What does that mean? I don't think it's all right."

"My wife and I have an open marriage."

"Oh, please!"

"No, it's true."

"An open marriage. That's so Hollywood!" I said in dismay. "That's not a marriage."

"It was her idea a couple of years ago. Because of our son, it's worked out for his sake."

"And our dinner, is she going to know about this?"

"Probably not, she gets jealous."

"And do you get jealous?"

"Nah, I don't care anymore what she does."

I was not sure what to do with this information. I had started to have feelings for this guy. I did not consider an 'open marriage' a marriage at all. If you do not have loyalty and trust, then what have you got?

Two weeks later, I got a call from Doug. He had finished editing the Kenny Rogers show and had some downtime. He wanted to know if he came to Maui, would I see him? I thought about it…then told him I would. This time he met my children, and they liked him and his high energy. He brought along a Super 8 camera and encouraged my ten-year-old son and his best friend to write a script. They wrote, "Big Time Jewelry Heist." I had a lot of my grandmother's costume jewelry. My youngest daughter played the 'napping girl.' She was to be asleep on the sofa when the robbers came in and would awaken in time to catch them in the act. The boys were consummate actors, the napping girl really fell asleep, and when we whispered to wake her for her part, she played it so well since she was still half asleep. Except automatically, she first walked to the refrigerator and had to be quietly redirected to the bedroom. Doug said he would take the film to California, edit it, and bring it the next time he visited. So there was to be a next time.

The new man in my life was a talented singer and musician; he played piano and guitar. The guitar he brought with him on the next trip. He gave me a cassette of songs he had written and recorded with his band. They sounded professional; I was impressed. For the next four months, he flew over for a week each month. I introduced him to *The Urantia Book*. Looking through it, he cautiously remarked, "This has to be the strangest book in the world."

"There is none like it and never will be. This is it. Take it or leave it!"

He took it. Later Doug's close friend, the bass player of the band, began reading a copy we loaned him. Shortly thereafter, he went out and bought his own.

In July, I took the children to the mainland to see my parents. I was staying for two weeks before going back to work; the children were staying for six weeks: two weeks with their grandparents and four with their father.

While I was there, Doug and I spent a lot of time together. One day he asked me to sit in on an editing session; it was for "The Danny Thomas Show." I was introduced to the director, the producer, and Mr. Thomas stopped in for a while. A segment of the weekly show featured a Pop singer. That week Gerry Rafferty was singing "Baker Street." During editing, Doug said to the director, "This piece looks boring."

I silently agreed. The director vocally agreed. Gerry Rafferty was not an exciting act. Doug asked the director, "How many different takes do we have?"

The director looked down at a schedule on a clipboard and said, "Four."

"Great, let's see what we can do with them."

Doug used all four camera angles, and within an hour, he brought Gerry Rafferty's performance to life. Everyone was happily surprised with the result. A new era was being born—the music video—Doug would be at the forefront.

I went back to Maui, and Doug came with me. There was no denying how we felt about each other. For the next year, I remained in Hawaii, and he traveled back and forth. The long-distance relationship was difficult. In the spring, we split up for a while. It was very painful and a hardship on both of us. On top of that, he had filed for divorce; it was not a pleasant time for him.

By summer, we came to the conclusion that if our relationship was going to succeed, I would need to move to the mainland. He flew to Maui and helped me pack. It meant that my two children would be changing schools again, but they would be close to their grandparents and father. My eldest remained at the private boarding school; it was her senior year.

My parents could not have been happier to have our family near them once again. Doug and I rented a nice suburban house in

Burbank, and my children got to know his son, who was living with his mother. He was a friendly, energetic boy, a lot like his father. It was good fortune that his age was just between my youngest daughter and my son. He fit into the family quite nicely and visited every weekend.

Chapter 16

At the beginning of 1980, Doug and I were married. We had a small wedding party. Amy was the maid of honor. Her brother-in-law married us. I knew him and Amy's sister well. The best part of the wedding for the boys was riding in a limo. They talked about it for days.

My ex-husband gave me an unpleasant wedding surprise; he sold the house on Maui. I asked him how he could do that since he had put the property in our children's name. Gosh… he had never gotten around to doing that. I asked why he needed the money. His answer was that he and his new wife were buying a vacation home in Oregon amid the beauty of nature. Astonished that he would even admit to such a selfish motive, I wanted to know where the money was I had spent building the house? He would pay me someday. That someday never came.

Doug wanted me to learn his business. I would often drive into Hollywood and meet him at the editing studio where he worked. Sometimes we would go together if it was not going to be a long working day. It was unusual for a wife to sit at the back of the editing bay observing, but directors never objected. I found that I enjoyed the editing process, the constant rewind and fast-forward of scenes until you got the cut just right. It made the end product worth the effort.

He was editing vignettes for "Hour Magazine" a daytime talk show hosted by Gary Collins. A vignette is a short piece inserted into the show. A director and crew would tape it either on a production set or go to the home of the personality of interest to the television audience. The taping was an hour interview; then, the piece would be edited down to three or four minutes. The director was in charge of choosing the editing shots, and Doug would follow his or her instructions, often making creative suggestions.

Soon after I started attending the sessions, I watched as the director made a young, pregnant starlet into a vegetarian. During the hour of taping, she had said that in the first three months of her pregnancy, she could not eat meat and, for those months, was a vegetarian. When the director got through with the vignette, it was edited in such a way that the television viewer would believe that the young woman was a lifelong vegetarian. The viewers would have no idea it was caused by her first trimester. On the way home in the car, I said to Doug, "You guys made that young woman into a vegetarian by your editing."

"I guess we did."

"No, I guess. You did."

"The director's a vegetarian. He thought it made a better story."

"But it isn't the truth."

A sarcastic smile crossed his lips, "That's the magic of editing, sweetheart."

The editing facility that Doug usually worked from was close to Los Angeles City College. One evening Doug and I were at dinner with another couple, friends of ours in the editing community. She was talking about her college years. It dawned on me that I did not have any college years, and maybe it was time. So I enrolled at the city college for the fall semester.

In the spring of 1981, Doug brought home a three-quarter-inch videotape that a fellow editor had given him at work. He interrupted the TV program the children were watching, completely ignoring their complaints, and put the tape into our professional VCR machine hooked up to the television. "Check this out!"

First on the tape was the music video "Video Killed the Radio Star." Then came "Elephant Parts," a video album by the ex-Monkee, Michael Nesmith. We all sat in rapt attention. Doug was excited. MTV had not yet launched its network, but he could see a bright future for the medium. He was tired of editing the same types of television programs. And with his musical talent, he knew there was a place for him. He wanted in. The children and I wanted to see the tape again.

MTV launched in August, playing videos that had originally been intended as promotional videos produced by record companies or the artists themselves for international distribution. Many were merely concert clips. On MTV's premiere program, the first video aired was "Video Killed the Radio Star," directed by Russell Mulcahy. Recording companies scrambled to produce material for the show.

Russell Mulcahy had started out directing low-budget videos in Australia. He then moved to London to work in earnest in this new music video genre with larger budgets. In London, he would only work with one particular editor, but that editor refused to travel.

When Mulcahy was hired to direct two videos for Billy Joel, "Pressure" and "Allentown" he needed an editor in the states. Doug was recommended, and a meeting was set with Mulcahy and his producer. Doug brought a reel of his work. They liked it, and they liked him. He was hired and became the editor for all U.S. projects.

Working with Mulcahy and Billy Joel brought Doug recognition. He started getting work with other directors. He continued to edit videos for Mulcahy, including Fleetwood Mac's "Gypsy." It was the most expensive video produced at the time. Doug took his son and my youngest daughter to the set on a day of shooting. They were tapped as extras in a street scene and were taken to the costume department to be fitted out as 1930s street urchins.

It was a cold day. Stevie Nicks took a liking to my daughter and kindly kept her warm by inviting my eight-year-old into her trailer to hang out with Stevie and her backup singers. That day both children came home wanting to grow up and be stars.

Life was cruising along nicely when one day, while I was at the bank on Hollywood Boulevard, the teller said to me, "Your husband called, and you need to go to your mother's house when you leave here."

I was not worried. My impetuous husband often summoned me for odd reasons at odd places. When I got to Mom's, Doug told me that the dermatologist tried to get a hold of us, and since we were not home, he called the emergency number, my mother. She called Doug at work. The day before, my husband had a mole removed from his back. The dermatologist sent it to the lab. He told us we would have the results in about a week. But here it was the next day.

The mole that the doctor had removed was not a mole but a melanoma. He was sending the report to Doug's physician, Dr. Frankel.

Within two weeks, Doug underwent surgery. A large diamond-shaped portion was removed from his back. The surgeon came in and told us that he believed he had gotten all the affected area and more, but with Melanoma, one cannot always be certain. If Doug passed the five-year mark, then chances of it ever returning were remote. He began six-month check-ups.

Doug was back to work within a few days. I could not keep him down. He cut red meat out of his diet, and I carefully shopped for natural foods. Wheatgrass was the new antioxidant with purported cancer inhibiting properties. We decided he should take it daily. The first time he drank it, he complained bitterly, "It tastes like licking the blades of a lawn mower."

"Really, Doug, when is the last time you licked the blades of a lawn mower?"

He gave me a rye look, "Very funny. You try it."

I did. He was right. But I was determined he should drink it. How could it hurt? I bought flats of the grass at the health food store and kept them on our patio. We worked it out, so every morning, I would get up while he slept, grind the stuff, and give it to him to drink just as I woke him up.

Life went back to normal except for his morning cocktail.

My eldest daughter was in her first year of college, and she usually brought a friend home from school. They had great fun going with Doug to video tapings or editing sessions. From time to time, I went with my husband.

One particularly memorable time for me on set was for a video with the Pointer Sisters, "I'm So Excited." Upon arrival, the producer introduced me to the three ladies. After a few long takes, they invited me into their dressing room. I discovered drinking fine Champagne did not interfere with their rousing performance.

In September, Doug and I took a trip to London. We met with many of our contemporaries in the music video industry and were shown a wonderful British time. The next time we would see them would be for the Irene Cara video "The Dream" created for the movie "D.C. Cab." I would write this video incorporating British cabs, which was a fun way to get a working trip to England.

Chapter 17

After a year working with different editing facilities, Doug and I talked about starting our own business. A fellow editor was selling his offline editing system. Editing a music video was an expensive venture for a record company. An offline rough cut could take up to two weeks—eighty to ninety hours. The online final cut usually only took twelve to fifteen hours and had to be done at a professional editing facility with its superior technological equipment. Booking a professional editing facility by the hour was costly.

We decided to set up an offline studio at home to do the rough cut, charge less but make a good profit. Our main expense would be a small business loan for the offline system. I went to our banker, completed all the paperwork, and got approval for the loan. Turning our den into an editing studio, we put up blackout curtains and bought secondhand comfortable leather furniture. Doug usually worked with the video director, and sometimes the artists came along.

I was still pursuing my college goal and now attending classes at UCLA, majoring in contemporary world history, particularly the communist revolution in Russia, the rise of Nazi Germany, and the Holocaust. It was this study that caused me to pay more attention to current events.

That spring, mass peace protests had broken out across Western Europe with demonstrations against NATO'S installation of American-made Pershing missiles. About the same time, President Ronald Reagan announced the Strategic Defense Initiative. The news media called it "Star Wars." Reagan wanted to build an anti-missile defense system. He believed that if America could put a man on the moon, America had the ingenuity to protect itself from nuclear war. I thought to myself, "Had things gotten so bad?"

I had grown up in the era of the U.S. vs. the USSR, fighting communism, bomb shelters, and dropping under my desk at the sound of an alarm when I was in grade school. I never gave it a second thought; it was just something you did at school.

My father worked as a cameraman in the movie studios. He was an informed union man and astute regarding world affairs. Politics and current events would often be the topic of conversation at the dinner table. Dad was not an alarmist and did not build a bomb shelter when it was in vogue. He told me that in 1949 when the Russians tested their first atomic weapon, it had a frightening effect on many Americans. He never believed it would result in a nuclear war because both countries could inflict such devastation upon each other.

But now, every night on the evening news, there were reports of an anti-American groundswell, demonstrations in Europe, the bellicose posturing of Soviet leaders, and the President not backing down. Doug and I were growing concerned. Was a nuclear war possible, and if so, would our children be safe? Would Los Angeles be safe? Would the Port of Los Angeles be a target? It was the busiest port in America, a vital hub of survival. As we were attempting to discern if the danger was a true possibility, Doug and I had a reinforcing experience.

Shortly thereafter, Mike came to the mainland to visit his mother in Long Beach and gave us a call. He wanted to come out to Burbank and see us. Mike and Doug had met on Maui and become casual friends before Mike moved to the Big Island, the island of Hawaii. When he arrived, the children were happy to see him. He was impressed with the editing room, and Doug showed him some of the tricks of the trade. We got into a discussion of the possibility of a war.

At first, Mike thought we were overreacting, but after a few thoughtful moments, he asked us what we thought about the safety of the Big Island. I had purchased some books on nuclear war and fallout. (There were many on the market at the time featured in the windows of prominent bookstores.) We looked up trade wind patterns of the island in relation to Pearl Harbor. The island of Hawaii was way south of it. Mike said, "Of course, nowhere is completely safe, I guess…anyway, you'd like it. I have some great friends there."

He looked at me, "Especially you would like the wife of one of my friends. You're a lot alike. She's a good lady. You guys should come over and check out the island."

Doug's eyes lit up. Just the mention of the islands put a smile on my overworked husband's face, and an island home was very enticing.

For the next two weeks, Doug and I considered the possibility. We had been planning to purchase a home in Los Angeles and had saved a down payment. The prospect of making that purchase in Hawaii seemed a better decision in any case.

I called my friend Jane. She was working as a real estate agent and was now divorced from Jim. I told her we wanted to buy a place on the Big Island, someplace with land. She did not share my concern when I mentioned the possibility of war, but she was eager to help us and have my family back in her neck of the woods. Setting us up with a fellow realtor on Hawaii, we made arrangements to fly over and see what the island had to offer.

Before we could leave, Doug was scheduled to direct and edit a music video. Directing was a big step up for my talented husband. During negotiations with a record company, it was the general practice to introduce two or three different concepts/scripts for the video. One night at dinner with Jeff, our friend and producer said to me, "You're a good storyteller. Why don't you write one?"

I was surprised, "You have to be kidding."

Doug agreed, "Why not? The record company executive makes the final decision, not us anyway."

The next day I put on headphones, listened to a tape of Rick Springfield singing "Affair of the Heart," and wrote a concept. It was submitted along with other writers' concepts and, to my surprise, chosen.

After Rick Springfield's video was completed, we were on a plane heading to the Big Island of Hawaii. We stopped in Honolulu, had dinner with Jane, then on to the Big Island the next morning to meet the realtor. In the meantime, I had called Marian, who was living on the island, and told her we may be neighbors. I confided that part of our decision was based on the belief of the possibility of a nuclear war.

MAP OF HAWAII

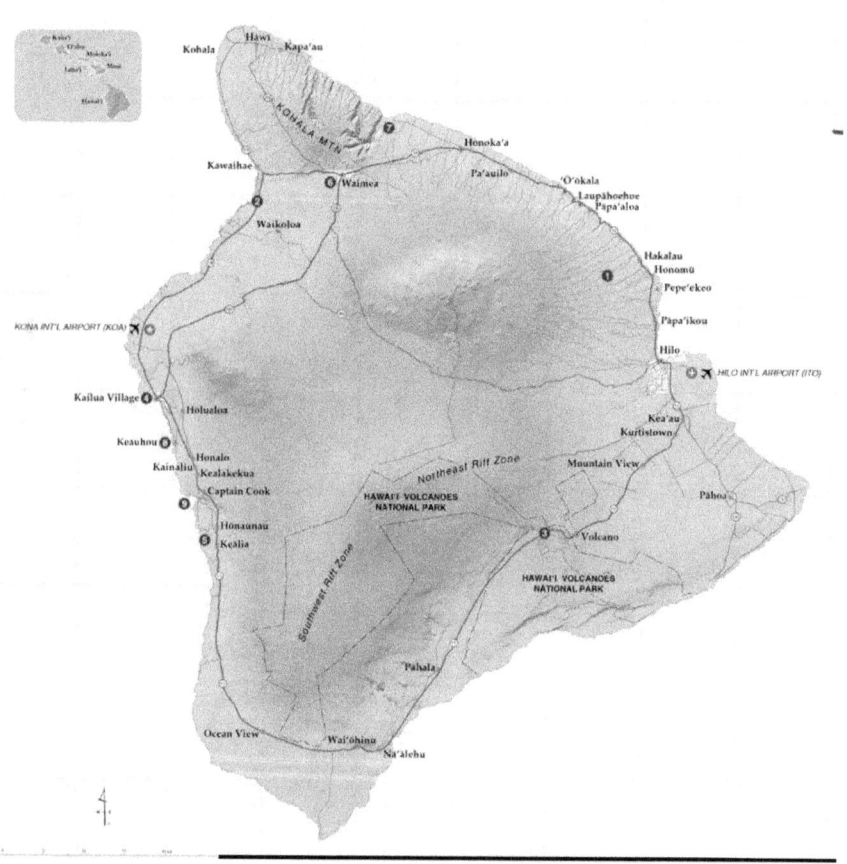

Chapter 18

Coming in for a landing at Kona airport, all we could see out the windows of the plane was a massive black lava-rock landscape. It was amazing, like being on a newly forming planet. The realtor met us at the baggage claim area, an outside carousel. Mark was a friendly man and chatted with us as he drove to the hotel where we were staying. The highway into Kona was landscaped every mile or so with brilliantly colored clusters of bougainvillea. The profusion of color was strikingly beautiful against the black backdrop of hardened lava. Doug and I already liked this interesting island.

Mark was ready to show us properties with farmland. After we dropped our luggage at the King Kamehameha Hotel and returned to the car, he said, "I'm going to show you three places. Usually...I save the best for last, but in this case...well, you'll see."

We drove east along Alii Drive, the ocean to our right. Once outside of town, and after fifteen minutes, we came to the town of Captain Cook. There was a fork in the road; Mark took the lower road. After another five minutes, he made a right turn onto Painted Church Road. Not far from the corner on the left, we saw a thick banana grove behind a low stone wall. Just beyond the grove was an open-gated, asphalt driveway with a large mango tree overhanging the entrance. Ripe mangoes littered the driveway. On the other side of the gate, the low stone wall continued; it bordered the entire property.

Mark turned left into the driveway. Immediately to the right, we saw a garden of pineapples growing in neatly lined rows. Behind the pineapples was a long aloe hedge in front of a huge breadfruit tree. Doug and I were silent as we continued up the driveway. On both sides of the road were mature avocado trees with oversize avocados hanging from green stems; there were eight avocado trees on the property. On the left, elevated above the land, was a large teal-green, wood-frame house with a high-pitched roof. A wide lanai spanned the entire front of the house. The driveway ended, and we parked. Directly in front of us were the most beautiful dark-green leafy trees loaded with macadamia nuts.

In a sort of daze, we got out of the car and climbed the wooden stairway up one floor to the residence door. Underneath the house, through wooden slats, we could see large beams supporting the house. Reaching the door, we were greeted by a balding older gentleman. Mark stepped aside while Doug and I entered into an open kitchen with a long, low breakfast bar separating it from a spacious living room. Hanging from the center beam of the high ceiling, a fan lazily turned. Windows stretched all along the front wall from the kitchen into the living room and turning the corner at the far wall.

The gentleman introduced us to his pleasant wife, who joined us in the tour.

The front door was on the windowed wall between the kitchen and living room. The couple took us through the door and out onto the large lanai with its extending roof, giving some shade and rain protection. This would be the dining room. Doug and I looked out over tropical fauna and could see all the way down to the ocean of Kealakekua Bay. Wow!

We looked directly below us and saw a manicured pebble garden with evenly spaced circles of rocks, centering hapu'u ferns. Orchids of white, purple, and yellow grew right out of the stalks of the ferns. At the edge of this private garden were two stone benches sitting under pink and white blossomed plumeria trees, perfect for making leis. To the right, the owner pointed out a screen greenhouse of tomatoes. There was a bird bath just before the greenhouse; yellow-headed finches and bright red cardinals with yellow bills were flapping around bathing. Monarch butterflies flitted through the breeze. Before we even saw the rest of the house, we knew this was the farm for our family.

Back inside, the wife took us through an archway just left of the kitchen leading to a hallway and two bedrooms with two baths, one off the master bedroom. Each bedroom had a sliding glass door that led onto private lanais. We stood on the master bedroom lanai and overlooked umbrellas of dark green macadamia treetops all the way to the end of the five-acre property.

Then the owners took us on a tour of the grounds. We discovered papaya trees, a small coffee grove, a garden of rich soil to the left of the house where strawberries, Manoa lettuce, and zucchini were growing. There were rubber snakes in the strawberry patch to keep the birds away. Every tree on the property, including starfruit and cherimoya, were growing right out of crumpled lava rock. The cherimoya tree with its vanilla custard fruit grew at the back of the property, a new species of fruit for us. Cherry tomato vines twisted along the black lava with their bright red fruit. There were also patches of vacant space where we would soon build a chicken coup, half-basketball court, and an additional larger greenhouse. The farm was the owner's labor of love, but he admitted he was getting too old to keep it up. We told Mark we did not need to see another property. He said, "That's what I figured."

We returned to the hotel and discussed an offer on the property. The farm was on leasehold land, which is common in Hawaii. The lease was $1.00 for ninety-nine years; there were sixty-nine years left on the lease. That was fine with us since leasehold property is much more reasonably priced. We came up with an offer. It was accepted. We went into escrow before the week was out, awaiting loan approval from First Hawaiian Bank.

I had spoken to Marian on the phone, but we had not seen each other in years. Doug and I rented a car and drove up to see her. She and her family were living in Waimea, the Big Island's version of Up Country. Although no forest of trees, there was beautiful sprawling pastureland. It was cattle country and boasted the largest privately owned cattle ranch in the United States.

It was great to reconnect with Marian. She had not changed, and we had a very talkative reunion. We stayed with her for a few days. She had taken to heart the possibility of a war, and Doug and I met with friends of hers and discussed preparation scenarios.

From Marian's, I called my mother in Los Angeles to find out how my father was. He had been ill for a year and was not doing well when Doug and I left. I could not reach her, so I called my sister. My father had been admitted to the hospital, and Mom was with him.

My father passed away the next day while Doug and I were flying back. When we arrived at Mom's home, my sister had driven up from San Diego and was with her. It was a sad time, even though predicted. In the last year of my father's illness, my mother asked if she could borrow my Urantia Book. I gave her one as a gift, and she began reading. The knowledge in the remarkable book brought her great comfort during this time and later.

Chapter 19

Doug went back to work at a feverish pace. We had plans for the house once it was ours. One of my favorite videos he edited during that time was "Stand Back" for Stevie Nicks. The director was a young choreographer, and he and Doug worked well together. Doug went to the taping. He and Stevie knew each other from working on "Gypsy."

My oldest daughter was in her second year at college. I told her we had bought a macadamia nut farm on the Big Island and why. I asked her what she wanted to do. Unbeknownst to me, she had already decided she was not going to return to the university she had been attending for the last two years. She wanted to take a year off. My other two children would be changing schools again, but it was back to Hawaii. Doug's son, who was twelve years old, wanted to come live with us. We were very happy with his decision. His mother was not, but she relented. The nightly news kept up the drumbeat of possible war because of Reagan's determination to bring down what he called 'the evil empire.'

In July, the property was ours. The whole family flew over and took possession, six of us now. We had a housewarming party, a Hawaiian luau, kalua pig and all. Jane came from Oahu, Mark, our realtor, was there with his son, and Mike brought along friends. Lei, one of the nicest women I have ever known, became a close friend along with her husband and children. They were the same ages as my stepson and youngest daughter. Mike also invited some construction buddies with their wives. Mike and these guys would build us four bedrooms, a rec room, and a bathroom, all on the ground floor under the main house.

Within six weeks, the children had their rooms, each with their own entrance along a covered walkway. Within two months, Doug and the boys were playing basketball on a half-court, and there were twelve hens laying eggs in what we named the chicken condo. My oldest daughter was in charge with the help of Lei when Doug and I traveled to the mainland for work.

United Airlines had a direct flight from LAX to the Big Island, which made everything a lot easier. We still had the house in Burbank and were looking around for a smaller place when my mother put forth a proposal we could not refuse. When my father passed away, my parents owned and were living in a four-unit apartment building just off of Sunset Boulevard in Hollywood. The building was built in the late 1930s, and like many on the wide boulevard, it was constructed in Art-Deco style. Each of the four units were two bedroom, two bath homes.

The tenants in the front unit had given notice and were moving out at the end of the month. The apartment was perfect for our lifestyle. Downstairs was spacious, and upstairs, we could turn one bedroom into an offline studio. Mom was living alone, and the arrangement brought her entertaining company. She knew I was concerned about a war and did not share my fear, although she was delighted to come visit Hawaii as soon as construction was completed.

The children started school, my oldest son, a senior in high school, Doug's son in eighth grade, and my youngest in sixth. They each had their farm chores.

Our neighbors across the street, a local family, introduced themselves and wanted to manage the commercial part of the farm, the macadamia nuts. We hired them, and they became friends as well as business partners. Our macadamia nuts would grace Mrs. Fields' white chocolate chip macadamia nut cookies. The company bought from the co-op we belonged to.

With our belief that the family was secure, Doug and I felt comfortable going back and forth to L.A. for work. His next job directing was a second video for Rick Springfield, "Human Touch." The record company approved my concept, and Jeff managed a generous budget. Doug and Rick Springfield got along well; they were both tall, likable men. With that video completed, I returned to Hawaii while he fulfilled other editing obligations. When those jobs were completed, he returned to the farm.

We spent as much time as possible on this beautiful land and with our family. One evening I was preparing dinner with my son as the sous-chef. My stepson had gone to the garden to pick the lettuce and tomatoes for the salad. While scooping out an avocado, my son asked me, "Why do you believe *The Urantia Book* is the truth? I know we've grown up with it, but how can you be so sure?"

Now I know you cannot give your faith to another, so I searched for the best answer for him, "You just have to read the book yourself."

And he did. It took him four months. He came to his own conclusion and became a faithful Urantian ever since.

Thanks to the direct United flight from LAX to the Big Island, living 'bicoastal' lives was stressless. That is except in the way my husband was notoriously a 'near-miss-mortal' regarding getting to the airport in L.A. just in time for our flight, no matter my nagging.

Doug and I were at an industry party one Saturday night when, for fun, I entertained our producer Jeff and other friends with a supernatural story of the Hawaiian legend of Madame Pele, the volcano goddess, and her destructive jealousy of her beautiful sister Hiiaka. I brought it into the present day, reincarnating Hiiaka and her handsome lover Lehua. (The character of Madame Pele was drawn loosely upon Sheila, and for Lehua, I used Rick Springfield.) To my surprise, our friends sat listening in rapt attention. Jeff encouraged me to write it into a screenplay, which gave my husband visions of directing a feature film.

Jeff was also meeting with MTV executives about a possible pilot project featuring thirty-minute theatrical videos. I wrote two: one for David Lee Roth and one for Billy Idol. A fellow video concept writer also submitted one. Eventually, MTV decided not to greenlight the project; they did not want to spring for the budget nor deal with record company executives.

Our life passed in a whirlwind. The threat of war had receded into the background of the media and our minds. Things were running smoothly; we now had a married couple as housekeepers on the farm. My oldest daughter was attending an East Coast college. My son was in the army. (Six months earlier, when he announced his decision to join, we were more than surprised.) My youngest daughter was at a private school up in Waimea and boarded during the week. Doug's son was happy to stay at the local high school, where he had a group of close friends.

Madonna had recently arrived on the scene; my youngest daughter went to school dressed like her. Before Madonna's first big hit, Susan Sontag had made the movie "Desperately Seeking Susan" which Madonna co-starred with Rosanna Arquette. The studio held up the movie release, but when Madonna turned into a rising star, and her audience was young girls, Sontag recut the film to give it a PG-13 rating. Doug edited the video to Madonna's song, "Get into the Groove," using nothing but movie footage. He had already been working with top film directors and producers using MTV for video trailers for their movies.

At the beginning of 1985, Doug directed a video with Bonnie Tyler, "Holding Out for a Hero." When he came back from the shoot, he kept praising her as a real trooper. He got a helicopter shot of her standing on the ledge of a cliff, belting out her song. He was nervous just being in the helicopter. She seemed cool as a cucumber with the wind of the chopper blowing against her in a full-length, white gown while standing on the precipice.

Meanwhile, I finished my first screenplay. Using his many contacts, Doug began taking it around to the studios for him to direct. Jeff was also shopping the script to executive producers. A prominent musician was at a party Jeff gave, and the script was lying on the coffee table. He picked it up and started reading. Upon leaving, he took the script with him to finish. He liked it so much that he went ahead and recorded its theme song. So I had a cassette tape of its opening credits music before I had a deal.

Doug had worked with the director Taylor Hackford on a Phil Collins video for the movie "Against All Odds." Mr. Hackford was just finishing up a film about a Russian dancer attempting to defect from the USSR. It was titled "White Nights." Lionel Richie sang the theme of the movie "Say You Say Me." Doug began off-lining the video.

The studio had sent over videotapes of "White Nights," minus the ending. It was a bit unusual for the tapes to be edited without the ending, but Mr. Hackford wanted to get the ending just right and traveled with a small crew to an Eastern European country. A film crew had previously been to the USSR for background shots of the movie. How Taylor Hackford managed those shots at that time is a trade secret. The Soviets would never have allowed any American filming a movie starring the dancer Mikhail Baryshnikov who had defected in 1974.

Doug could not finish the video until the ending was delivered. When it arrived, he edited shots of the ending at the beginning of the video. He always went for the best dramatic effect, no matter the sequence of the film.

In the editing process, you watch the tape over and over again. I never tired of sitting next to Doug and interjecting my advice (often ignored) while he edited Baryshnikov and Gregory Hines's dance.

One afternoon, Lionel Richie came to our home to watch the inter-cut of his performance of the song into the movie clips. I made sure they were comfortable in the edit studio with snacks and went to my mother's apartment. My mother and I could talk for hours. In the early evening, Mom decided to celebrate something. We opened a bottle of champagne and were having a glass when the phone rang. The phone sat on a table next to her La-Z-Boy recliner. She answered, then pointed the receiver at me, "It's your husband."

I walked over and took the receiver, "Hi, what's up?"

"You have to come down here," he said gleefully.

"Why? You're busy editing," I wined.

"Just come."

He hung up. I told my mother I would be back.

Our apartment front door opened directly into the living room. Sitting on the sofa opposite the door were Lionel Richie and his wife. Doug was sitting to the right in the only other chair and on the floor in front of the coffee table, turning toward me as I opened the door, sat Stevie Wonder. I am sure I did a double take. Doug introduced this friendly man. His driver and assistant sat on one of our dining room chairs pulled into the living room. I sat on the floor with Stevie Wonder and joined the conversation centered on the driving skills of the blind singer. He liked to drive his car around his estate driveway. His assistant was telling the story laughingly, claiming that sitting in the passenger seat directing Stevie was a bit hair-raising.

As the others went on to a different topic, Stevie turned to me and told me that he was not born blind. He was a premature baby put into an incubator at birth. I knew that around the time of my birth, incubators were a new technology and that the amount of oxygen pumped into the incubators mistakenly blinded the babies they were trying to save. I wondered to myself if that had not happened, would Stevie Wonder's life have taken a totally different direction, and the world would not have the works of this unique and talented man?

A few minutes later, Stevie said to Lionel, "I want to play that song for you."

He had come to our home to play a song he had just composed for Lionel. We had a piano that Doug often played. The assistant got up from the dining room chair and led Stevie the short distance to the piano. For a brief time, we had our own private Stevie Wonder concert.

The next day Doug was working and asked me what I thought about an edit. He leaned back in his chair and crossed his arms, watching the replay. Feeling a lump on the outside of his left bicep, he said, "Feel this."

I put my hand where his was; there was a hard growth slightly raised above his skin, the size of a nickel. "It must be a cyst or something."

The next week, I noticed the cyst had grown and made an appointment with Dr. Frankel's office. He was on vacation, but his associate would see Doug.

Chapter 20

While sitting in the doctor's waiting room, I was reading a magazine. Removing a cyst is not supposed to be a long involved process. After thirty minutes, I began to wonder what was taking so long. After almost an hour, Doug emerged looking grim with a white gauze bandage on his arm. "The doctor said he couldn't get it all."

"What does that mean?"

"I have to have some X-rays. Talk to the nurse and make an appointment."

The X-rays were scheduled in a week. Dr. Frankel unexpectedly called the next day, saying he was adding a CAT scan, but we should not worry. Worry, we did.

Doug went through the tests and was told Dr. Frankel would call with the results. Three days later, we were sitting in Dr. Frankel's office. The doctor, in his mid-thirties, the same age as my husband, looked visibly shaken.

"Doug, the melanoma has metastasized."

The test results showed that he had five tumors, one on his brain, in his lung, on his spleen, and so on.

Doug asked, "Is there anything we can do?"

"You could try chemo, but it would only prolong your life months, not years. There is no cure."

"I don't want chemo…how long do I have?"

"…Six months."

I could not believe the words that were being said; tears involuntarily began running down my cheeks. I could not even feel them. My husband reached over and wiped them away.

He looked at me, "It'll be all right."

"No, it won't," I thought.

We went home. Doug went upstairs to finish the offline version of the "Say You Say Me" video. We were scheduled for the online editing session that night.

Within a week after Dr. Frankel gave the prognosis of six months to live, Doug went into denial. After all, he was not sick. Yes, he had noticed a lack of energy lately. But he was too young to die, and his future could not have been brighter.

When friends learned of his illness, they were lovingly supportive. A production designer called a meeting at our home. She and four friends arrived on a Friday evening to convince us to travel to Chicago to meet with a well-known Chinese homeopathic doctor. It was reported that he had been responsible for the remission of many who had malignant melanoma. We, of course, were willing to try anything. As a loving gesture, they handed us two open-ended round-trip tickets to the windy city.

Doug's energy was intermittently lagging, and occasional pain was setting in. But he was still strong and hopeful when we boarded the plane at the end of October. We had not told the children yet.

The appointment with the Chinese doctor was set. Arriving in Chicago in the evening, we checked into a nice older hotel. Our friends had booked us into a suite with a small kitchen for two weeks. The next afternoon we took a taxi to the Chinese part of town.

The doctor met us in his office. I was mentally analyzing him as he was interviewing us for twenty minutes before he took Doug into an examining room. For me, the doctor passed scrutiny; he seemed the real deal, but whether he could help us was yet to be seen. He told us that he did have patients in remission, but there were no guarantees. The wound on Doug's arm from the attempted cyst removal, which was a tumor, had not healed. The doctor wrote out a prescription for herbs to make into a tea and drink three times a day for the melanoma and another for the wound. Then, he turned to me and said, "I can help you too."

I had not said a word. I had been suffering painful symptoms ever since Doug's diagnosis. The doctor told me where in my body the pain was and gave me herbs also. I do not know how he knew.

We took our written prescriptions to the Chinese pharmacy. It was something I had never seen before. Rows and rows of small, shellacked wooden drawers were embedded up to the ceiling in a long wall behind the pharmacist's counter. A smiling, slightly built Chinese gentleman read the prescriptions and began to pull out appropriate drawers, some he had to reach with a rolling library ladder. It was quite a show. He mixed my husband's herbs into packets and mine as well. He also gave Doug a bottle containing a yellow powder to be applied to the open tumor wound on his arm.

We bought two Chinese ceramic teapots and cups, stopped and bought a saucepan, then returned to the hotel. The herbs had to be cooked for twenty minutes, then cooled to drink, and taken three times a day. Our hotel room smelled interesting.

Within two days, I was pain-free. The wound on Doug's arm was healed from the magical yellow powder, and his energy was higher, but still pain would come and go. We saw the doctor every three days, and he would make adjustments to my husband's herbs.

On the seventh day, we were walking on the broad promenade by the Chicago River when Doug said, "Isn't the Urantia Foundation in Chicago?"

Nodding my head, "Yeah, it is."

"Do you know the address?"

"I'm sure it's in the phone book."

"Should we go?"

"Why not? Marian told me that visitors are always welcome."

"Then let's check it out."

My husband had not changed. Get a bright idea and follow through; the sooner, the better. We were both eager to actually see where it all began and to visit for a moment with someone working there.

The next day we hailed a taxi and gave the driver the address. Doug was feeling well. He was not in any pain and had his usual energy. We arrived at a turn of the century, three-story building with a stately portico. Walking up the few steps, we knocked at the front door. Receiving no answer, we felt comfortable going on in. To the right of the entry was a large comfortable reading room with worn sofas and chairs. No one greeted us, so we went on to the back offices to say, "Hello, we are Urantia Book readers."

An older woman was bustling down the hallway. She passed us by without any acknowledgment. Then she was gone. We went to another office with the intention of introducing ourselves. A man sat busy at his desk. He looked up at us then went right back to what he was doing. We went back into the living room and up a flight of stairs. A couple of other people were preoccupied at work, and no one gave us any notice. It had to be obvious to these people that we were strangers. My husband and I looked at each other, feeling like unwelcome guests, so we walked back down, through the entry, and out the door.

After walking a block in cold, windy Chicago, we turned to face each other and said almost instantaneously, "That was weird."

It was not what we had expected from people at the Urantia Foundation, members of a Brotherhood. Were they reading the same book we were? Some kind of friendly gesture, at least a hello, would have been in order even if they were terribly busy. We couldn't help but be reminded of how Jesus, no matter what subject he was discoursing on or how important the topic, he would stop to take time to answer the apostle Philip's foolish questions, or anyone else's for that matter. We walked away with the impression that these people did not practice what they preached. It was just a typical busy business office.

That night we received a call from Taylor Hackford's assistant. They had learned of Doug's illness and that we were in Chicago for treatment. By coincidence, "White Nights" was opening the Chicago Film Festival two evenings hence. We were invited to attend. When we arrived, the fanfare was entertaining, and to see

Baryshnikov and Gregory Hines portray their roles on the big screen was a momentary break from reality, a welcome diversion. That was the last evening that Doug would ever again be pain-free.

After our time in Chicago, we returned home for a few days and then on to Hawaii. The Chinese herbalist would ship Doug's prescription weekly to the Big Island. My husband still had hope the herbs would work. We had not told his son and my youngest daughter of his illness. We wanted to do that in person. I had written to my son in the Army and called my daughter in college. At the farm, our little family gathering was very difficult. Doug was honest and told them he might not make it. The children's reactions went from bewilderment to sadness to hope. But after a month, the hope began to fade.

My husband lived for another two months; he passed away on February 6, 1986. He was thirty-four years old. In January, he had come to terms with his death and tried to help his son and my daughter do so also. During that last month, I was living inside a gray cloud; it surrounded me wherever I went. I could tell the sun was shining, but it truly never pierced the cloud.

We were both so grateful that Doug spent his last days on earth on the farm. He loved the place. The summer we had taken ownership, he stood at the top of the gently sloping property, spread out his long arms, and said, "This is my kingdom!"

He was home in his kingdom up until the last six days, where he died in the small community hospital in Captain Cook. His attending physician was the same doctor who had set my oldest daughter's broken arm when she was eight years old at the Kahuku Hospital on the North Shore of Oahu.

Chapter 21

Doug was gone. He was not only my husband but also a friend and fellow spiritual traveler. He never doubted that an eternal journey lay before him. We both knew we would be seeing each other again. The hit song by Dire Straits, "You're So Far Away from Me" was in rotation on the radio. For some reason, singing along helped my sadness which I kept to myself; to do otherwise would not do anyone any good. My greatest comfort was in knowing that my husband's intense pain was over. His body was riddled with thirty-two tumors on the day he died.

Our island friends organized a small funeral ceremony. We walked over a field of black lava, carrying an urn of Doug's ashes, and entered an ancient lava-tube cave that ended at the mouth of a cliff with the sea below. We said a prayer, then I opened the urn and poured Doug's ashes. As his ashes dropped below upon the surface and floated atop the deep blue water, we all, one by one, took off the beautiful flower leis we had made and threw them onto the ashes. The current slowly took the white and gray ashes encircled by the colorful rings of yellow, pink, white, and turquoise blossoms, floating out to sea.

Less than two weeks after my husband's ashes mingled with the sea, I received a call from a film producer. The phone rang, I answered, and when the caller identified himself, I was quite surprised. The man was someone I had met two, maybe, three times.

159

Best I could remember was at a party. He wanted to know how I was doing. My answer was a bit cautious since I hardly knew the guy, "I'm fine."

"Good. I'm glad to hear that. But I think you should know that Doug has not left the earthly realm, and he wants to make love to you one last time through me."

Did I hear him correctly? "Excuse me?"

He repeated his bizarre claim and added, "I am willing to fly over and reserve us a hotel suite wherever is convenient for you."

I had been propositioned in Hollywood before, but this one takes the cake!

Forcefully I replied, "My husband and I left no issues unresolved. I think you have the wrong spirit connection."

He stammered on the line. I hung up.

In March, Jeff came over to the to stay for a couple of days. Before he left, he said to me, "Let's take a walk."

We walked down the winding driveway onto Painted Church Road, "When are you coming back to L.A.?"

"I'm not. I am going to stay here."

"What about your writing?"

"Doug's son has another year and a half of high school. I want to stay until then."

He stopped and faced me, "You know, in our business 'out of sight, out of mind.' You'll lose your momentum."

"The boy has just lost his father; he can't lose his home and friends. If I don't stay, I would have to sell. Anyway, without Doug, it's not the same."

He shook his head in disagreement, "Your decision."

Walking back up to the house, I noticed for the first time that the beautiful farm was overgrown. With Doug's illness, I had not been paying attention. I was going to need help other than just friends. A pile of bills was stacked on the built-in desk in the kitchen. The kitchen faucet was leaking, and something was wrong with the solar panel connection.

Through a trusted friend, I hired a handyman. He already had a job, but his hours fit into a schedule where he could help with the farm, working for room and board plus a small salary. Together we made my soldier son's room into his. He was a nice person, never any trouble.

Life during the following year and a half was never lonely, between teenagers, my wonderful friends, and running the farm. Our financial situation was a challenge. The farm was not a large working concern; it was more a five-acre gentleman's farm. Doug's income had supplemented its happy existence. After my stepson's graduation, he remained for the summer, and then he returned to his mother's home in Los Angeles.

I knew I was going to have to either sell or find renters to cover the cost of the mortgage. I did not want to give up on the farm just yet, so I leased it. Returning to my rent-free apartment was the best option. My youngest daughter had two more years of high school. She wanted to continue to board at the school in Waimea. My eldest daughter graduated from college and began her career as a software engineer for a company in Braintree, Massachusetts.

By September 1987, I was back living in the city of my birth. Within a month, my mother was diagnosed with breast cancer. I was glad that I could be with her through her surgery and chemotherapy recovery. My sister came up to help but having one daughter able to be with Mom full-time during this difficult period was a great comfort. My experience dealing with a cancer patient made my mother's difficult ordeal a little easier. Fortunately, she was finally pronounced cancer free.

Once Mom regained her health, I began working on another screenplay. This one was based on the true story of an SS Officer in Hitler's Nazi Germany. He had saved the lives of many Jews.

When I attended classes at UCLA in 1983, one of my professors was Saul Friedlander, a renowned lecturer, and writer on the destruction of the European Jew. One afternoon, he spent the class time telling the story of a Waffen SS Officer. At the end of the class, he asked the students by a show of hands if the German should be considered a war criminal or a courageous individual. Two-thirds of the class raised their hands for war criminal, one-third for courageous. I was among the one-third.

After class, I went up to Professor Friedlander with additional questions. He gave me the name of the book that he had written on this unusual man and also the title of a book by another author, "The Spy of God." Both books were in the UCLA Library, and I checked them out. After reading the man's life from two different authors, I knew there was a story to be told. Telling the story to Doug, he too had become excited about it and encouraged me to write. Before returning the books to the library, I photocopied every page. Realizing I needed a lot more background knowledge of the entire period, I began to read other books on the subject. Now, I had the time to write the story.

In June, my youngest daughter came to live with me. Her best friend was killed in a car accident near the end of the school year in Waimea. It was a terribly sad event for her. She no longer wanted to continue school in Hawaii. She would attend my Catholic alma mater. Later, after her first week at the all-girls high school, she told me how much she appreciated wearing a uniform. Her mornings were free of decisions.

On July 4th, we not only celebrated Independence Day but also the arrival of my eldest daughter to add to our all-girl menagerie. She had quit her job on the East Coast. A friend of ours set her up for a job interview with an independent production company located on the Universal Studios lot. She was hired as the production secretary because of her computer skills. Within a month's time, they promoted her to production coordinator. One evening she came home and said, "Mom, we have a shoot tomorrow, and we don't have enough extras. Will you be one? You'll get paid."

My husband had often put me in his music videos, and I knew extras did a lot of standing around waiting. I smiled, "Sure, Honey, how early?"

"You can leave with me at 7:00 a.m."

It was worth it. I got a chance to see my daughter handle her job with extreme proficiency.

In the past, I had observed many others in her position. Within the next few months, the company promoted her again to production manager.

Working on a screenplay does not pay the bills. A close friend, Leslie, wanted to help me. She was producing a low-budget video for the first album of a group called NWA. I had no idea who they were. She hired me as the AD (assistant director). I was the wrong person for the job. In fact, I was an abject failure. The artists looked and sang like they had just been released from the penitentiary, which at least one of them had. It was the first Gangsta Rap video. I should have been embarrassed by my inept job performance, but I only felt sorry for Leslie. Especially when the director took her aside, and I heard him ask, "Where the hell did you get her?"

What had happened in the last year and a half in the music industry? Where was Duran, Duran?

One would have thought Leslie would have given up helping me, but she did not. Her boyfriend's mother owned a casting agency and answering service for the stars. Actually, the stars were professional extras and older actors that could no longer afford full-time personnel and did not want to use an answering machine. I interviewed and was hired for the night shift. I worked alone from 10:00 p.m. until 6:00 a.m. with an old-fashioned switchboard like one that I had experienced using at a summer job when I was sixteen. I was the Lily Tomlin character on "Laugh-In."

The job brought needed extra cash, and I was able to use my mother's car. The agency hours enabled me to be the morning carpool mom for my daughter and two other girls; then, I went to bed. I did not get much sleep during that period. But I did have some entertaining conversations with one older star when she was having her last drink before going to sleep at 1:00 am or so.

A longtime friend, the son of Holocaust survivors, knew the story of my screenplay. In September, he invited me to a conference being held at UCLA—Children of Holocaust Survivors. It was a three-day event that held my interest from start to finish. On the last day, I was seated next to a man who engaged me in friendly conversation. He was Israeli and was curious about me since there were no gentiles at the conference that were not spouses. His name was Dov.

After class, he walked me out to the quad, and we sat down on a bench in front of vending machines. I was thirsty and got out some change from my purse and purchased a Diet Coke. Between sips, I told him I was writing a screenplay about a member of the SS during the war who I considered heroic for risking his life when he could have taken the safe route and done nothing at all. I knew that the officer did not survive the end of the war, but his widow could still be living in Germany. To my great surprise, Dov told me he was studying in Germany and was returning in October. He was a symphony conductor and furthering his craft under a famous German maestro. The sun had set while we were talking. He asked if I would like to have dinner in Brentwood. Without hesitation, I said, "Yes." Tossing my empty Coke can in the trash, we walked off campus.

During dinner, I told him the story of Kurt Gerstein, the German who had joined the SS to work against the Third Reich from the inside. Obersturmführer Gerstein was clandestinely connected with the Confessing Church during his time as a Waffen SS Officer. The Confessing Church began its existence in 1933 in opposition to the German Protestant Church that became politicized by the Nazis; its leaders effectively appointed by Hitler. By 1935 ministers of the Confessing Church were being arrested by the state. (Dietrich Bonhoeffer was one of them.) Consequently, its members continued their activities underground.

Kurt Gerstein was the first to report to the outside world the existence of the death camps through a Confessing Church connection to the British press. His report was not believed.

Dov listened attentively and asked probing questions.

After dinner, we walked back to my car in the UCLA parking lot. The next day, Sunday, he was to be the guest conductor at a concert in Costa Mesa and invited me to attend. Since I would need to drive down myself, he suggested that I bring a friend.

Leslie and I traveled to the Costa Mesa symphony hall in Orange County. Our tickets were waiting at the call window. While people filed in, the cacophony of musicians tuning up their instruments reverberated throughout the hall. At 2:00 p.m. sharp, the concert hall grew quiet. Dov, wearing a black tuxedo with tails, walked onto the stage with his graceful baton in hand. The audience clapped. He bowed and then turned to the orchestra; his black hair fell just below the collar of the black tux. With a dramatic wave of his baton, the orchestra responded. Whether one is a fan of classical music or not, a live orchestral performance is something extraordinary.

After the concert, Leslie and I waited in our seats. The hall was nearly empty when Dov bounded down the side stage stairs and over to us. I introduced him, and he asked us both, "Did you enjoy it?"

"Very much so."

My friend was a little starry-eyed but managed to agree enthusiastically.

For the next month, Dov and I saw each other often. The evening before he returned to Germany, we were talking about Kurt Gerstein again.

"When I get to Germany, I'll try to find his wife if she is still alive."

That was so unexpected; I was speechless for a moment, then managed to stammer, "…that would be like looking for a needle in a haystack, don't you think?"

"Maybe, but when I have time, I can give it a try."

"It just doesn't seem likely."

"We'll see."

Chapter 22

On a Saturday in November, my daughters and I were arriving home from a movie. While I was putting the key in the door lock, I heard the phone ringing. I hurried and reached it just before the message machine picked up.

"Hello."

"Hi, it's Dov."

"Where are you? Are you here?"

"No, I'm in Germany. I found her. I found Kurt Gerstein's widow."

"No way, she's alive?"

"Very much so. I spoke to her on the phone. I told her about you and the screenplay. She seemed guarded but gave me the number of a family friend. I called him. He's an opera producer and knows the maestro I study under."

Did I just hear him correctly? I could not find my tongue.

"Look, you should come to Germany. Let's pursue this."

I found my tongue, "Are you kidding? I'm on my way."

"I'll call tomorrow, and you can give me your flight details."

"Oh, Dov, I don't know what to say."

"Just get here; this is exciting!"

The next day I was at the United Airlines ticket office on Sunset Boulevard. Using a credit card, I purchased a round-trip ticket to Munich.

Landing in Germany, Dov met me at the airport, and we took a taxi to his apartment. He did not own or need a car. He told me people were being very protective of Frau Gerstein, and maybe we would have more difficulty interviewing her than he originally thought. A meeting had been set up for us with a retired Protestant minister in the next two days. He lived not far from Munich. We rented a car, and since we had some time, we first traveled to Dachau. Although I had been studying in books, the experience of the museum was unfathomable evil to me. All the lives that were taken, and all the souls that were twisted.

When we drove out to the minister's home, I was a little nervous; we both were excited. Finding the address, we parked on the street. There were two little girls playing hopscotch on the sidewalk in front of the house. As we went up the few steps to the front door, they watched us and started softly chanting, "Bibelstudium, Bibelstudium."

Dov translated, "They're saying Bible study."

We knocked, and an elderly white-haired gentleman answered the door. His manner was friendly. Our visit lasted about a half-hour with Dov translating. Dov and I must have passed the first test, for the minister went to the telephone and made a call. An arrangement was made to meet with the opera producer in the city of Mannheim.

Dov called friends who lived in Stuttgart, halfway between Munich and Mannheim and asked if we could stay the night. He had rented their extra bedroom in the past. With my suitcase and Dov's in the car trunk, we drove to Stuttgart. Reaching the apartment after the dinner hour, we climbed the stairs to the third floor. A regal young woman answered the door; she was a professional ballerina and looked the part. Dov had brought a good bottle of wine that we shared with her and her boyfriend. The three conversed in German. I did not understand a word but smiled and nodded my head occasionally.

The next morning when we awoke, the couple had left for work. During the night, the first snow had fallen over the city. I opened a window and looked down upon a blanket of white covering clustered, red-pitched roofs that glistened in the morning sun. What a fairy tale image!

The university town of Tubingen had played a major role in Kurt and Frau Gerstein's life. It was next on our itinerary and only a short detour from Stuttgart. We toured the charming city that had not been bombed during the war. Thus by the time we reached the opera house in Mannheim, we only had a few minutes to spare before the appointment. Both of us changed into fancy clothes in the car. It was not a very big car. We were hurrying, bumping each other, and laughing the whole time.

We arrived at the stage entrance looking presentable and were shown in. Performers were rushing around, getting ready for the opera. The producer greeted us in a pleasant manner, and we sat across from him on the bench of a long table in the middle of the hustle and bustle. He started asking me questions in English and German. Dov translated the German. After about ten minutes, the man confided that Frau Gerstein's friends were very cautious because a Frenchman had interviewed her a couple of years ago under false pretenses. Then, he wrote a scathing thesis of lies. I expressed puzzlement, "Why would anyone do that?"

The producer informed us that the Frenchman was out to prove the Holocaust was a Jewish hoax and had to discredit Gerstein's reports during the war. I assured the producer I only wanted to tell the truth as best as I knew. We had a frank discussion, and I learned more about the courageous personality of Kurt Gerstein. The producer said he would arrange a meeting with Frau Gerstein for us, and he did.

When the heavy red curtain in the gilded opera house rose, Dov and I were seated in VIP seats from where we enjoyed the opera. (Actually, Dov enjoyed the opera, it was my first time and did not make me an instant fan.)

Meeting the widow of Kurt Gerstein was a great honor for me. This woman's life had been extremely difficult not only because of the double life her husband led during the war or the hardships of the war itself as the mother of young children, but after the war the German courts denounced her husband. Many years later, that decision was reversed.

Driving up a wide sweep of a curving driveway through a park-like setting, Dov and I saw a rambling one-story retirement home. It was painted soft green with white trim. We parked in a lot just beyond the entrance. Walking into the lobby, we were greeted with "Gruss Gott." (Gruss Gott is a greeting used in some parts of Germany instead of Guten Tag. Directly translated, Gruss Gott is Greet God instead of Good Day.) Dov told the receptionist we were there to see Frau Gerstein. The friendly woman remarked that we

171

were expected and walked us down a windowed hallway, gently knocking on a room door.

Frau Gerstein opened the door. She was a small, pretty, elderly lady. Introductions were made as she invited us into her spacious rectangular room. To the left was the bedroom area with a double bed made up in feminine décor plus a nightstand and a tall bookshelf. Across from the door, two large windows offered the light of day through opened curtains. A comfortable seating area was off to the right; two upholstered armchairs were against the wall and faced toward the bed. On a coffee table sat a bowl of sugar, a small pitcher of cream, tea cookies, plus a fine china teapot with matching cups and saucers. She motioned us to the comfortable chairs and asked if we would like some tea. We accepted. I watched this unassuming woman and felt so fortunate to actually be able to speak with her.

After handing us our tea, she sat across the coffee table in a straight-backed chair. There was some small talk as we gently worked into the interview, Dov acting as interpreter. I had a list of questions prepared and took a notebook from my purse. The questions were about her husband and some about her. I knew what I wanted to know, and she knew just what she would tell me and what she would not. Therefore during the interview, she gave me information I did not have, but often she politely refused to answer a question or claimed she did not know. Her husband would not have jeopardized her safety by telling her things that could put her in harm's way. His close confidants knew that he always carried a cyanide capsule on his person. He had said, "Under torture, everyone eventually talks."

I could tell behind her keen eyes that she was not giving me answers to some information she wished to withhold. And I understood why. It was 1988 when we were together, and some complicit Germans, who had managed to melt into the background after the war, were still alive. I had no doubt it was possible that someone could act treacherously towards her or perhaps toward her grown children and grandchildren. I was grateful for any answers.

Overall, I received a deeper insight into the relationship of this remarkable couple. She was his trusted mortal partner; God was his trusted spiritual one. During the war, when an esteemed minister of the Confessional Church expressed anxiety to Gerstein about the danger he was in, he had replied, "Do not worry for me. I cannot fall further than into the loving hands of God."

When it was time for us to leave, Frau Gerstein rose from her chair. Walking over to her nightstand, she opened a drawer and withdrew a piece of rose stationery. On the paper was written the name and telephone number of another close friend. She told us we were welcome to call him. So, we passed another test, the most important of all.

We checked into a hotel, and Dov called Herr Helmut Franz. We were set to meet him at his home in two evenings. Early the next morning, we were on the road again. Reaching the city of Mainz, we stopped. Dov wanted to see St. Stephen's Church built during the Middle Ages. The Jewish artist Marc Chagall had been commissioned in the 1960s to create new stained-glass windows.

We walked into the empty church and sat near the front. The beauty of its simple elegance was striking. White concave walls created a perfect backdrop for Chagall's tall, narrow, stained-glass windows set in iridescent tones of blue with occasional splashes of vibrant primary colors. It seemed a perfect expression of man for an awesome place to worship.

From Mainz, we drove further north, checking into another hotel. That evening we followed Herr Helmut Franz's directions to his home. At 6:00 p.m. Herr and Frau Franz welcomed us. Dov, once again, was the interpreter, although Herr Franz was a businessman and spoke some English. The Franz's were a merry couple, and even though we often needed a translation of words, we did not need translation of feelings.

Herr Franz was a boy when Gerstein, a young youth counselor, led a Christian camp on the island of Sylt in the North Sea. Kurt became a good friend to Helmut's older brother and remained close to the Franz family. Herr Franz told stories of his relationship with Kurt before Hitler's rise, giving me another window into the character of Gerstein.

Herr and Frau Franz took us to dinner at a fine local restaurant. We shared a good bottle of Riesling with our meal and an aperitif for dessert. When we returned to the home, Franz asked if I had a copy of my screenplay. I did. A copy of the screenplay traveled with me wherever we went in Germany. While Dov went out to the car to get it, Franz went into his study and brought out a book he had written and published the year before about Kurt Gerstein. We both wrote inscriptions on our inside covers and traded works.

Franz had one more surprise for us. It was arranged that I would be allowed inside the archives of the Confessing Church and given access to documents relating to Gerstein: his commission and orders by the Third Reich, personal letters written during his time as an SS officer, and other writings and documents of Herr Gerstein's. Dov's wide brown eyes grew wider when he translated this to me. The documents were stored at the Landeskirchliche Archiv in Bielefeld, a town in the northern German region of Westfalen.

Driving back to our hotel, Dov and I were chattering excitedly. It never occurred to either of us that such a place existed. And to think, Dov made this all possible by his first telephone call. I had been studying Kurt Gerstein and the epoch he lived in for five years. I felt like I knew him, and it was becoming more and more personal.

The Landeskirchliche Archiv was a modern three-story, window-walled building in the center of Bielefeld. A tall blonde gentleman greeted and introduced himself, then took us upstairs to sit at a dark-wood table with chairs. He put a short stack of files on the table. His instructions were that we could read and take notes. If we wished to make a copy of any document, we should set it aside, and he would decide if permission would be granted. When we were finished with those files, he would bring others. It was a treasure trove to me. Dov translated, and I took notes as we read each document, many on official Third Reich stationery. From Gerstein's personal letters, we deduced they were often written in some kind of code. He sent coffins to hospitals for the dead, yet it seemed that the coffins contained smuggled supplies to towns to survive the war. I had already written in my screenplay how he smuggled food and other goods into concentration camps through accomplices or bribery. Setting aside various documents to copy, we were only allowed a fraction. But by the end of our time, about four hours, the briefcase where I had carried my screenplay now contained the documents that we were allowed to copy. We thanked the gentleman who assisted us and left.

Stopping for a late lunch, we were soon headed out of Bielefeld back to Munich. It was a seven-hour drive. I drove while Dov translated the documents into my notebook. It was my first foray onto driving the Autobahn—quite an experience. I quickly learned to stay out of the left lane when a Porsche came upon me in an instant. It grew dark; then rain turned into snow.

We arrived late and tired to Dov's apartment. My plane was scheduled to leave at 7:00 a.m. the next morning. We had not meant to cut things so close, but then we had no idea how successful the trip would be. With little sleep, I said goodbye to my Israeli friend. We would not see each other for another year, and then he would be in love with a Sephardic Jewess.

Chapter 23

The new year brought a new rewrite, actually three by March. I was ready to have people read it. Leslie was the first. She highly approved, except she thought it was long for a screenplay. An average script is one hundred and twenty pages; mine was one hundred and fifty. I had so much information. There were so many dramatic events in this man's life; it was difficult to decide. She took it to a vice president at Universal Studios. He submitted it to the script department for analysis. While I waited, another friend whose judgment I trusted read it. He liked it but was not sure how to market it. The Holocaust was a sensitive issue; claiming that an SS officer was a courageous character was a tough sell.

An entertainment lawyer I knew well read it and then took it to an independent producer. He was not interested.

I contacted a personal friend, a film director. He knew about my project and wanted to read it when finished. We met for lunch, and afterwards, he took the script with him. One week later, he called and was very enthusiastic. He said the script was too long, but he had some ideas and wanted to know when he could come over and discuss them. I was excited. We set up a time for the next day.

The next afternoon he was at my door. He came in and put the script on the coffee table. Sitting on the sofa, he began to leaf through the pages, advising me that the script needed tightening. I told him I could not decide what to keep and what to lose. I was hoping a good director would be able to help me once the screenplay was greenlighted. He shook his head, "You've never had a script brought to the screen. You have to do it yourself."

He gave me a trick of the trade. "Take 3"x5" cards, and on each, tag it with a scene heading. Then go through the cards and decide which can be eliminated without jeopardy to the whole."

"Thanks. That's a great idea!"

Then he shocked me, "Look, if you turn the character into a modern-day Macbeth, I think I can get it done."

"Macbeth? Macbeth had blood on his hands."

"Right."

"Kurt Gerstein risked his life saving people."

"Sure, but… He was a member of the SS, and nobody has heard of him. It will never be believed that a member of the SS was a good guy. To be a marketable story, he has to come across as conflicted, you know, a Macbeth-type character."

"But he wasn't." I shook my head, "No, I can't do that."

"Look, you've been working on this a long time. You want to see it made, don't you?"

"Of course, but I won't do that to his character."

"It's the only way I can interest a studio. Just think about it and let me know."

When he left, I was extremely disheartened. The following week, Universal sent the script back. Rejected!

Now reality slapped me in the face. I never called that director and decided to put Kurt Gerstein on the shelf. I would try again later.

Not long after my bitter disappointment, I met an engaging gentleman. A good friend introduced us at a party by saying, "I think you and Ted have an interest in common." We did.

Ted was a self-educated scholar on Nazi Germany, a confirmed bachelor with a full head of graying hair and a sardonic wit. On our second meeting, I drove to his home, where he cooked me an excellent meal. I discovered that besides his historical library, he was also a music buff with an extensive collection of albums. We began seeing each other frequently and exchanged knowledge with stimulating conversations while listening to eclectic music. Ted did not work in the entertainment industry, although his uncle was Norman Lear.

One evening Ted was at my apartment, and I showed him *The Urantia Book*. I had spoken to him about it before, but he was seeing the actual book for the first time. He took it in his hands and, after a few moments, said, "I know this book. My uncle's wife, Lyn, has it."

That was noteworthy; there were so few readers in the world.

In May, my youngest daughter graduated from high school and would be going on to a university in September. My son, out of the Army, had gone on to Hawaii to start a business. He aided me in selling the farm. It was time.

At the end of the summer, Ted took me to a family gathering for Norman Lear's birthday at a relative's condominium. Ted and I arrived after dinner. He introduced me, and we sat down among the group in the living room while everyone pleasantly chatted. Lyn Lear sat on her husband's lap during the evening. She was a very attractive blonde about my age. After a half-hour, she got up and headed through the dining room. I met her a few steps into the room and took the opportunity to greet her personally, "Lyn, Ted tells me that you are a reader of *The Urantia Book*. So am I."

I did not get the reaction I had expected. An intense look crossed her face, "Do you know that there are serious problems between the Brotherhood and the Foundation?"

I shook my head, "I didn't know."

"There's going to be a meeting next Saturday, downtown, between the Trustees of the Foundation and the Executive Committee of the Brotherhood. You should go."

She gave me the name of the hotel where it was to be held and the time. Then she walked into the kitchen to get the birthday cake for her husband. I returned to my place next to Ted and spent the rest of the evening wondering what was going on.

The next day I told my eldest daughter of my encounter the night before and asked if she wanted to go with me to the event. She was as curious as I.

That Saturday, I drove my daughter up our street and turned onto Sunset Boulevard, heading toward the entrance to the Hollywood Freeway, music playing on the car radio. My daughter reached to turn down the volume and said, "I'm confused. What's the difference between the Urantia Foundation and the Urantia Brotherhood? You've never really talked much about these people. Though, I do know the Urantia Foundation publishes the book; it's on the copyright page."

"That's right. It was first published in 1955. The Foundation also owns the trademarks: the word Urantia and the three blue concentric circle symbol on the cover."

"The same on the *Banner of Michael.*"

I smiled, "See, you know something."

"What about the other stuff?"

The Foundation was established in 1950. It was set up by what's called The Declaration of Trust."

"Is that where the Trustees come into it?"

"Yes. There were five men appointed."

"Could there be a woman Trustee?"

"Of course. When anyone becomes a Trustee, they swear an oath to uphold The Declaration of Trust."

"Meaning?"

"There are various duties contained in it, but the most important duty is to keep the text of the book inviolate."

"Inviolate…means unchanged."

"Exactly as it was originally revealed by the Revelatory Commission."

"And they are?"

"Some of the authors of the Papers."

"You know, when I was in college and would read the book sometimes before I went to sleep, my roommates would notice and ask about it. If I told them that it was written by different celestial beings, they usually thought I was joking. So how do *you* explain it?"

181

"Good question. It depends. If someone is sincere, then I encourage them to read it for themselves and find out."

"Good answer. If I hadn't read it myself, I probably wouldn't believe it either... You know, Mom, when my classmates and I would get into a discussion if there really was a God, I would ask: 'How could there not be?' It's funny, but that would usually end the discussion.

"And as you mature, you will see more and more of His hand in your life."

"I like the fact that there are angels here to help."

"They are actually closer to you in the physical sense."

"Except I wish I could see them."

"People have. Any more questions?"

"What about the Urantia Brotherhood?"

"I don't know much about them. The Foundation set it up as its social entity to foster study groups and do conferences. I went to one of their conferences a long time ago. I liked it; it was well organized."

"So, do they have Trustees too?"

"No, only the Foundation has."

"Who runs it?"

"Don't know. Let's find out."

"Let's."

My daughter reached to the radio, turned up the volume, and blasted Axl Rose singing "Welcome to the Jungle."

On Saturdays in downtown Los Angeles, there is not much traffic. My daughter and I arrived, parked the car, walked through the lobby, and found the conference room with rows of folding chairs and people milling about. At the head of the room, on a moderately raised stage, were two tables, each long enough for four people to comfortably sit looking out at the audience. One table faced forward, the other table was to the left at a slight angle, giving the men at both tables the ability to see each other when they spoke.

The men at these head tables were not all seated; some were standing and talking with others. I saw Lyn Lear and went up to say hello. She was gracious but busy, so we left her to her work. A woman was passing out copies of the agenda. When she handed one to my daughter, we noticed that she was wearing a small azure blue concentric circle pin on the lapel of her jacket. My daughter commented on the pin; she liked it. The woman proudly stated that they were given out by the Brotherhood if you had read the book in its entirety.

The meeting was called to order. People took their seats. Few chairs remained empty. From our vantage point, my daughter and I were able to closely view all the debaters at the two head tables. And that is what it turned out to be, a debate. The acoustics in the room were excellent.

The participants introduced themselves to the audience. At the table directly in front sat three Trustees of the Foundation. The angled table had four men who announced themselves as the Executive Committee of the Brotherhood. Of the three men from the Foundation, I recognized two of them, the banjo player at the

1973 conference in Brentwood, Richard Keeler, and Martin Myers from his speech at that conference. The Brotherhood Executive Committee had a President; he was a light-haired, somewhat younger man. His name was David Elders.

My daughter and I had no particular expectations. When the discussion turned heated, I was surprised. The atmosphere caused me to focus more on the demeanor of the two groups rather than the substance of the issues. David Elders was often argumentative, not deliberative, and the other three members of the Brotherhood group groused with him. It was disconcerting. The men at the Foundation table were no shrinking violets in answering back, but not in such an emotionally charged manner. When the meeting was adjourned with seemingly nothing resolved, my daughter and I left. We did not stay around for refreshments.

As we drove home, I asked my daughter what she thought. "I liked what Martin Myers had to say; he made the most sense. What did you think?"

"I thought Richard Keeler did his best to act as peacemaker toward the Brotherhood representatives."

"What about the guy David Elders?" she asked.

"He made me feel uncomfortable. I found what the entire Brotherhood group talked about disturbing. Their wanting to use advertising to sell the book is wrongheaded. I know the original mandate was to introduce the book on a person-to-person level. That was one of the things that attracted me in the first place."

"Why do you think they are so set on changing it?"

"Well, it's a lot easier to sell a book, then to interest someone by living its teachings."

"Doesn't look good."

"No, it doesn't."

Chapter 24

My finances, or lack thereof, made it clear that it was time for me to focus on getting a real job. Although my typing skills were good, and I had been using the dot-matrix system for my screenplays, the new computer software was a mystery. My computer savvy daughter offered to teach me Microsoft Word. I bought a how-to book, and she let me practice on her work computer after hours at the production company.

Now I needed transportation. My sister was buying a new car, and instead of using her older one as a trade-in, she generously offered it to me. Mom and I drove down to San Diego, spent a weekend with family, and I drove the 1982 silver Nissan Maxima diesel home.

That next week I signed up with a temp agency that specializes in the entertainment industry. My first temp job was at Paramount Studios in the offices of Eddie Murphy. I did not get to use my new software skills much. Mostly I was answering the phone and sending out fan mail, pictures of the star. The next job was at the Walt Disney Studios for two weeks. Here, I began to learn the Disney intercompany system.

After that, there were two more Disney jobs: one for a producer developing a screenplay that would be made into the movie "Captain Ron" starring Kurt Russell, the other in the screenplay submission department.

As a temp, I was usually filling in for an assistant or a secretary on vacation, and my duties were never very demanding.

My next call was for one of the Disney legal departments. Disney had its own DVD distribution division, Buena Vista Home Entertainment. The attorney I began working for was newly hired and had come from an academic background, not entertainment. We worked well together, and my background in the industry impressed him to the point that he told the personnel department that he wanted to hire me full-time. The head of personnel had someone else in mind for the job and gave him a hard time, but he insisted. I was hired.

On a beautiful autumn day, Marian flew from Hawaii to L.A. She was a masseuse, and a client that lived in the Malibu Colony had hired her for two weeks. I picked her up at the airport. She stayed with us overnight. We got into a conversation regarding the problems between the two Urantia organizations. Marian was always a font of information.

"The Brotherhood wants more autonomy. They are fighting the Foundation over commercial advertising and pricing of the book. They think it is too expensive, and the price slows dissemination."

"It's an expensive book to publish and worth every penny. Actually, it's priceless," I commented.

"It is priceless."

"Please explain to me the hierarchy of the Brotherhood. It's confusing."

"There's the Executive Committee, plus an additional group of thirty people in the General Council who support and advise the Executive Committee."

"Lots of cooks," I quipped.

"There are. The Executive Committee has fourteen members, David Elders is President."

"I remember him from a Urantia meeting my daughter and I recently attended at a hotel downtown. So where's the problem?"

Marian confided, "David Elders wants to get rid of the Trustee Martin Myers."

"On what grounds?"

"He's interfering with the actions of the Brotherhood."

"How?" I questioned.

"I haven't heard all the specifics, but it seems personal."

"He was there at the hotel meeting too."

"The Executive Committee even sent a letter to the Foundation demanding Martin's resignation."

"How could they make that happen? Trustees are appointed by fellow Trustees."

"They can't, actually."

"It seems futile. The Foundation owns the copyright and the trademarks. What leverage could the Brotherhood possibly have?"

"Don't know. Though I heard that David said the angels were on the side of the apostle Paul, not Abner."

"Really? He's privy to the activity of angels? And is he supposed to be Paul?"

Marian laughed.

"What a shame! Do any of these people read the same book I read?" I lamented. "Where is truth, beauty, and goodness?"

The next day, I drove Marian down Pacific Coast Highway into the gated community of the Malibu Colony. In my music video days, I had been there to parties at night but never in the light of day. Her client had an expensive home with a raised terrace over the beach. I sat in a lounge chair sipping iced tea while she gave the woman a massage. Every home I could see had a large terrace. Nobody was on the sand.

Marian came out to join me. I said, "Let's walk on the beach."

We soon discovered why nobody was on the beach. The shore was the substitute for walking one's dog. Marian and I had to navigate between dog poop in the wet sand and gently lapping waves. Our jaunt did not last long.

At the end of the year, Marian called to tell me that the two Urantia organizations had officially split. She informed me: "The Foundation has de-licensed the Brotherhood. They can no longer use the name Urantia or the concentric circle symbol and have to move out of the Foundation building."

"Why? What happened?"

"The Brotherhood held a general meeting and unanimously passed a resolution making itself an independent, autonomous organization. They informed the Foundation that they would no longer jointly fundraise or even share the membership list. On top of that, they wanted more space in the Foundation building in Chicago."

"Wait a minute. They wanted what?"

"They lease part of the first floor. They wanted to lease the whole floor including all the offices so they could expand. Oh…and hang their own sign on the building."

"Are they nuts? What an odd demand! They're saying we don't want to have anything to do with you anymore, but we want more of your space."

Marian agreed, "How did they expect the Foundation to react?"

"Now, no more Urantia Brotherhood. What a mess. It's so sad."

"It's a mess, all right."

"Well, it's over," I added.

"We'll see. By the way, how are you doing? Still seeing that guy Ted?"

"That's over."

"Oh, sorry."

"It's nothing to be sorry about. It just fizzled out."

"Well, knowing your life, someone else will come along. Men take to you like bees to honey."

Chapter 25

When I worked at CBS, it was in the department of Business Affairs. My boss was an attorney, but his job was making deals with talent agents, not writing contracts. Often it was necessary to go to the legal department to pick up a contract. Watching those secretaries typing legal documents, I would think how I would never want to be one. Now I was, and grateful to be employed. Copyright and trademark law are integral to the release of Disney DVDs into the marketplace. It was an interesting legal education that has served me well. And I enjoyed the company atmosphere.

When I stepped outside for lunch onto what was referred to as 'the campus,' it made for a lovely break in the day. Employees walked along paths between swaths of freshly mowed grass in a park-like setting and saw chipmunks scurrying from tree to tree, real or cartoon, depending upon your mood. Streets were named after Disney characters. You could take Goofy Lane down to the backlot, where movie sets sat idle, and enjoy your lunch sitting on a bench. My favorite quote from the master visionary Walt Disney is one he wrote for Tinkerbell, "All you need is faith, trust, and a little pixie dust."

Through my youngest daughter's doing, I met her boyfriend's uncle, a divorced gentleman. The gentleman and I began seeing each other on a regular basis. One evening we were talking about my screenplay. He wondered why I did not submit it to Disney. I explained that company policy was not to accept unsolicited scripts from employees. Everyone wanted to be a screenwriter in Tinsel Town.

All the documents I had gathered in Germany, plus Helmut Franz's book sat safely in my credenza. Dov had translated the pertinent ones, but I wanted to be able to read them all myself. I decided to study the German language. Finding a night class twice a week at the San Fernando Valley Community College, I enrolled. From Burbank, the home of the Walt Disney Studios, I could easily travel to the college in the Valley. In the spring, I took a seat in the front row of German 101.

My relationship with the divorced gentleman was moving along nicely. The possibility of marriage was discussed. Although, he often expressed curiosity in just why I was studying German, since my script was completed. He had a pilot's license, which I had an interest in. He offered to pay for flying lessons if I would quit my German classes. I found that a strange proposal. It seemed he felt threatened in some way. I gave it some serious consideration but decided to turn down the offer. Little did I realize the future would show his concern was prescient.

The year 1990 passed quickly. My baby girl had graduated high school and was on to college. My eldest daughter became engaged to a talented director of photography, and she moved out to live with him. They would be married the next year. My son maintained a partnership in a business in Hawaii.

Dov returned from Germany and introduced me to his fiancée. The three of us had dinner together, and I learned that a Sephardic

Jew was of mixed Spanish and Moor descent. From time to time, Dov and I would meet for lunch, and we tried to converse in German, but after five minutes, he was back to English. It took a lot of patience to follow my broken German conversation. So, to improve my conversation skills, I added a class at the Berlitz Language Center in Westwood on Saturday afternoons.

During a New Year's Eve party to ring in 1991, my divorced gentleman introduced me to a woman, an old family friend. Maybe it was the champagne, but she seemed to be more than a family friend, and she was not that old. By the end of January, with no champagne, I discovered she was a *very* close family friend. "Fool me once, shame on you. Fool me twice, shame on me." I ended the relationship. It hurt, and some tears were shed, but trust issues are a big deal. (I have always believed that a broken heart hurts more than a broken leg. I have had both.)

On Saturday the day before Easter, my mother was in San Diego with my sister's family. I was alone, feeling sorry for myself when the phone rang. It was Dov. He asked if I wanted to go to a party that afternoon in the Pacific Palisades. I told him I could be ready in an hour. He picked me up, and we drove down Sunset Boulevard to Pacific Coast Highway, turning into the Palisades.

Pacific Palisades is a community of exclusive homes built on a bluff overlooking the big blue Pacific Ocean. After finding a parking space a block from the Spanish-style house, we walked through the open front door. Just inside was a long foyer. Against the right wall was a table spread with hors d'oeuvres and an open bar. On the left was a step-down living room with guests mingling with drinks in their hands.

Standing alone in the middle of the foyer was a man who looked sad. The lone figure was dressed in black: black silk sports jacket, black turtleneck, black slacks, and black Bally loafers. His considerable light blonde hair noticeably contrasted with the black clothing.

I said to Dov, "Let's go talk to that guy. He looks lonely."

We went up and greeted him. He smiled a little and, with an accent said, "Hello, my name is Joe, I come from Germany. I don't speak English."

No way! I was thrilled and immediately introduced myself in German and said a few sentences. He looked at me quizzically. I did not seem to be making myself clear. Maybe it was my accent? Dov joined in, and they engaged in a short, friendly conversation. From what I could understand, they were talking about cars. "Typical," I judged.

More people came through the door, and the party started picking up. Dov and I left the German and mingled for a couple of hours in the many-roomed mansion with two large patios from where guests could watch the California sunset.

With the fading sunlight, a quarter moon became visible. Dov and I had split up, talking to different groups. When he found me, he said we should be leaving soon.

A plan popped into my mind. I went into the bathroom, took a piece of paper and pen from my purse to write my name and phone number. My hands were a bit shaky. I had never given my number unsolicited before, but I convinced myself I had nothing to lose. Joe seemed like a nice fellow, and if he invited me to dinner, he would have to converse with me in German. I went looking and found him on one of the patios smoking a cigarette. I was so nervous, I don't remember what I said, but attempting to act cool, I smiled, slipped the paper into the upper pocket of his sport coat, and added, "Auf wiedersehen."

As Dov and I were walking to the car, he asked, "Did you give your number to that guy?"

It was a strange question since Dov and I were not involved. I said, "What guy?"

"The German that looked like he just stepped out of Central Casting."

For some inexplicable reason, I lied and said, "No."

Late Wednesday afternoon, my mother returned from San Diego. I told her to come to my apartment, I would fix dinner. She brought a bottle of champagne, and while she poured, I told her about my Saturday and meeting a German guy. I added, "He probably won't call."

Mom smiled, raised her glass in a little toast, and said, "Maybe."

I was busy taking a roasted chicken out of the oven when the phone rang. I asked her to get it. The phone was in the dining room on a side table. She picked it up and said, "Hello."

She walked into the kitchen with a big grin on her face and handed me the receiver, whispering, "It sounds like him."

It was, and after a few minutes, we managed to make a dinner date for Saturday.

Saturday evening at 7:30 p.m. sharp, the doorbell rang. I hurried down the stairs putting in my earring. When I answered the door, I took a closer look at him and was pleased with what I saw.

Joe had been in Los Angeles for two months and was learning his way around. He asked if I would like to go to a French restaurant. French was fine. He opened the door of a white Porsche, and I sat in the bucket seat of the sports car. During the short drive to the restaurant not far from my apartment, I said, "Your name can't be Joe, that's English."

"My name is Josef."

"Well, that was easily translatable."

He gave me an amusing quick smile.

When we entered the restaurant, the maître d gave us a wide grin and asked, "Table for two?"

"Yes, please."

The restaurant was large and at the very center was a gazebo raised three steps above the floor with one table. The maître d seated us there; it was like being on stage. Joe and I spent the entire time through wine and dinner communicating in my bad German and his sparse English, including many hand gestures. It was fun.

While waiting for dessert, I went to the lady's room. On my way back, for the first time, I noticed the other diners—*all* the other diners. We were in a gay restaurant. Joe and I were the only heterosexual couple in the place. I should have known. It was on Santa Monica Boulevard in West Hollywood. No wonder we were in the gazebo. I asked him if he had been here before. He shook his head no. It was quite tricky explaining the dining clientele, but when he looked around, he understood and laughed. He had driven by the place quite often on his way from his apartment to a business he and a partner owned. The restaurant's name in French was prominently displayed on the awning.

Every time I saw my German friend, he was driving a different European car. He had come to California on a business visa to buy high-end used cars to ship back to Europe. California cars had no rust since there was neither snow nor chemicals on the roads to melt snow. He bought the cars at auction or from private parties. When he had enough cars for a shipping container, he would send them to a partner in Brussels who sold them to dealers throughout Europe. Joe's second partner, whom I later met, was from Austria. Together they had a foreign car repair shop in Altadena. The partner had been in California for a year, and his English was very good. Through Joe's business dealings, his English was rapidly improving.

We had been dating for over a month when one evening, I drove down to his apartment in Marina del Rey, an upscale harbor community. We walked to the Chart House for dinner and then to a disco. Afterward, we returned to his apartment and were going to take a walk along the boardwalk, but first he wanted to check his cell phone. It was the first cell phone I had ever seen, a Sony black box with the hand piece in a cradle. It had to be carried by a strap like a handbag. He used it for business, and it was also his personal phone. He listened to a message and then excused himself and went into the bedroom to make a call.

I waited, sitting comfortably on a balcony chair where I could view the marina full of yachts with their tall masts, listening to the

197

tinkling of bells as they swayed in their boat slips. The call did not last long. He came out and told me that we would not be taking a walk, and I should go home. Was I surprised! He ushered me out the door. I made my way to the car by myself and drove home quite dismayed.

The next morning, I was having coffee with my mother and told her the disconcerting story. She did not know what to say. All I could think of was that maybe another woman had called and left a message that she was coming over. I was disappointed and sighed, "He was too classy for me anyway." She gave me a look I could not read.

Not enough time had been spent between the German and myself to say that the incident caused me heartache, but I did have feelings of rejection.

MAP OF THE CARIBBEAN

West Indies

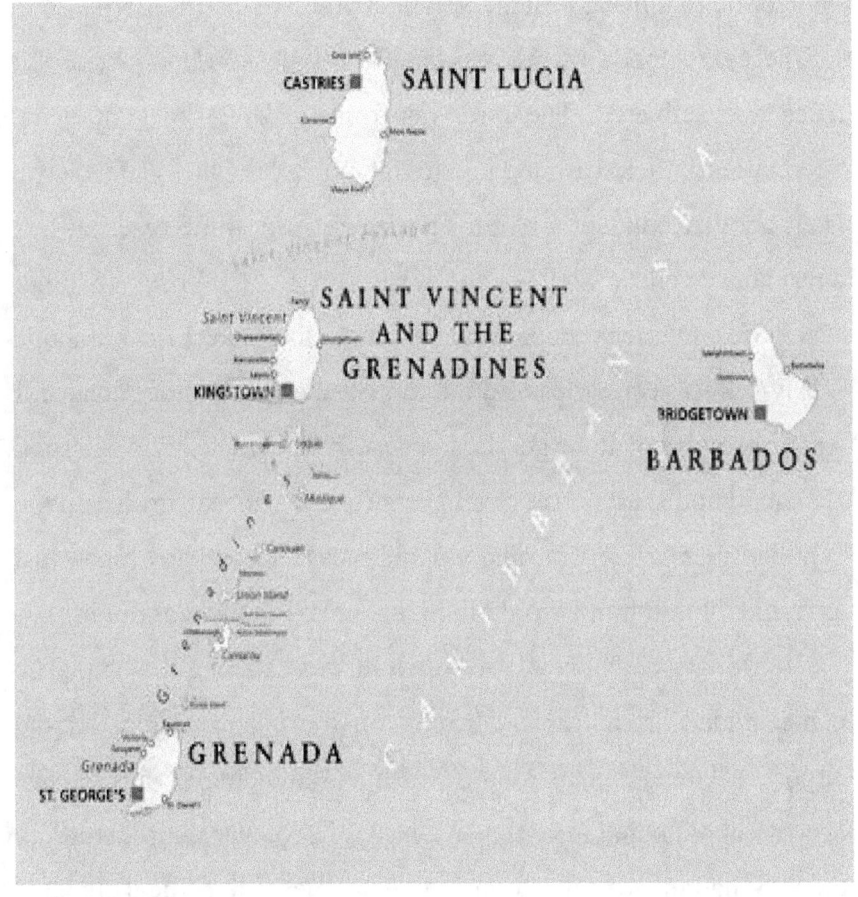

Chapter 26

A couple of weeks later, I received a phone call from the divorced gentleman. He wanted to patch things up between us and invited me to dinner. I said, "No thank you."

The next Monday while working at my desk, a bouquet of red roses was delivered. The card was from the divorced gentleman. Secretaries gathered around my desk. Ooooh, how lucky! Two days later, another bouquet arrived. This time it was white roses. A few days later, yellow and so on. I was giving the roses to other secretaries. Our legal department began to look like a flower shop.

My fellow secretaries told me to give the guy another chance. I was not so sure. But the gentleman was sly and knew my weak spot. He called and said he had two tickets for a Caribbean cruise on the Windjammer Cruise Line and would I please accompany him—just as friends. I told him I would think about it. I thought about it.

We flew to Grenada where we would be catching the ship. The plane landed amid tropical beauty on the island nation. At the airport, a Grenadian man stood with a Windjammer sign. I was nervous about being in Grenada. During the Reagan administration, the U.S. had invaded the country to get American medical students who were being held hostage by government troops. Another issue was an airfield that had been constructed using Cuban labor and Russian money; it was long enough to land large military aircraft. The invasion had been big news in the U.S. media.

I spoke to the Grenadian man holding the Windjammer sign and told him that I was an American, and since we had invaded his country, maybe I should never mention my nationality. He laughed and said, "You didn't invade us. You rescued us. Those Cubans treated us like dogs."

I felt a little better, but I did not completely trust his answer. After all, he was making a living from tourists, many of them Americans.

We had one day on Grenada before boarding the ship. My friend rented a car, and we drove the roads of the "Spice Island" known for cinnamon, nutmeg, and mace. Visiting a marketplace, it was obvious the people were poor, but they were busy selling what they farmed. We decided to drive to a waterfall recommended to us by a hotel clerk.

The topography of the island is volcanic. Driving up a steep incline, ahead of us, just before a sharp turn, was a large concrete wall. Without it, if you went straight, you would have driven off the cliff. On the entire length of the wall was one line of graffiti, the only graffiti I saw on the island. It read, "We love President Reagan."

When we reached our waterfall destination, there were a few curio shops. In one shop, with very few items to sell, a portrait painted on velvet of Ronald and Nancy Reagan was hanging on the wall. It seemed so out of place in the little room. I was curious and asked the woman how much it cost. She looked at me offended and said, "Not for sale. It belongs to my family."

I felt compelled to buy something in the shop and left with several little gunny sacks of island spices.

The entire drive back to the hotel, I was thinking about how in the states, the 'invasion' had been reported and was still reported years later. My early editing days with Doug and that director who slanted the truth about the 'vegetarian starlet' came to mind. From then on, I vowed to take the reportage of any news with a healthy dose of skepticism.

In the late afternoon, we took a taxi to the port where our cruise ship was docked. Our ship, the *Fantome*, was a romantic four-masted schooner. We were told that originally Aristotle Onassis built the ship as a wedding gift for Princess Grace and Prince Rainier, but they neglected to invite him to the wedding, so it was later sold. It sailed today with a manifest of eighty-four passengers. Our stateroom was tiny with bunk beds and a typical marine head. I slept on the bottom bunk with the porthole to the sea as my window to the voyage.

From Grenada, we sailed to the islands of Carriacou, Petit Martinique, Palm Island, and the uninhabited islands of the Tobago Cays belonging to St. Vincent and the Grenadines. We spent our days snorkeling and our evenings socializing and drinking rum punch aboard ship. The last island we visited was Bequia, a small well-populated island also part of St. Vincent. It was *the* party island, and at night we danced at a "Jump Up" intermixed with locals. A Jump Up was a weekly scheduled outdoor island disco with a live steel band playing reggae music and also covering popular top-forty songs. "Red Red Wine" is a staple tune of the Caribbean.

Every morning at sunrise, the young British Captain, standing on the bridge of the ship in his starched white uniform, ordered the raising of the sails of the four tall masts. Heavy white canvas flapped in the wind as the black crewmen, dressed in white pants and blue and white striped cotton t-shirts, pulled aloft the sails to the music of the sailor's prayer *Amazing Grace*. Awesome! At night, the sky was crowded with stars, and the Southern Cross glittered visibly. Magnificent! Although the cruise did not rekindle a romance with the gentleman, it did ignite a romance with the Caribbean Islands.

On June 28, an earthquake rocked Southern California. I thought of the German and how he had probably never experienced an earthquake. At work that morning, I decided to give him a call.
He answered, "Hello."

"Hello wie gehts, it's Carole. I was concerned about you with the earthquake."

"Oh hello, I'm okay. I'm living in Pasadena. Things fell off the shelves and broke."

"Pasadena? Why do you have the same phone number?"

"My cell phone."

"Oh right…Pasadena is near the epicenter of the quake."

"It's bad. There's no electricity, and I can't play my music or have my coffee."

"I am glad to hear you're okay."

"Thank you."

"Well, goodbye. Tschuess."

"Tschuess."

I sat at my desk, shaking my head. An earthquake woke him up, things fell off the shelves, and he was worried about music and coffee. What a character!

The character called me within a few days and made a dinner date. I drove out to Pasadena and met him at the restaurant. Enjoying a glass of wine, I asked him why he was living there. He told me it was close to the European auto shop that he and his Austrian partner owned.

Dinner came, and as we ate, I pressed him, asking what happened the last time we had seen each other. He was hesitant but finally told me that the telephone call he had received was bad news, very bad. He had loaded a shipping container the month before with cars that had cost him over a million dollars. The container never made it to Brussels. Somewhere along the line, it was stolen. I asked if he had insured it. The answer was no. I thought to myself, "Boy, that was a costly mistake."

"When you left, I made more phone calls. The autos were gone. Then I went to the liquor store, bought a bottle of Jack Daniels, and went to the beach."

"I'm so sorry."

"When I woke up on the sand, the sun was in my face. I had a bad headache. I thought okay, Joe, you must keep up."

"Keep going," I corrected.

"Yes, keep going."

And he had. He moved out of his expensive Marina del Rey apartment to a guesthouse in Pasadena. I liked him better. Before he seemed arrogant. The arrogance was gone, although he was still a self-confident man.

After dinner, we were sitting on the small patio of his bungalow when I told him about my trip to the Caribbean and how I was saving money to go back and live there for a while. He confided that the Caribbean had been his goal in life. In fact, he had spent his business life working toward attaining enough money to move to the Caribbean and buy a restaurant or some other business. When in Germany, he owned a bistro while he was the VP of Marketing for a major German automaker. Often, after work, for fun, he would be the chef at the bistro.

I said, "I guess it's not your destiny now."

With a sad look on his face, he nodded his head.

I left and did not hear from him again until September when he called and asked if I was still planning to go to the Caribbean. Figuring I would have enough money by the end of November, I said, "Yes."

My plan was vague, but I believed I could find work there, although I was not sure where there was just yet. He asked if he could come over to talk. I said, "Sure."

The next evening, he came to my apartment, and we discussed the islands. I told him which ones I had visited. Our conversation lasted a couple of hours, and at some point, the pronoun "we" began to be used. By the end of the evening, we were going together. His partner would buy him out of the auto shop, and he would have some start-up money, nothing like what he had originally planned but maybe enough. First, he thought it best for us to find work on an island.

By the end of October, I had given notice at Disney and sent my youngest daughter to live with her brother on the Big Island. She did not want to continue with college, and I did not want to leave her at our apartment. During the last semester, our place had become *the place off of Sunset Blvd* for her sorority sisters. The rock-n-roll scene was big and fun, and too inviting.

On November 11, 1991, Joe and I were on a plane, destination Barbados. With layovers, it took over ten hours. Landing at the airport outside of Bridgetown, taxi drivers were waiting at the baggage claim area to help tourists with luggage and take them to hotels in the area of St. James.

We were greeted by a friendly Barbadian man and followed him to his taxi. As he was driving us to the hotel, he circled in a roundabout where at the center was a large statue of a black man literally breaking his chains against slavery. It was an expressive work of art. The driver gave us a little history lesson: The statue was of a Barbadian hero, a slave named Bussa, who led a slave revolt in 1816.

The tourist area of St. James was one very nice hotel after another on the island coastline. British families going back to colonial days owned the hotels. Barbados is part of the British Commonwealth.

After spending one day there, we made an appointment with the hotel manager to inquire about employment in the area. During the meeting, we gave oral resumes of our qualifications. Did he have any suggestions? The man listened to us and said, "You don't really want to live on the island."

Of course that struck us as odd. We rented a mini-moke and traveled into the interior and around the island. The people were not friendly. The Brit was right, we did not see any opportunities.

Back at the hotel, sitting by the pool, we discussed where to go next. I thought of Bequia, the Grenadine Island of St. Vincent, the last island on the Windjammer cruise. The people were friendly, and the harbor was filled with yachts. (Any boat over thirty feet is called a yacht in the Caribbean.)

St. Vincent and the Grenadines was mainly a yachting destination. People from Europe, Australia, and the US converged to enjoy the easy sailing from one island to the next. Many sailing tourists rented yachts at the neighboring island country of St. Lucia and sailed south to the Grenadines. Others sailed their own yachts. Some avid sailors caught the winds as far north as The British Virgin Islands. Commercially sponsored regattas were frequent during the winter season.

We flew into the small airport on St. Vincent near the capital Kingston. We were not traveling light. I had two suitcases; Joe had three. After exchanging money into EC (Eastern Caribbean money), we took a taxi to the Bequia ferry landing, only to discover we had missed the ferry by five minutes. The taxi had deposited us and our luggage on the concrete wharf. The sun was beating down, my blouse was beginning to stick to me. I was tired and not happy at the thought we would have to look for another taxi to take us to a hotel in town and try again the next day. I always keep in mind one of the admonitions in the book: *Mortals only learn wisdom through adversity*. But it was not working its usual magic on me.

Joe was not deterred, he walked around talking to local men to see if there was a way we could get to the island. He found the captain of a trading boat that was delivering boxes of frozen chicken thighs and drumsticks to Bequia, and he was willing to take us along for $10 EC. We climbed aboard his vessel. His men loaded our luggage. On the way over, we sat on deck on boxes of frozen chicken that were covered by a thick blue tarp.

About fifteen minutes into the voyage, I was feeling better about it all and decided to walk to the bow. In order to go up front, I had to go through the pilothouse. Coming out of the bright sun and into the shaded pilothouse, I took one step and fell through a dark open hatch down into the engine room. I landed on the shoulders, then into the arms of a very strong black man. After his great surprise to find me in his arms, he said, "Da white lady, she land on me!" Ha, ha, ha.

It was quite amusing for everyone, even me as I was being helped out of the hold. Yet, in the back of my mind was the fact that if he had not managed to break my fall and catch me, I am sure I would have broken something.

On Bequia, we took a taxi to Lower Bay. We had already checked hotel rates, and a guesthouse at Lower Bay was the most reasonable. It was a long clapboard building with sixteen rooms on the second floor. There were two communal bathrooms for guests, one at either end of the hall, cold showers only. We lugged our suitcases to the room. There were two windows open to the breeze, but no screens on the windows. (We didn't see a screened window the whole time we were in the Caribbean.) After unpacking some things, we changed into more comfortable clothes and went to look for dinner.

Walking down the only road, we came upon an open beach café called Da Reef and ordered fresh grilled fish and a lobster salad for a total of $7 EC, including a Hairoun beer for Joe. The exchange rate was about $3 EC for $1 US. We were the only diners except for an older gentleman with a British accent and a young surfer-looking guy with a ponytail. We would get to know both of them well.

That night, fair-haired, fair-skinned Joe was a magnet for the mosquitos that came through the open windows while we slept. I had a couple of bites; he was covered. After a continental breakfast with other well-bitten guests, we all walked into town and bought mosquito repellant.

The next day things got busy on the island. Season was on. Lower Bay had a sandy cove. Down the road, closer to town was Princess Margaret Beach. During our stay, we made friends that remain close to us today. There were a lot of wild and crazy vacationers there with us, four couples banded together and partied hardy.

One day we pooled our money and hired a yacht and its captain to sail us to one of the deserted islands with a white sand beach. The island was deserted except for a wooden table used by local fishermen to clean their fish. We overstayed our chartered time and were an hour late leaving the island. The captain was none too pleased. On the way back, we encountered rough weather, or the captain and his mate just kept tacking; either way it was a rough ride. Then going into the Bequia harbor in the evening, the boat's engine would not start, so the captain had to sail zigzagging between many moored yachts. When the vessel slowed, dragging its anchor to a halt, we did not wait for the dingy and just jumped overboard and waded the short distance to the beach. Later we met up at Da Reef for dinner. It was all great fun, but in the end Joe and I had to get serious. Our new friends were vacationing; we were looking for work.

In the only St. Vincent newspaper, we had posted an ad with short resumes looking for employment. We gave the telephone number of the Lower Bay guesthouse. After a couple of weeks, the owner of the Wallilabou Anchorage, a restaurant and yachting harbor located on St. Vincent at the port of entry into the country, left us a message. I called the number (Joe's English not being as good as mine) and spoke with the owner Mr. Russell. An appointment was set for January 2.

On New Year's Day 1992, we said goodbye to our new friends and boarded the ferry to St. Vincent. Joe was down to two suitcases. He had given away some nice clothes to the workers at the guesthouse. Upon debarking, a taxi took us to a hotel that Mr. Russell recommended. He picked us up the next day, and we drove out to a large colonial-style home. We met Mrs. Russell, a Canadian. She led the interview in her office. She told us that Wallilabou was losing money, it needed competent management.

The Russells also owned the Coca-Cola bottling franchise for St. Vincent and the Grenadines. After the interview, we sat at a grand dining room table for lunch with them. They offered us the prospect of staying at the harbor for ten days to observe the restaurant and the concession that rented out moorings for yachts. Joe told them that we would draw up a proposal.

Our host took us on a long drive to Wallilabou through outlying villages. Traveling by boat would have been much quicker. Mr. Russell, a Vincentian, was a bit eccentric and carried a small 22-caliber pistol in his glove compartment. He showed it to us. It gave us pause, but the locals paid him no mind, even when he brandished it at the boat boys. Boat boys were village teens, some even younger, on surfboards who paddled out to the moored yachts and generally pestered the yachtsmen. But they also provided a service and brought fresh produce and other grocery items to sell to the sailors.

We stayed at Wallilabou for the ten days, witnessing numerous problems. There were many yachts moored in the bay since it was the port of entry, and they came in for the day before heading across the Grenadines. Wallilabou should have been making a profit. Upstairs over the restaurant was the office. Sitting atop a desk was an old manual typewriter. Joe drew up the proposal; I typed it.

Local ladies, two cooks, and one waitress were running the restaurant. The former manager, a Canadian woman, had fallen in love with a handsome Vincentian and ran off with him into the jungle, or so the gossip went according to the ladies.

On the seventh day of our stay, a boat with an outboard motor steered by a young black man pulled up to the dock. His white passenger, a trim, nice-looking man jumped out. Joe and I were standing near the seaside entrance to the restaurant. Chuck came up and introduced himself. He, an American, and his wife, a Canadian, owned an eco-type resort just two bays over. He had heard about us through the 'coconut wireless' and invited us to go with him to see his place. We got into the boat. I enjoyed traveling in this open boat, skirting the beautiful tropical shoreline. It was a different perspective on the brilliant handiwork of the architects of our Father's universe.

The couple's bay was a tropical garden with palm trees surrounding its sandy cove and an island-style restaurant. Hidden among the lush foliage of the hillside were twelve large, over-sized tents with queen beds, private outdoor bathrooms, and patios overlooking the bay. It also had moorings for four or five yachts in its small harbor.

We sat at an outside table of the couple's restaurant and had an interesting conversation with them. The restaurant seated twenty diners. During our visit, from a yacht moored in the bay, three people got into a dingy and came ashore for drinks. Joe offered to fix an appetizer for the yachters. Chuck said, "By all means."

Joe went into the kitchen and found large tomatoes, cream cheese, and fresh basil growing just outside the kitchen door in an herb garden. He invented plates of 'Caribbean' Insalata Caprese for the three yachters, plus Chuck, his wife, and me by sprinkling olive oil and balsamic vinegar on the salads. Everyone was impressed. Joe knew he was interviewing; I was oblivious and just along for the ride.

While Chuck was motoring us back to Wallilabou, he mentioned that if things didn't work out with Mr. Russell that he and his wife would be interested in hiring us. Joe said, "I'll keep that in mind."

Our six-week visitor visas were set to expire. When we brought this to the attention of Mr. Russell, he said he could handle it. He boasted that he had been a member of the government and knew people well. It seemed he did know people too well. He was a prominent member of the opposition party from the one in power. We quickly lost our naiveté to island politics when we sat with Mr. Russell for a very long time in the office of a government official and left with no visa in hand.

A few days later, we decided to try on our own. Mr. Russell advised we might have better luck. We did not, and when the Vincentian passport official wanted to keep our passports, Joe said, "No thank you." We left the office.

Joe contacted Chuck and told him we were leaving. He suggested that we leave the country and go to St. Lucia, the closest independent island. After ten days, we could return by applying for another visitor visa, and then he would get us work visas if we wanted to work for them. We were on the plane to St. Lucia the day our visa expired.

Chapter 27

St Lucia is the next island nation and a beautiful yachting destination as well. We stayed at a simple guesthouse overlooking Rodney Bay, a renowned marina with slips for both large and small yachts from around the world. After ten days at the docks, meeting some interesting foreigners, we returned to St. Vincent.

Coincidently, the same official who wanted, twelve days before, to keep our passports was one of two officers manning passport control when we returned. I recognized him and told Joe we should get into the other guy's line. But it was too late. Joe stood out in the crowd of few tourists and majority locals. But we did get into the other line. When it was our turn, the official joined our officer and took our passports. He angrily said to Joe, "You're that world-famous chef. I spoke to you before. Your visa expired." (Things can get exaggerated on an island.)

He took us to the sidewall of the small airport, where we sat on a bench, not knowing our future. I understood that the man was doing his job. Nonetheless, while we had been on St. Lucia, we had run into a British fellow we knew. He had been managing a resort on Bequia at Friendship Bay. The Brit had overstayed his work visa at the request of the Vincentian hotel owner, yet he had been arrested and put in jail on the island. He was not released until some yachting folks heard about his plight and arranged to take him off the island, sailing to Rodney Bay. I seriously wondered what the inside of the women's jail looked like. It could not be good.

Joe and I sat there for an hour before the officer returned with our passports. We were not allowed to re-enter the country. After paying a considerable fine and the cost of two plane tickets, we were escorted by two uniformed officers onto the last plane leaving for St. Lucia. They boarded us last after the other passengers and sat us in the two front seats of the small aircraft. We were rejected VIP's.

Back to the Rodney Bay guesthouse we went and were in daily contact with Chuck. He and Sharon were serious about getting us back to their establishment. We liked these people, and their bay was beautiful. Working for them for a year or two would give us a real feel for business on the island. So, we waited to see if Chuck was able to move the visa office in our direction.

With all this back and forth, we were seriously running out of money. Joe's Austrian partner in the business back in Altadena, California had paid him some of the money for the split, but he still owed him a considerable sum and was supposed to have wired it to Barkley's Bank on St. Vincent. Now we were on St. Lucia. Joe called, and the partner guaranteed the money would be sent there to Barkley's. Every day we went to the bank to see if it had been sent. Not yet! And every day we were hanging out at the Marina. Things were getting dicey, very dicey. We were in effect homeless and near broke.

Sitting on a bench at the Marina with the splendid yachts displayed before my eyes and all the different nationalities represented, I watched while these men and women went about their lives, totally unconcerned with the couple uncertain if they had enough money to stay one more night with a roof over their heads. I wondered if that was how homeless people felt in cities, standing by the side of a road or a freeway off-ramp as commuters drove by on the way to their busy lives.

By now, I was carrying on a constant inner dialogue with my individual spirit of the Father, *The Urantia Book* calls our Mystery Monitor, but nothing seemed to be saving my sanity. Just as we were walking along the boardwalk and toward the small grocery store that serviced the harbor, I noticed, for the first time, a bulletin board on the side of the yacht harbor office. I stopped to read the notices.

There before my astonished eyes was an ad looking for a Girl Friday for a tugboat operation to do office work: correspondence, bookkeeping, etc.

Joe and I memorized the telephone number. We stopped at the market and bought a can of Campbell's Tomato Soup. That was to be our dinner. After checking with the bank again, we returned to the guesthouse, and I called the number.

On the phone, the man identified himself as the captain. He had been looking for someone for a while and asked if we could meet that evening. I told him I had no transportation. He asked where I was staying and said he would pick me up. At 6:00 p.m. I was waiting outside when he drove up, and I got into his car. Safety was in the back of my mind, and I decided to keep it back there since something seemed to say it was all right.

While we were driving toward his place of business, he asked if I had eaten dinner. I thought of the canned tomato soup that Joe was going to eat alone. I answered that I had not. We stopped at, of all places, a Kentucky Fried Chicken, and I waited until he came out with the meal. We drove up a hill to his place, which doubled as his home and office.

I walked into a house on a cliff with windows all around, looking out at the Caribbean Sea. The scene was magnificent and afforded a view of the main harbor. The interior was wood paneling like a large cabin. He took me to the patio to meet his multicolored parrot. Opening the cage, he reached in as the large bird got onto his hand. He spoke some words to it. It answered back. Putting it back into the cage, we walked through the living room and sat at a small dining table off the kitchen. My first bite of The Colonel's fried chicken was delicious!

The captain was the owner and operator of the only tugboat on the island. He navigated every large ship into and out of the main harbor, including freighters and cruise ships. His appearance matched his profession. He was a stocky, muscular, early fifties, ex-Merchant Marine. I judged him as a straight-up guy, who seemed thoughtful. We talked about my responsibilities; all of which I could certainly manage. Then I mentioned my boyfriend was with me.

He had gotten up, gone to a cupboard, and retrieved a bottle of rum which he brought to the table with a couple of glasses and a bottle of Coca-Cola for mix for me. As he sat down is when I mentioned my boyfriend. (The timing was purely innocent on my part, there was never any intention to obfuscate.) After a pause, he poured us drinks: his straight up, mine mixed with Coke. "I have to say, that changes things... I'm really looking for a single gal with no attachments."

"But I can still do the work."

"Yes, but you see my experience has not been reliable under those circumstances."

He poured himself another shot of rum as I sipped mine. Then after a few long minutes, he asked, "How much are they charging you at the guesthouse?"

"$50.00"

I did not tell him that tomorrow would be our last $50.00 unless Joe's partner came through.

Shaking his head, "That's too much. Let me show you downstairs."

The bottom floor of his house was like a whole other house. It could have been a rental. It was sparsely furnished with some living room furniture, a double bed in the one bedroom, a kitchen with a small fridge and a stove, a bathroom, plus its own entrance.

"You and your boyfriend could stay here."

This was an offer I could not refuse. "That would be really nice of you."

So it was arranged. Tomorrow afternoon he would pick us both up at the guesthouse, and we would be his guests.

When I got back to the guesthouse, Joe was sitting in the kitchen looking forlorn. Before I was able to tell him the good news, he told me his not-so-good news. He was hungry. He had opened the can of Campbell's Tomato Soup, put it into a pan, and heated it up, but it was so thick it was not even edible. I got the can and read the instructions to him. He was supposed to fill the can with water and add it to the soup. "Oh." It was his first experience with American soup. In Germany, what was in the can was what you ate. But it was too late, he had thrown it down the sink. We looked at each other, and for some reason, he started to laugh. I joined him. Then I told him about the captain, and we now had a place to stay.

"What do you think of the guy?"

"I like him. I think he is on the level."

Relief spread across his face.

Staying with the captain was an adventure in itself. He gave us a tour of his amazingly powerful tug. The diesel engines took up the entire vessel with only the pilot house and a powerful winch. When he started up the engines, there was no doubt this vessel could maneuver a freighter.

One morning the captain was to bring in a cruise ship and invited Joe to go along. Joe was ready at 4:30 a.m. and just as the captain was starting up the engines, he took a pint-size bottle of rum out of a lower cabinet and took a big swig, then offered the bottle to Joe, who felt obliged to do so also. That was the first time Joe downed a swig of rum before dawn. The ride was certainly memorable in many respects.

To our good fortune, the captain had chickens that ran loose in the yard outside our windows. He fed the chickens rice which he had in bulk. We bought chicken bouillon cubes and 'borrowed' some of the rice to mix it with the soup. We did not have to go hungry. Nor thirsty, the captain invited us up in the evenings and always offered us rum with coke for me.

The money that was supposed to be at Barkley's had still not arrived. Joe had confided his predicament to the captain, so the captain offered the use of his phone. For the next three evenings, Joe called his partner only to get an answering machine. This was not looking good.

Then on the fourth night, the partner answered. There would be no money. His excuse, real or not, was that the IRS had frozen the bank account because he had not paid the taxes. He was closing up shop and going back to Austria. "Auf Wiedershen!"

We were stunned. I asked Joe if he believed the story. He just shook his head. "It doesn't matter, does it?"

Once again, a business deal had blown away into thin air.

Now what? My mind was in a quandary, I honestly could not think straight. Thankfully, Joe could. The next morning he said, "I think you should call your mother and see if she can help us get out of here."

Call my mother??? Through all this, that option had never entered my mind. Don't know why my mind had just skipped that beat. What a fabulous idea! We walked down to town. Using a pay phone, we called collect only to have her answering machine pick up. We walked around the town that we were getting to know quite well. Coming back to the phone, I called again. Answering machine. It was 11:00 a.m. California time, and very unusual for Mom not to be home. (It turned out she was at my sister's.)

Joe suggested that I call my eldest daughter and explain to her our dire situation. She came to the rescue, scolding me for not calling sooner. We went to the American Airlines ticket office and booked the tickets for the next day. They called her and took her credit card number. Joe and I gave in to great sighs of relief. Yet it was still a little premature.

The next morning the captain drove us to the airport. We thanked him. He told us he was glad to have helped. (What a nice guy.)

Down to two pieces of luggage, not having money for extra bags, we went up to the airline window with our tickets, expecting a seat assignment on the first plane in the journey. The ticket agent informed us there was an exit tax to leave the country. A WHAT? The tax to leave the country was $32 EC. We searched our pockets we had $5 EC. "Sorry," said the woman at the window. "Not enough."

She was adamant, we could not board the plane. Joe just looked at me, now what? We were holding up a line of people behind us, I turned and went begging, "We need EC to get out of the country, could you please help?"

And the people did. Now, not only could I add being homeless to my variety of experiences, I could also add begging. I would not recommend either.

My daughter picked us up at LAX. Joe and I had only been gone for three months; it seemed like three years.

Chapter 28

We counted ourselves extremely fortunate to have my apartment to come back to. I had loaned it to a friend while she was waiting for escrow to close on a house she was buying. It had closed a week before, so she was just moving out. My mother was sorry things didn't work out for us, but she was happy to have me back. Joe moved in too, and a friendship quickly developed between the two of them. Both of his parents were deceased. His mother had died a few months before he moved to the United States, so Mom became a surrogate.

Yet Joe was angry. Angry that his dream had slipped through his fingers and especially angry at another business deal gone wrong. I asked him if he wanted to drive out to Altadena to see if the partner had moved out yet. His answer was no. He knew it could have ended in an altercation; it would not have been pretty. Nor would that have recovered his money.

I went back to the Hollywood temp agency. My first job landed me back at the same department, Buena Vista Home Entertainment at the Disney studios. I began working for a newly hired, young, black, female attorney. Saying hello to my old friends and previous boss was interesting. The young woman and I worked well together, and within a month, I was once again part of the Disney family.

Joe befriended a neighbor, a humorous, good-natured Israeli, and an ace mechanic. With my mother's Sears credit card, Joe turned our apartment garage into a mechanic's shop, and the Israeli and he went into business together buying used European cars, fixing and reselling them.

One evening Joe and I talked seriously about my screenplay. I had first mentioned it when we were dating. He had made no comment, so the subject never came up again. Now that we were back in L.A. and understood each other better, I reminded him of the good SS officer. His reaction was swift, "There were no good SS officers."

I argued, "There was."

He would not believe me. I retrieved my screenplay from the credenza and tossed it at him, "Your English is good enough now, read it yourself. If you get stumped on a word, look it up. Use my German dictionary."

He read it and changed his mind. His critique was that it needed to be more dramatic. I brought up the 3"x 5" index cards idea, and we began to play around with the scenes. We reworked it, shortened it, and made it more suspenseful. I gave it to my son-in-law, the director of photography, who I trusted for an honest critique. After reading it, he said, "This should be made."

With company policy, I could not submit it myself. But if a vice president did, of course, that was different. I went to the vice president of our department, who by this time I knew well, and asked if he would allow its submission. He agreed to send it to the script department. Two weeks later, I got it back. Rejected!

The vice president asked me to come to his office. Sitting across from his desk, his words stung, "Sorry, but we know that Spielberg has a project in development at Universal along the same lines. There isn't room for two."

One year later, "Schindler's List" was released.

Shortly after our return from the Caribbean, I received a phone call from a man introducing himself as Wilshire Wood. He said he was with the Urantia Foundation and that he was having a get-together. He lived in Santa Clarita, a forty-five minute drive from my apartment. Would I be interested in coming? We talked for a few minutes, and I decided, why not? When I got off the phone, I told Joe and wondered, "Where did he get my phone number?"

Joe knew the importance of the Urantia Papers in my life. He had faith in God, but, at that time, was not curious as to the why or how. I invited him to come along, but he was not interested.

It was a beautiful California day when I arrived at the Santa Clarita home. Cars were parked everywhere, and I had trouble finding a spot. Stepping up the walkway to the large home, I rang the bell. It was answered by a tall, broadly built man whose head was turned talking to a group of people behind him. When he looked my way, he said, "The door is unlocked, you could have just come... Oh, sorry, I'm Will Sherwood. We don't know each other."

"No, but you called me." I introduced myself.

"Yeah, sure. Come in and join the party. We'll be calling a meeting in about an hour when all the Trustees are here."

I realized I had made a mistake with his name. It was not Wilshire Wood but Will Sherwood.

The interior of the home was even larger than the exterior portrayed. I went into a house full of people. I did not know anyone, but in a group of Urantia Book readers, it did not matter. We all had one thing in common with few others in the world. I got myself some punch and mingled. Everyone seemed to know each other.

Walking through to a large backyard where people were chatting, I joined a small group. They were talking about a lawsuit the Urantia Foundation was pursuing against a woman named Kristen Maaherra. I learned she had typed the entire book and put it onto CD format, distributing copies for free. The Foundation had threatened her with legal action, but she ignored them. The group was tsk tsk'ing the Trustees for being so litigious. This was not their first lawsuit to protect the copyright.

From my experience in legal matters at work, I knew that what she had done was copyright infringement and brought this up to the group. A woman spoke up, "But she is only a poor housewife. How can she afford a lawyer?"

I did not feel it was my place to comment upon the logic of why her financial status had anything to do with copyright infringement. I also wondered how poor she could be, if she had the time to type a 2,097 page book with approximately 650 words per page, and then have it copied onto CD's to distribute. That cost was significant in time and money. (There were no self-burning computers at that time.) But I did ask, "Why did she do it?"

The answer was that the book needed to have an index. I said, "What about Clyde Bedell's *Concordex*? It indexes the book and is more helpful on topics than a straight index."

225

The woman gave me an unpleasant glare. The whole group gave me a closer look. Realizing they had never seen me before, they walked away.

I stood alone, curious by the group's seemingly rude reaction when a nice looking, dark-haired young man came up to engage me in conversation. "Hi, I've never seen you before. Are you with the Fellowship or the Foundation?"

"Hello…Who is the Fellowship?"

"The Fifth Epochal Fellowship. We used to be the Urantia Brotherhood."

"I belong to neither. Wilshire, I mean Will called and invited me to this gathering."

The young man introduced himself, and out of the blue, he said, "I channel Gabriel."

I had not heard the term 'channel' in many years, going back to the time I dabbled in the Occult. Friends of mine and I used to play around with an Ouija board at parties. There was supposed to be a spirit guide channeling through the moving piece, spelling out predictions. But it never told us anything useful, so I realized it was a dead end. (Pun intended.)

I questioned him, "Are you talking about *the* Gabriel, the Bright and Morning Star, the chief executive?"

"Yes, Gabriel."

As kindly as I could put it, I said, "Isn't Gabriel awfully busy helping to run a local universe? Does he really have time to talk through you?"

"It's Gabriel, all right."

My heart went out to this unfortunate young man. But clearly, he was wacky! And people like this could only hurt the reputation of the book, inhibiting a serious person from giving it a chance. What was he doing being a member of the Fellowship? In the future, I would learn how all-inclusive the Fifth Epochal Fellowship could be.

The meeting was called to order, and we went inside. A sizeable rec room had been cleared of furniture and set up with folding chairs. For the third time in twenty years, I found myself in the midst of a large group of readers. This time the Trustees were completely in charge. They stood in front of the group. I recognized Richard Keeler, who everyone called Rich. I did not see Martin Myers. But I recognized the third man who had been at the L.A. debate, his name was Hoite Caston. There was another Trustee, Patricia Mundelius. She was a pleasant looking, older woman, her white-blonde hair pulled back in an unruly bun, reminding me of a kindly school teacher. I learned she was the granddaughter of Dr. William Sadler and Dr. Lena Sadler. The couple who dedicated their lives to publishing *The Urantia Book*.

Once the meeting was brought to order, accusations started flying at the Trustees. Once again, the behavior was more interesting to me than the subject matter. A tall man with a short gray ponytail seemed to speak for many of the group when he stood up demanding that the book be printed in a cheaper format so more people could afford it. "How did the Foundation expect to spread the book among the less fortunate? How else would the truth be

227

known?" Once again, I witnessed an angry man focusing on the sale of books, not on living its teachings.

There seemed a strong proselytizing quality to this man's demands. This kind of murmuring spread throughout the group. It sounded as if these people were approaching the Urantia Papers as necessary to one's salvation. Were we reading the same book? Nowhere in the book did it support or even hint that it was necessary to read the book in order to be 'saved.' Quite the opposite! Spiritual growth did not depend on the words of a book, but on one's heartfelt attempt to find God. Beautiful writings could spur on one's soul, but they were not necessary. The Urantia Papers were revealed for those who wanted a deeper, more scientific explanation of the workings of the wondrous, loving Father and his Son, and all the multitudes of beings in the almost endless panoply of the universe.

After the meeting was over (to no one's apparent satisfaction), people began to leave. I was curious to speak to others. To a Hispanic woman, I brought up the evangelistic attitude and that it was not the intention of the book. I will never forget her blank stare.

I began feeling very alone in my point-of-view when Will Sherwood came up to me and asked if I could spare a few minutes to speak with Hoite Caston. He took me upstairs to a room where the Trustee was sitting in a straight-backed chair. I sat across from him.

Hoite was friendly and asked me different questions, including how long I had been studying *The Urantia Book*, what it meant to me, and how I felt about its dissemination, which I believed should be on a person-to-person basis. Then we chatted about my job and the entertainment industry. He told me that when he was no longer a Trustee, he was going back into the field. He had been a producer. I thought to myself, "That might not work out so well. Once out, it's hard to get back in." But I kept that thought to myself.

I went back downstairs and was about to leave. Apparently, all the Fellowship members had left. There were only a dozen or so people still at the home. In his study, Will was speaking with a handful of them. He came out and asked me to join this group. I learned the Urantia Foundation was setting up an international organization to replace the defunct Brotherhood.

This new organization was called the International Urantia Association (acronym IUA). Included within the IUA would be international and regional associations. Will Sherwood and the Trustees were busy establishing an association for Southern California and Arizona. It became known as the Southwest Urantia Readers Family (acronym SURF). Other regional IUA associations were forming across the United States and in other countries throughout the world.

Will and Trustee Patricia Mundelius asked if I would volunteer to be the membership co-chairperson of SURF which was to be one regional part of the IUA. I accepted, not having a clue what I was doing.

A month later, I attended the first SURF meeting. At the event, the name Harry McMullan was mentioned. He was an independently wealthy man who devoted his time and money to the Fellowship and was providing funds to Kristen Maaherra, the woman who was distributing the CD of the book. The Fellowship had also created a special fund for donations toward the woman's legal fees. If she won the court case against the Foundation, then the copyright of *The Urantia Book* would be ruled invalid and go into the public domain. I could not understand why anyone would want to break the copyright, even if, as was stated, many Fellowship individuals hated the Trustees of the Foundation. Did these people not understand the possible ramifications? And what was hate doing here, anyway?

On New Year's Day, Joe and I drove down Sunset Boulevard to Gladstones, a famous fish restaurant on Pacific Coast Highway. As we were going in, Charlie Sheen was coming out.

My relationship with Joe was growing stronger every day. We sat at a table by one of the many windows and watched seagulls swoop over the ocean. A sunny winter day in Southern California has a certain pristine light. While we were waiting for our lunch, I brought up the subject of marriage. Joe looked at me in all seriousness and said, "A marriage certificate is just a piece of paper."

"Okay, then…"

Chapter 29

The Trusteeship of the Foundation was in flux. Through the efforts of Rich Keeler and the vote of the other Trustees, Martin Myers was removed from the board. He turned around and unsuccessfully sued the Foundation to reclaim his position. All this turmoil was beyond me. Why could these people not get along?

The California/Arizona association, SURF, was growing to the credit of Will Sherwood, its president. The other membership co-chair and I worked well together, but Will's guidance was important. The meetings were always well run, and then the group would study a topic from the book.

Life on this planet is fraught with challenge. There is always something else around the corner. My youngest daughter returned from Hawaii. She had decided she wanted to go into the theater as an actress. An actress! Oh my! In high school, she had acted as leads in plays and had fun with it. But to me, it was not serious. I guess to her, it was. She had friends in San Francisco who worked in theater, and that is where she was going to move and find work. Joe, myself, my mother, and her father tried to dissuade her but to no avail. So Joe and my daughter went shopping for a car and bought a used, white VW Jetta. Then she was off to the city by the bay. She found a job as a waitress on the San Francisco pier.

Believe it or not, within a few months, she was successful and was in a play with a large supporting role. Joe, Mom, and I drove up to see her and meet her new boyfriend. After the play, we all went to dinner.

The next day we were visiting at her apartment when I went into the tiny kitchen and saw hanging on the refrigerator with magnets an embroidery of a passage taken from the Urantia Book. I recognized my older daughter's handiwork; she had sent it to her. It was from Part IV, *The Life and Teachings of Jesus*, titled: *The Young Man Who Was Afraid.*

When Jesus was twenty-eight years old, he was hired by an Indian businessman to travel to Rome and act as an interpreter for the man and a tutor for his teenage son. The three traveled for two years visiting cities and countries along the way. The passage on my daughter's embroidery took place on the island of Crete. Jesus met the downcast and depressed young man up in the hills. Among the loving advice given was: *My friend, arise! Stand up like a man! You may be surrounded with small enemies and be retarded by many obstacles, but the big things and the real things of this world and the universe are on your side. The sun rises every morning to salute you just as it does the most powerful and prosperous man on earth.*

My daughter came up behind me as I read, she said, "Can you imagine what it's like for Jesus to call you friend?"

From then on I stopped worrying, my youngest child knew she was in good hands.

Joe and I were getting ready to celebrate our second Christmas together, and the same disagreement arose regarding Christmas traditions. In Germany, one puts up the tree on Christmas Eve, opens presents, and then goes to midnight mass. I contended that the tree needed to go up before, presents were opened on Christmas morning, and midnight mass could be postponed until Christmas Day. Since he was in the United States, I won half the battle. The tree went up a week before. Besides, my mother was on my side, and Joe loved my mother and vice versa.

On Christmas Eve, Joe received the best present he could have ever wished for. Chuck called and told him that his St. Vincent work visa was cleared and good for one year. Joe was so happy; he went out and bought the most expensive bottle of champagne and took it to celebrate with Mom. My visa was still pending. Of course, we agreed that he would go on ahead.

Joe made flight reservations to leave on January 20th. That would give him time to wrap up the business he had with his Israeli partner. They would finish the cars they had together, and the partner could continue to use the tools and garage for his own work. This was fine with Mom.

Three days before Joe was to leave, in the early morning hours, we were awakened by what seemed like a deep rumble with a severe undulating motion of the bed, like a disturbing wave under our mattress. It was barely light, and I knew instantly that it was an earthquake. I grabbed hold of Joe's arm to keep him in place. His first reaction would have been to jump out of bed and run. But he lay still beside me. I listened to the creaking sway of the building, especially for the cracking of plaster on the ceiling. If I heard that, then we would have to run. But it was holding.

I was born here in Southern California and had experienced earthquakes. I knew that many injuries occurred from crashing furniture and falls. I made sure we held together until it was over—maybe 20 seconds. Once we did rise, we found the heavy bookcase that had been against the wall had fallen over onto the stairs; it blocked our descent. That could have a caused a major injury.

People were freaked out and in the street immediately. Some of our neighbors were Russian Jews, and this seemed a first for them. The aftershocks were unnerving. This would be named the Northridge Earthquake since that town was the epicenter. There was great damage all the way down to Santa Monica where an overpass of the 10 Freeway had collapsed, killing a motorcycle cop and a truck driver. There were a few fatalities, but because of the time of 4:30 a.m., many more did not occur.

Our building escaped structural damage, but Joe and I were busy putting ours and Mom's apartments back into order.

When Joe boarded his plane for the Caribbean, he was not too sad to leave Southern California behind. It was a long flight with three connections to St. Vincent. When he arrived, he called to say, "I love you. I'm tired and getting ready to cook for dinner guests."

I remained at Disney. Being alone in the evenings, I began to attend Urantia study groups: one in the San Fernando Valley on Tuesday evenings, and one in Santa Monica on Thursdays. Will Sherwood attended the Santa Monica study group sponsored by a member of the Fellowship. Will and I were the only Foundation loyalists, which I had become. I just could not fathom the act of breaking the copyright. Why? The study group usually stuck to the script and studied the book. But the guy that channeled Gabriel was a member. That still struck me as curious.

During the next SURF meeting, when the members were enjoying refreshments, I asked Will about the 'Gabriel' guy. He informed me: "There is a whole group of them. It's a growing movement, and the Fellowship doesn't put a stop to it. The channelers call themselves the Teaching Mission."

He explained: "Our 'Gabriel' guy is a little different because the Teaching Mission 'receivers' channel beings who have gone on to the mansion worlds."

"You mean ghosts."

"No, they claim that they are students advancing through the mansion worlds and have come back to help."

"Okay, then they were once mortals and lived on an evolutionary material planet."

"Yes."

"Well, that makes them ghosts. Mansion world students or not."

"I never thought of it that way. You're right."

[Jesus Christ stated: "*In my Father's house there are many mansions.*" There are actually seven mansion worlds which are the initial destinations of surviving mortals.]

"The book explicitly states that no one ever comes back as a spirit or otherwise. No haunting allowed," I joked.

We both laughed at my haunting joke, but it was really not funny. Will continued, "They have very interesting names too, like Ham or Thorn or something."

"And the Fellowship allows this?"

"Yes. They even have a link on their website to the Teaching Mission."

"What do these supposed channeled beings say?"

"That is the dangerous part. They use concepts from the book, and it makes them sound like they are delivering something new. Especially to people who don't read the book for themselves. And I've heard they often get the concepts wrong. They also give advice."

"Like?"

"Like…oh, one of their favorite words is 'stillness.' You know, like practice stillness. Stillness is the way to get in touch with your higher self. They even council things like don't forget to write to your uncle."

"Oh please! Who falls for this? How can you read the Urantia Papers and fall for this?"

He groaned, "Don't know? Makes people feel special that a celestial being would talk to them, I guess."

"But it's not a celestial being. Mansion world students are not celestial."

"Right!"

"It's just a new con on an old game?"

"What do you mean?" asked Will.

"Mediums. Those special people that channel the spirits of the dead."

"It's a con game for sure."

On St. Vincent, Joe was running the restaurant from 6:00 a.m. until 11:00 p.m. The kitchen had to be open for breakfast for the in-house guests. At lunch and dinner, yachting visitors moored in the bay joined them. He had two very competent Vincentians working for him: Janice, a sous chef, and Dennis, a young man who waited and bussed tables. Chuck's wife helped out when it was busy. Joe worked hard, but he enjoyed it; he felt he was beginning to build something for the future. His dream was within reach. At the end of March on a Sunday phone call, he said, "I have something I want to ask you. Please don't say no."

"Okay."

"I'm down on my knees."

"What? You're where?"

"On my knees. Will you marry me?"

"I guess absence makes the heart grow fonder."

"What?"

"Oh please, get up. Yes, I'll marry you," I said laughing.

In May, I flew to St. Vincent, and after signing all the proper government paperwork in the capital Kingstown, Joe and I said our vows in front of a Vincentian judge in her office. My bouquet was red Anthuriums. Chuck and his wife were our witnesses. When the judge said to Joe, "Do you take this woman to be your lawfully wedded wife?"

He hesitated a moment, then said, "I take this woman to be my lovely wife."

The judge repeated, "Do you take this woman to be your lawfully wedded wife?"

"I take this woman to be my lovely wife."

Then the judge shook her head and slowly stated the sentence once again. When he answered, "I take this woman to be my…"

Chuck, his wife, and I said in unison, "Lawfully."

Joe said, "Lawful? I thought you said awful, and my wife is not awful."

Everyone laughed, including the judge. Joe repeated the traditional pledge correctly.

Our coach was the hotel truck used to transport supplies. It had a blue canopy and was decorated with tropical flowers. We rode down the main street of Kingstown to the best restaurant in town, sitting on its bench seat.

We honeymooned in the guest suite of the eco-hotel, a large comfortable tent with a queen size bed and private outside bathroom with bright yellow trumpet flowers hanging down the enclosure of the walls. The patio off the tent had the finest view of the bay.

The tourist season was over at the beginning of June, so Joe and I returned to L.A. together.

Chapter 30

In mid-summer, the IUA (International Urantia Association) sponsored its first conference. It was held in Nashville, Tennessee. Victoria, a member of SURF, and I flew there together. She was my roommate at the event.

It was a wonderful three days spent meeting one hundred and fifty readers and attending topical classes where discussion flowed freely. There were no Fellowship members; they were holding their own conference. When the split occurred, only one-third of the readers stayed with the Foundation. The majority followed the ex-Brotherhood.

In October, Joe went back to St. Vincent. Two months later, my work visa came through. I said goodbye to SURF, my job, friends, and family to join my husband and begin our Caribbean life together. For the first time, I became his working partner and a waitress. It takes a special skill to be a waitress; I did not have it. But I kept a smile on my face because I was happy. I think I managed to fool most of the people, most of the time.

By the side of the restaurant was a very large tree that lit up with fireflies at night. There had to be many hundreds. As the tree was flashing these tiny lights, some of the fireflies would go foraging for food and fly through the patio eating area. A French family of five came from a yacht for dinner. They had a six-year-old boy who was fascinated by the sight. As I was serving them, the mother told me her son had never seen such a sight and wanted to know more about the flying lights. Since my entomological knowledge was zero, I made up a story about all the families of fireflies living in the tree. The fathers would go out searching for food while the mothers took care of the little fireflies to make sure they were happy waiting for their daddies to return. Then when daddy firefly brought food, it was mommy's turn to fly free of the tree. And that is why the tree stayed all lit up, and the little boy saw so many others flying through the patio and onto the bushes around. The French father was translating while the face of the little boy stared at me entranced. The parents thanked me, but they need not have. It was just as enjoyable for me to watch the little boy's eyes in wonder at my firefly family fairytale.

Our Caribbean adventure together was short-lived. After only two months, my mother became ill again. When I talked to her, she said she was fine, but she did not sound fine. My eldest daughter, now married with a young son, drove from her home in Studio City to help her grandmother. My daughter told me not to worry, she could handle things. But Joe called our son-in-law to get to the truth. After the phone conversation, he said, "We are going back. Make us plane reservations."

It seemed our Caribbean adventure might be over.

Within two weeks of our return, my mother had another surgery and recovered quite quickly. But it was obvious that at Mom's age, we needed to be there for her. Joe soon found a job with a friend of my daughter who owned a craft-service company that provided food and drinks during film shoots. He went to work cooking at commercials, television specials, and, of all things, music videos. It was his turn to meet the stars!

One evening, he came home from a video shoot for Janet Jackson. He could not believe the star treatment. When he was setting up first thing in the morning, in rolled two Winnebago trailers to be used for Janet's dressing room. One was pink, and one was blue. He asked a production assistant why two in different colors. He was told they were not sure if Janet would be in a blue or pink mood.

Through a friend, I got a part-time job for The Jay Leno Show's accountant three days a week. The accountant and I got along very well; she was a good person. This enabled me to spend time with my mother. Rejoining SURF, I was elected Secretary.

The second IUA conference was held again in Nashville in July 1995. My son flew in from Hawaii and traveled with Joe and me to the city of Country Western music. The conference had double the number of participants than the first IUA conference, many more from abroad. My friend Marian was there, and I introduced her to my husband. Joe met Seppo, a brilliant Finnish scholar of the Papers. He spoke German with my husband when they enjoyed a cigarette outside away from the group.

On the second day of the conference, one of the committee members who had been tasked with developing the IUA came up to me and asked if we could talk. Tonia was someone I had met at the last conference. She took me to a room where Trustee Patricia Mundelius and Cathy Jones, a spirited older woman whom I had met at Will Sherwood's home, awaited. They talked to me about my role in SURF. They discussed associations that had formed by country within the IUA: Finland, France, Australia, and New Zealand, and the four in the United States including SURF. The Foundation wanted to put all U.S. associations under one umbrella organization, the United States Urantia Association (acronym USUA). At this same time, another meeting was being held with a potential president for this new organization. Patricia Mundelius asked if I would consider becoming its secretary. By the end of the meeting, my answer was yes.

After the meeting, Cathy Jones came up to me smiling, "I recommended you to the board for secretary."

A little unsure, I said, "I guess I should say thanks then."

"Don't worry. You'll do great."

I was then introduced to Rick Brinkman, who had accepted the position of president. I liked him immediately, and the feeling was mutual. He was a handsome, sixty-something gentleman with an outgoing, forthright personality. We were asked to choose our vice-president and treasurer.

I left that conference with an additional position, and three new friends, Tonia, Cathy Jones, and Rick Brinkman. There was a strong camaraderie between Tonia and I. She was my age and lived on the island of Maui. Cathy Jones was an easy woman to like and dedicated to the Urantia movement.

Rick and I started with only a list of readers and went from there to organize the USUA with the help of others. There would be fourteen regional associations within a year. It was a lot of work, but we enjoyed it. Tonia suggested we start a quarterly newspaper. I became the editor. Surprisingly, my husband joined in to use his marketing and design skills. By mid-August, we were up and running. The first USUA news quarterly was published four months later with submissions by members.

I also joined the editorial board of the IUA Journal, the international quarterly periodical. Previously, I had written articles for the Journal. Seppo, my husband's Finnish smoking buddy at the Nashville conference, was the Editor-in-Chief. With the assistance of Will Sherwood, we redesigned the quarterly.

In February 1996, the copyright infringement trial of the Urantia Foundation v Kristen Maaherra was held in the District Court of Arizona. The court ruled in Kristen Maaherra's favor and invalidated the copyright. We were shocked! The Urantia Foundation began an immediate appeal of the ruling. But for now, *The Urantia Book* was in the public domain.

The Fellowship lost no time in executing its plan. The Executive Committee, including Mo Siegel, Gard Jameson, and Harry McMullan, voted to print their own book, defiantly giving it the same name—The Urantia Book, even though the Foundation was the legal holder of the trademark Urantia. A publishing company, Uversa Press, had been formed. Mo Siegel was the only person who I was familiar with. He had been the redheaded entrepreneur with the entourage pointed out to me by Marian at the 1973 Los Angeles Conference.

On July 15, the Fellowship book from Uversa Press was released for sale. The text of the book was mostly identical to *The Urantia*

Book except the set-up of the book and the cover were startlingly different. The interior pages were set in two columns like the Bible. With numbered, quotable verse paragraphs, also like the Bible. Across the front cover, in full color, were three pictures. The first was a mature female angel in repose with full-on feathered wings; the next picture was the planet Earth in partial shadow; and the third, a mystical, wimpy picture of Jesus.

The winged angel and wimpy Jesus were dishonest contradictions of the text inside this book. A reader would find: *Seraphim do not shed physical tears; they do not have physical bodies, neither do they possess wings.* The second picture was a NASA Earth view. The third picture, the wimpy picture of Jesus (a copy of "Christ at 33" by Heinrich Hoffman), is also a gross contradiction of the truth. *The pictures of Jesus have been most unfortunate. These paintings of the Christ have exerted a deleterious influence on youth; the temple merchants would hardly have fled before Jesus if he had been such a man as your artists usually have depicted. His was a dignified manhood; he was good, but natural. Jesus did not pose as a mild, sweet, gentle, and kindly mystic.*

Both quotes within the Uversa Press book are accurate to the original Urantia Book. But not all remained the same. Text has been added that was not in the original. Why? To make it more commercial? Whatever their intentions, it is against the direction of the Revelatory Commission. If mortals think they know better, maybe they should think again!

Just as it was coming off the press, Mo Siegel, with his superior, business marketing experience, went to work on book distributors throughout the United States. Hawking his book as a superior deal—only $18.95 and "One that research had proven spiritual book shoppers would prefer, plus it would increase profits for the distributors." But it was all to no avail. Their book was never a success and languishes today. I saw it at a Costco a few years ago on a table of marked-down sellers.

Many loyal readers of *The Urantia Book* were upset but believed that the Foundation's pending legal appeal would prevail. Yet Hoite Caston was done fighting, he resigned as Trustee. Rich Keeler proposed a Frenchman, Georges Michelson-Dupont, to take his place. Georges had played a role in revising the French translation, Le Livre d'Urantia. I had seen him give a talk at a plenary during the first conference in 1994 and was introduced to him at that time.

Chapter 31

In July, my new friend from the conference, Tonia, and I were talking on the phone when she told me that she was going to take the position of Director of the business office at the Foundation in Chicago. We had developed a close relationship ever since she had been part of the committee appointing me to the role of Secretary of USUA. She wanted me to consider moving to Maui to take over her large study group. Knowing Joe's restaurant background, she dangled the prospect of opening an establishment in Lahaina. I thought about my mother. If I could get her to move with us, we would consider it. First, Joe wanted to visit Maui and see the proposed restaurant.

Once again airborne, I was looking forward to showing my husband the beautiful islands of Hawaii, two of them at least. We landed on Oahu. I had called Jane, and she met us for dinner in Honolulu. We enjoyed a pleasant evening together. The next day we drove out to the North Shore to stay with Robyn and her family. A reminder of that time in my life of my fondest memories.

Boy, was I in for a surprise! Robyn had warned me, but what I saw did not seem possible. Instead of mile after mile of pleasant beach houses along the beautiful coastline, most of what we saw was mile after mile of high walls built around estates. An access pathway from time to time gave us a glimmer of the beach. We stopped at Waimea Bay, with its perfect curling waves where surfers sat atop their boards waiting for the next one. Their rent had to be a lot more expensive.

Joe and I drove by the school in Kahuku. It still looked bright and shiny in my eyes. Robyn told me that Steve was married with a young daughter and had opened another school. I was happy for him.

Next, we flew to Kahului on Maui, rented a car, and drove to Kihei, where we had reserved a condo. After checking in and calling Tonia, we drove to her home a few blocks away and met her husband. The four of us went together for dinner, enjoying fresh seared Ahi and great company. Tonia had set up a meeting with her business friend in Lahaina to talk about the restaurant.

Lahaina had been an old whaling village and still sustained that ambiance. It is a major tourist draw. The businessman greeted us in his office. After a friendly yet serious discussion, he took us to the location in the heart of a Hawaiian-style tourist center. There had been a restaurant before, but it had closed. It was an open area with a bar well in the center and tables and chairs positioned within a low stone wall, covered by a thatched roof. The businessman left us there. Joe talked through different scenarios for possible success while we observed the traffic and tourist clientele for about an hour. He came to the conclusion it would not work for us.

That evening Tonia took me to her Urantia study group. I met a lot of good people but did not think I would be moving to join them.

The next day Joe and I drove Up Country to the parcel of land where I had built the A-frame. The journey was the same beautiful drive with sugarcane fields on both sides of the highway, and the ocean could be seen below from the road. The little town of Makawao looked unchanged. Traveling up Piiholo Road, halfway to the top, we took a right turn onto a smooth concrete street, no longer the packed dirt which I remembered. Large homes with fenced enclosures, corralling thoroughbred horses, now took the place of Eucalyptus Trees. Everything had changed so. I felt nostalgic and counted myself fortunate that I had been able to go through life's experiences on such a modest budget.

At dinner that evening with Tonia and her husband, Joe told them we would not be moving to Maui. Tonia said, "Well, I tried."

We talked about her upcoming position as Director at the Foundation. I would write an article in the USUA news quarterly announcing her appointment. Tonia wanted me to include a picture of her with the article. We had never printed anyone's picture before, but I told her I would ask the board.

In October, another Trustee resigned. It would be a while before a Korean gentleman, Dr. Kwan Choi, an economics professor, filled the vacancy. Dr. Choi had spearheaded the translation of the book into the Korean language.

At the beginning of 1997, I was elected President of SURF and served until leaving California at the end of the year.

Tonia called for a special meeting for SURF members and stayed with us.

We drove to Marina del Rey for the meeting on a motor yacht owned by a member. It felt like home to Joe since the marina was his first residence in the states. Tonia had many items on her agenda to discuss, one in particular was to ask our group to host the first conference in California for members of the USUA. We all agreed to coordinate the conference.

My mother had been re-diagnosed with cancer. This time it was terminal. I had often spoken of Tonia fondly, and Mom wanted to meet her. Tonia was respectful and kind to her. They discussed the teachings of the book and Tonia's work at the Foundation.

Fortunately, Mom did not suffer much pain for the last three months of her life; the living force just slipped away, and she could feel it. She would drum her fingers on her La-Z-boy recliner, impatient to leave. I sat with her and read aloud the Papers on the mansion worlds. She especially loved the Gardens of God. She also found the aea of glass on the capital inspiring. *The Edentia sea of glass is one enormous circular crystal about one hundred miles in circumference and about thirty miles in depth. This magnificent crystal serves as the receiving field for all transport seraphim and other beings arriving from points outside the sphere; such a sea of glass greatly facilitates the landing of transport seraphim.*

Mom asked me if I thought that mansion world residents could skate on the Sea of Glass? I really had no idea, but since it had always been a dream of hers to ice skate like an Ice Capades star, I answered, "Sure, why not?"

On one of her last days, while speaking briefly to my sister on the phone, Mom told Sis not to be sad, since she would soon be skating on that crystal lake.

Rick Brinkman had chosen for vice-president of USUA, Bruce Porter. He was from the Northwest. Bruce called to tell me he had the perfect place for the USUA conference. It was the Glen Ivy

Conference and Retreat Center in Corona, California. He was convinced it was the right place. Rick Brinkman flew in from Florida, Bruce came down from Washington, and my husband and I drove out to Corona to meet them. Bruce was so right! It was a beautiful, serene oasis between Los Angeles and San Diego. Palm trees and brilliant-colored Bougainvillea graced the lush, manicured grounds. Bungalows and meeting rooms surrounded an auditorium and large dining room with excellently prepared meals.

The theme of the conference was to be "An Eternal Perspective." One of the members of SURF had been working on a topic of the book for over a year, "The Fruits of the Spirit." When she showed me what she had done, I was elated. It was tailor-made for the conference and fit right in with living one's life from an eternal perspective where mortal death is only the beginning of a universe adventure. I took her work with me and presented it to Rick and Bruce. We booked the resort that day for mid-May.

Joe was a big help in organizing. He created an enticing, colorful registration form, making a collage from pictures he had taken plus cutouts from the Glen Ivy brochure. Our organization's treasurer, Bart Gibbons, also proved to be an enthusiastic partner.

The first USUA conference gathered eighty-five participants. We rented two vans to pick up guests at the local airport. Joe and my son were the greeters and drivers to the resort. Rich Keeler, and the new Trustee, Dr. Kwan Choi, attended. It was the first time most of us had met Dr. Choi. He was gracious and somewhat awestruck; this was all new to the professor. Tonia was there with Cathy Jones. On Saturday night, a live band performed, and I nearly lost my husband to Cathy. She would not let him off the dance floor. Cathy was in her seventies, but one would never have known it. The three-day conference went off with nary a hitch. All the hard work paid off.

On June 10, 1997, the Appellate Court case of The Urantia Foundation v Kristen Maaherra was adjudicated: The United States Court of Appeals, Ninth Circuit Court ruled:

> Maaherra argues that the Foundation's claim is nevertheless barred even under the holdings of these cases because the Foundation intended to defraud the Copyright Office when it stated it was the "Proprietor of a work made for hire." Maaherra asserts that the Foundation did not want to reveal to the Copyright Office that the "authors" were celestial beings because the Copyright Office would have rejected the application.
>
> There is no merit to this contention. The Foundation deposited two copies of the Book with the Copyright Office. The Book clearly describes its own origin as having been created at the instance of: "Planetary celestial supervisors [who initiated] those petitions that resulted in the granting of the mandates making possible the series of revelations of which this presentation is a part." We conclude that there has been no fraud on the Foundation's part and no prejudicial reliance on Maaherra's part.
>
> We therefore hold that the Foundation's renewal copyright is valid and that Maaherra infringed it.

For the foregoing reasons, the decision of the district court is REVERSED and the case REMANDED for further proceedings on damages.

After the verdict, in lieu of damages, including legal fees, the Trustees agreed to forego all monies if the Fellowship agreed to discontinue publishing and selling the Uversa Press book. (It seemed like a lopsided concession to many of us. The legal fees were considerable, and legally they could no longer sell their book anyway.) The Executive Committee of the Fellowship agreed to cease selling their book and accepted the Foundation's offer of forgiveness of the legal fees. But we soon learned that they did not honor their agreement, nor the ruling of the court, and continued to market and sell their book with the contradictory cover and the added text.

Plus, the court drama did not stop. Once again, the Treasurer of the Fellowship, Harry McMullan, supported Kristen Maaherra in filing a further legal petition to have the case reheard. Eventually, the court denied the petition.

Chapter 32

My sister and I inherited the apartment building when Mom passed away. We decided to sell, but first her husband and Joe knew they had to make improvements. One of the apartments had been rented for the last twenty years by a reclusive woman who would rarely let anyone in for repairs. She was also a hoarder. It was under rent control, and we knew we could not sell the building with her there. Gratefully, her brother came and moved her to a retirement community but left everything else. It was amazing how each room was packed to the ceiling with useless junk. Stuffed brown bags lined the hall. Basic repairs and upgrades had never taken place since my father died. It would take months with Joe doing much of the work since he was on-site. My brother-in-law, a contractor, came many weekends to offer his expertise and join in with the upgrades.

I went back to the temp agency. My third assignment happened to be for Buena Vista Home Entertainment. The Walt Disney Company in Burbank is a very large studio with many divisions and many employees. When I landed back at the same department, the senior vice-president who had come down from the sixth floor for a meeting, saw me sitting at a desk and said, "You again? You keep turning up like a bad penny." I was not sure what that meant, but I hoped it was good.

This time I was temping for a vice president that had come over to Disney from ABC Television Network when the two companies merged. He was not an attorney, so my job was different. One day a screenplay crossed my desk, "Tale of The Mummy," to be directed by Russell Mulcahy, the British video director that Doug had gotten his start with. It was written by a fellow video writer who was sometimes my competition back then. I had to smile at how the world turns. Now I was an assistant whose boss was in charge of greenlighting the project. Reading the script, I wondered if it would get made. It did but went straight to video, Buena Vista Home Entertainment, of course.

My sister and I never had to put the apartment building on the market. Just as the work was completed, the tenants in one of the apartments wanted to buy it. They were two gay men who had been renting for about five years. They were friendly neighbors. Sometimes Joe and I would share a bottle of wine with them in their apartment.

One night while discussing the sale, one of them told us a story. When he first came to Hollywood years ago, he was walking down our street with its broad avenue and islands of palm trees down the center. He came to where the road narrows, which is where our building was built back in 1939 during the art deco period. From the sidewalk, someone can actually look through the rounded windows into our dining room before skirting the building. He loved the building and said to himself back then, "If I could live there, I know I will have made it in Hollywood."

Now, not only was he living in one of the apartments, he was about to become an owner of the building. Life is such a trip for us all.

After escrow and the completion of the sale, Sis and I deducted the cost of the upgrades and paid off a small mortgage my mother had taken out a few years prior, the remainder was ours to split. Joe and I had been considering what we would do next. Should we buy a house in the San Fernando Valley and continue in our professions? Or take another leap. He had asked me what I thought about going back to the Caribbean, but this time the U.S. Caribbean, the island of Vieques, part of the territory of Puerto Rico. He had been researching the island, and we talked about starting a hydroponic farm business. I was not against the idea. Joe had thoroughly researched the subject, and even had a meeting with a member of the Business Council of Puerto Rico in Los Angeles, who encouraged him. I did not want to stand in the way of a dream that my husband had given up for the sake of my mother, plus it was a viable business opportunity. After an earnest discussion, the decision was made. We were bound for the Caribbean Island of Vieques.

Before we left, Tonia came for a visit. The Foundation was once again in turmoil. Patricia Mundelius and another Trustee were resigning. That would leave Rich Keeler and Georges Michelson-Dupont and Kwan Choi. Tonia told me that Rich was talking to Mo Siegel and Gard Jameson to fill the vacancies. I was incredulous, "No way! How can that be? Those two were part of the Executive

Committee of the Fellowship and were instrumental in publishing the counterfeit book."

"Well, Rich is talking to them."

The next evening Patricia Mundelius called Tonia at my home. After the conversation, Tonia told me that they had decided the two Fellowship men would be the next Trustees. Again I objected, "But why?"

"Pat says the Foundation needs money, and they are bringing a very large donation. Also, they pledged that the Fellowship would discontinue selling the Uversa Press book."

"They said that before." (And like before, that never happened.)

I did not trust myself to speak any further. Where was faith? Where was spirit-led courage? Where was the ability to stay the course in tough times? Had they finally been beaten and given up? The Urantia Foundation was being operated like a material business in a material world with no acknowledgment of spiritual help. The copyright fight had cost the Foundation at least triple the money those men were willing to donate back. It was too ironic. And wrong!

L.A. traffic was so snarled that when my daughter dropped us off at the airport, Joe and I were glad to be leaving the city. The plane took off on time. Sitting by the window heading to Puerto Rico, I watched as we climbed a clear sky, passed through a bank of cumulus white clouds, and then broke through into the pale blue atmosphere. I was grateful to be away from the scene of Mo Siegel and Gard Jameson being sworn in as Trustees to give an oath to uphold the text of the Urantia Papers that they had violated with their own book.

Evil had infected the Fellowship, and now it took itself right on into the Foundation. The first thing evil did was remove the *Banner of Michael* from the dust jacket of the book—gone was the white background with the three azure blue concentric circles.

The explanation was that a more commercial dust jacket was needed to attract book buyers who perused bookshelves. The policy of person-to-person or spiritual guidance was no longer the focus; it was pure and simple marketing. It took time to convince a Trustee, Frenchman Georges Michelson-Dupont, and some IUA members. In order to sidestep concerns, a professional designer was hired at considerable expense, and three designs were presented to the membership at large, cleverly giving them a democratic voice in the matter. All were asked to vote on their favorite, and the majority ruled. "You can fool all the people some of the time and some of the people all the time, but you cannot fool all the people all the time." This seemed a time when all of the people were fooled.

At the end of 2000, the *Banner of Michael* books were finally all sold, and the new books with their dust jackets of descending tones of blue adorned the shelves of physical bookstores and online booksellers in 2001. Sales plummeted by one-third and continued their drop, never to recover.

By 2007, the fact that the new jacket was not causing Urantia Books to jump off bookshelves, more money was spent hiring design firms to develop another dust jacket. That design boasted a more commercial appeal with its earth tones. But just as with the cover of the Fellowship book with its falsehoods of a feather-winged angel and a wimpy Jesus, the truth was not a consideration in designing the second Foundation commercial attempt. For glaringly at the top of the dust jacket are the words INTERNATIONAL BESTSELLER. Does selling somewhere over 600,000 books since 1955—fifty-two years—qualify it as an international bestseller?

In March 2013, there was yet another design change. According to the Trustees, after hiring a research firm to survey almost 700 spiritual book buyers and presenting these buyers with a choice of seven different jackets, two cover designs were "significantly preferred." Both covers still boasted INTERNATIONAL BESTSELLER.

And today, in 2022, there is only one—with a little green tree on the cover. Whatever is that supposed to symbolize?

MAP OF PUERTO RICO

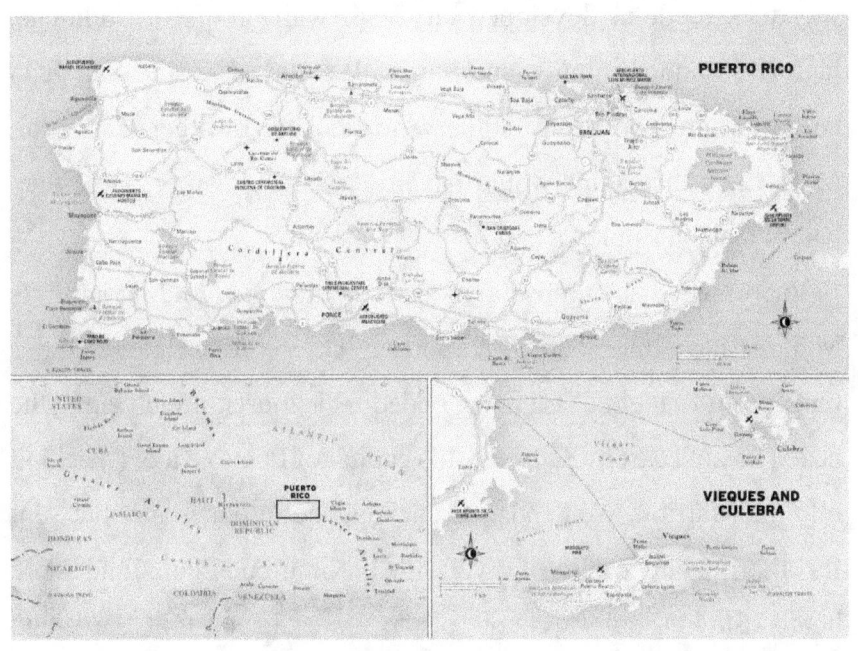

Chapter 33

The island of Puerto Rico came into view from my window of the aircraft. It was far different from any Caribbean destination we had yet encountered. The blue sea and green landscape quickly gave way to a modern, developed city with white roofs of buildings, high-rise condominiums, and hotels. We flew over the San Juan harbor where two cruise ships were docked. In other Caribbean ports, the cruise ships would have dwarfed the harbor. Here they barely made a ripple.

Puerto Rico is almost a modern continent. Landing at Luis Muñoz Marín International Airport on Isla Verde, we gathered our luggage and caught a taxi into Condado, the tourist stretch along the beach located east of San Juan, the capital of Puerto Rico. Checking into the Marriott, we deposited our luggage in our room and went for a stroll on Avenida Drive with its high-end shops and more hotels. Staying only a couple of days, we did not tour the island figuring there would be plenty of time in the future.

The ferry to Vieques departs from the harbor of Fajardo at the east end of the island. After taking a forty-minute taxi ride from our hotel, we purchased tickets, paying extra for luggage. We stood in line to board the sleek air-conditioned ferry. Our suitcases went into a hold at the front of the passenger seats. The trip took an hour.

Debarking at the small port of Isabel Segunda, as previously arranged, the owner of the SeaGate hotel picked us up and drove to her establishment, built upon one of the higher points of the island. On the way, we passed a young man riding a horse down a paved street. She explained there were wild horses on the island that had been left behind by the Spanish. It was not uncommon for a young man to claim one and use it for transportation.

Her hotel was quaint, comfortable and had a long, narrow patio where guests gathered for a continental breakfast. The patio overlooked lush green hills, the historic Spanish Fort Conde de Mirassol, and of course, we could see the sea.

The SeaGate van made daily trips into the main town, Isabel Segunda. After a leisurely breakfast talking with fellow guests, Joe and I went with the van to town. It was a small charming place, and we were anxious to see the entire island. The only car rental business was across the island at Esperanza, a seaside strip of restaurants and shops with one small hotel owned by Americans.

After a few days at the SeaGate, the hotel arranged for a local guy to taxi us to Esperanza. We took a room at the hotel. Renting a jeep, we toured the island.

Joe decided it would be best to live in Isabel Segunda for our purposes. That was fine with me. The town's main street was Munoz Rivera. We found a local real estate office and made our first friend, a woman who had been born on the island but had spent most of her life in New York. She was bilingual as are many Puerto Ricans. Only dealing in vacation rentals, she suggested we walk to the end of Munoz Rivera and speak with the widow Señora Morales.

The Señora owned an apartment building at the end of Munoz Rivera. We walked the two blocks and came to the building. It was a sun-bleached yellow, three-story, cement-block building. Interestingly, the sea had claimed the first floor, and the rental units were on the second and third floors. Señora Morales lived in a house just before the building. A waist-high chain link fence surrounded her home. Joe opened the gate and went to the door, and knocked. There was no answer. We waited near the building at the harbor.

About ten minutes later an elderly, but spry woman came towards the house carrying two bags of groceries. When she got to the gate, Joe realized it must be Señora Morales. He opened her gate and offered to carry her groceries. They hit it off and would become friends.

The Señora told us that in a week, one of her apartments would be vacant. It was two bedrooms, one bath, and a small open kitchen with a microwave and a gas stove top but no oven. It was on the ocean side. The bedroom windows looked directly out to sea. The water came right up and splashed on the building; it was like being on a stationary ship. The landing for the front door was a covered patio overlooking the harbor. We were happy to get it and painted the place before moving in. At night we fell asleep with the gentle lapping of water against the wall below us on the first floor. During storms, it was louder, but the building was as solid as a rock, and we were never concerned until later when the hurricane came to town.

Before we left California, while I was at work at Disney, Joe packed up our possessions. He gave a lot of things away since we had no intention of returning except to visit. The possessions we kept were in boxes stored with my daughter and son-in-law in their garage. We left them ready for shipping when we were settled. So Joe had them ship our computer, stereo, and the other things. They arrived two weeks after we took possession of the apartment. He had already begun to pick up the Spanish language by osmosis. Being from Europe, he already spoke two European languages and knew some Italian. But I was another story, although I had taken Spanish in high school. Before leaving the states, I bought a computer program for learning the language.

Once the computer arrived, I began spending a couple of hours a day studying, besides trying to communicate with patient locals. Often they would break into English before I could finish my Spanish sentence. I did not possess my husband's natural language aptitude.

We decided we needed a car, so Joe took the Fajardo ferry over to Puerto Rico and walked the entire auto sales district, finally buying a three-year-old, four-wheel drive Chevy Blazer. He drove the truck to the main harbor and caught the cargo ferry, also bringing a television he bought to watch the World Soccer Cup in Spanish, of course.

Our new realtor friend and her husband operated a small restaurant on their expansive home property on a bluff overlooking the sea further down the coast of the island. He boasted that he made the best conch fritters in the entire Caribbean, and he did. We became regulars both as paying customers and also as invited guests. It was not long before we knew most expats on the island.

One evening at the restaurant of our realtor friend and her husband, she told us that she had a client who owned a villa up in the Santa Maria area where many villas, both large and small, were built by gringos from the East Coast as vacation homes. The East Coast owners came sporadically making the properties targets for local thieves. She asked us if we would like to house-sit one of the villas she managed.

We were not really interested until she took us to see it. It was a lovely home having three bedrooms and two baths with an open kitchen and a large balcony overlooking a panoramic ocean view. On the patio below was a small infinity pool. In addition, there was a library with a book-shelved wall filled with paperbacks. There was no TV or stereo since twice they had been stolen.

Joe and I spent much of our time there, reading from the library in the evening or playing gin rummy and listening to our Sony portable boombox. Steven Tyler's Aerosmith song, 'Don't Want to Miss a Thing,' rotated often. It was exactly how we felt at the time. The villa was a great place to invite our island friends for parties.

Since no cruising malcontents knew when we would or would not be at the villa, the thieving stopped. Although, not before Joe's Speedo trunks, left on a chaise lounge by the pool, disappeared. I guess it fit the last thief.

Our apartment in town was only three blocks from the Catholic Church, and we attended Sunday Mass. We enjoyed the Spanish mass, and it proved another gateway to friends. Our social life was fulfilling, but our work life was not off the ground. We knew it would take time, but it was not far from our thoughts that money was going out and nothing was coming in.

From time to time, my realtor girlfriend and I would take the ferry to go shopping in San Juan. At Fajardo, car rentals were available for a day. After filling out the paperwork and splitting the cost of the car, we crossed the street to a local shack that served Cuban sandwiches and delicious Puerto Rican coffee. Then off we went to shop at the Super Wal-Mart, also hitting a few boutiques and bookstores.

Sometimes our husbands accompanied us, and our friends would drive us around the island to sightsee and lunch in a place we would never have found on our own. There is a lot of beautiful coastline around the large island of Puerto Rico.

Joe was forming friendships with people connected to the local government of Vieques. They were interested in his hydroponic proposal. Señora Morales had a son on St. Croix with knowledge of the business, and while visiting her, he met with Joe, and they discussed the ins and outs of hydroponic farming.

Friends of ours that we knew from the Caribbean island of Bequia lived in Pittsburgh. The couple came to get away from the winter. They had visited us when we lived in L.A. We were together there the night Princess Diana was killed and sat up that night watching the news.

On Vieques, we entertained the couple at the villa. The four of us spent the days at one of the beautiful beaches, then returned to the villa for a dip in the pool, the setting of the sun, rum punch, fresh fish, and barbecued breadfruit salad (my specialty).

One of our excursions was to Blue Beach. It was under the ownership of the U.S. Navy, and they often held maneuvers there.

Part of the land was used for bombing practice, but not the beach. It was only open when nothing was going on. It was actually the most beautiful and pristine beach on the island. But it was isolated since the land belonged to the military.

On a day the beach was open, we drove there with our guests. There was not a soul around but us. For some inexplicable reason, my husband decided to drive our 4-wheel over a sand dune off the road. Well, he got stuck, and no amount of fiddling could unstick the truck. The area was deserted, and there was no way to call a tow truck for help. Joe said he would be back and started walking to who knew where? The three of us sat on the beach, wondering when we would see my husband again.

Twenty minutes later, he returned at the head of a parade of a few navy guys and a huge tractor being driven behind them. The guys chatted with us as the tractor driver hooked up our car and pulled it out of the sand onto the road. We were gratefully rescued by the United States Navy.

(There had been occasional local demonstrations for years against the Navy. The people wanted the land back. During George W. Bush's administration, there was a demonstration, and he ordered the Navy to leave and give the people back their land.)

Time flies when you are having fun, but our business plan was not moving forward. Joe began developing another idea, but before he could implement it, Hurricane Georges came to change everything on September 15, 1998.

Two days before the hurricane was forecast to hit the island, we were having dinner with a couple who had befriended us from church. He was Puerto Rican; she was from the states. They had built their home on the island to withstand a hurricane. The majority of homes on the island were built in a similar manner. The island had gone through Hurricane Hugo in 1989. Most of the populace had rebuilt in concrete block with flat cement roofs.

That evening they invited us to stay with them through the coming storm. We thanked them but figured we would be safe hunkered down in our apartment. The next day as the hurricane was making its way toward the island, churning up the sea with increasing winds, our friends called and asked us to change our minds. Joe had just come from the market where locals told him not to ride out the storm in our apartment. We accepted the offer.

It was a good decision. Actually, it was a great decision! I had come from earthquake country, not hurricane and not a category 4. What a wild ride it was. And to be with friends in a large, well-prepared home was a godsend. The eye of Hurricane Georges went directly over Vieques then on to Puerto Rico, where it caused $2 billion in damage and eight deaths on the main island.

Our friends' home was so well built we were able to watch from the louvered windows as palm trees bent to the ground or were uprooted and flew through the air. The wood roof of an A-frame home sailed down the middle of the street landing in one piece. And it was so loud. People have likened it to the sound of a speeding freight train going by. It was like being in the Wizard of Oz with the Wicked Witch flying by on her bicycle. It raged through the night.

Early in the morning all was dead calm, not a bird chirped, nor an insect buzzed. People slowly began opening doors to come out of their homes to assess the damage. It felt like Munchkin Land when the Good Witch Glinda says, "You can all come out now."

Then the wind slowly began swirling in the opposite direction. The Wicked Witch was returning. It was only half over. We were in the center of the eye. It was strange. Certainly not something I would ever wish to experience again.

The day after, we drove with our friends in their jeep across the island. The Navy had cut through downed trees, clearing the road and, in some places, making walls on the sides almost two stories high. The beaches at Esperanza were gone, only coral remained. The entire tourist strip was badly damaged including the hotel where we had stayed.

The island was without power and water for two weeks. Our apartment lost the patio roof, and the interior tile floor was sloshing in water. It was frightening for me to think what it would have been like if my husband and I had stayed there alone.

The lovely villa had broken glass and water throughout, which we swept. Debris floated in the pool. We had half-gallon plastic containers that we filled with pool water and used to flush toilets. We jumped in the pool for a quick bath with our bathing suits on, chlorine was still in the water, but who knew what else.

The island of Puerto Rico was in far worse shape than Vieques. Ships were piled one atop another on land around the harbors. So

Vieques was on its own. It was such a strange experience to be on this island with no communication to the outside world: no phone, no electricity, no running water, no ferry, and none of the usual small airplane traffic. All inhabitants were in the same boat, we were all castaways together.

Then two weeks later as Joe and I were standing on our roofless patio looking out at the harbor, we caught sight of a cargo ferry making its way to port. The deep sound of the ship's horn was welcome music to our ears. What a feeling! Civilization!

Within a month, everything was almost back to normal, except no passenger ferry. Only the cargo ferry was docking each afternoon and leaving the next morning.

One morning I had just risen when my early bird husband returned from the bakery with fresh bread. "Good morning," I greeted. I had woken up in a sunny mood.

"I had the craziest dream. I was working at Disney and was so happy about it that I still have that feeling…And you know how much I *never* want to go back to office work."

But Joe was preoccupied and only half-smiled. After making coffee, we sat down to a breakfast of fresh bread, butter, and guava jam. He took a sip of coffee, "We're going back to the states."

"What? We're moving?"

"The hurricane helped me decide. I've been thinking about it for a while."

I sat silent for a few minutes…"Then, we should call Rick and take him up on his offer."

"I thought of that."

Rick Brinkman, the ex-President of USUA, told us before we left that if things did not work out for us in Puerto Rico, we should come stay with him. Rick had retired to Sarasota, Florida.

"Florida?"

Joe looked up from staring into his cup of coffee, "What did you say about a dream?"

I related my dream. The happy feeling it left me with was fading, "I guess I'm going back to Disney for a fourth time, only in Orlando."

"Looks that way."

I could not help but wonder why my life was so different, so not normal. It just did not seem to be able to stay in one place for very long. I loved my God and asked him why, but the only answer I seemed to get was—time to change.

I called Rick. He was more than gracious and said, by all means, we were welcome at his home as long as we needed. Joe arranged for our Chevy Blazer to go by the cargo ferry to Puerto Rico then be shipped to Port Everglades in Fort Lauderdale, Florida.

Two weeks later, friends gave us a Bon Voyage party, promising to visit us. We did not get much sleep and were at the dock before sunrise to board the cargo ferry. About ten minutes into the voyage, standing on the outer deck, the sun began to rise over the Atlantic. It was a cloudless morning, and as the golden sphere ascended from the other side of the planet, I put on my sunglasses, thinking a new day was dawning on an unknown future, again.

Chapter 34

It was noon when we landed at Miami International Airport. Our luggage arrived safely—lost luggage is such a pain. Joe hailed a taxi to take us to the cargo company at Port Everglades. We arrived at the guardhouse. Joe got out of the taxi while I waited inside in the air conditioning. He came back with a relieved smile on his face, "Our Chevy and our stuff are all here."

We had packed the truck with our stereo, computer, and other items. The shipping company would not guarantee its safe arrival. We decided to take the chance.

We loaded our luggage and left the Atlantic coast of Florida. Sarasota is on the Gulf Coast of the state. Driving through Alligator Alley, I tried to spot an alligator in the many water culverts along the way to no avail. We reached Rick's in three hours. His house was a very nice, typical Florida home painted a soft, light yellow. The interior had white square tiles on the floor throughout, a tropical flower print décor, and a screened-in backyard, enclosing a living-room patio and large pool. He and his long-time girlfriend, Vonnie, welcomed us. Coincidently Vonnie, a lively, caring woman, was originally from Puerto Rico. We stayed in one of the guest rooms.

Rick and I were of like mind when it came to the politics of the Urantia Foundation. He had been a member of the old Brotherhood and knew the cast of characters well. When the Trusteeship of the Urantia Foundation fell into the hands of Mo Siegel and Gard

Jameson, he left the organization. He maintained a study group that met weekly but no longer offered his services to the Foundation, although he remained friends with some members.

Rick told me that Harry McMullan, still treasurer of the Fellowship and past supporter of the Kristen Maaherra lawsuits, was about to break the copyright again. He was in the process of printing Part IV, *The Life and Teachings of Jesus* word for word from the book. I could not see how it would succeed. There would be terminology confusing to anyone reading Part IV that had been explained in the first three parts. I asked Rick, "I don't get it? What motivates this guy? He knows the original publishing instructions were never to separate the four parts. The Revelatory Commission admonished us that the book must never be separated, must remain whole."

Rick shrugged, "It is strange how bound and determined he is to break the copyright. Keep in mind when Mo and Gard became Trustees, they left ole Harry behind. The three had been good buddies. Maybe he had visions of becoming a Trustee himself."

"I guess that means another expensive lawsuit."

"That would be my reading of it. And you know Harry can easily afford it."

"Doesn't he have anything better to do with his money?"

"Apparently not."

When Harry McMullan released his paperback book for sale, "Jesus—A New Revelation," the cover did not reflect the teachings of *The Urantia Book* or Part IV. Just like the cover of the Fellowship Urantia book, McMullan's cover misrepresented the text. On his cover was the Salvador Dali painting "Christ of St. John on the Cross." Although the painting is remarkable and moving, it is a depiction of Christian theology as "Jesus the Redeemer," the last sacrifice offered to his Father for the sins of the world, the ultimate blood sacrifice to cleanse us all of Adam and Eve's Original Sin— the Atonement Doctrine.

Harry McMullan knows *The Urantia Book* disputes such dogma. What causes these people to perpetrate such unholy deceptions? Is it ignorance? A desire to sell their own published books at any cost? Or something more nefarious?

It could not be more clear than in Part I, Paper four: *The barbarous idea of appeasing an angry God, of propitiating an offended Lord, of winning the favor of Deity through sacrifices and penance even by the shedding of blood, represents a religion wholly puerile and primitive, a philosophy unworthy of an enlightened age of science and truth. Such beliefs are utterly repulsive to the celestial beings and the divine rulers who serve and reign in the universes. It is an affront to God to believe, hold, or teach that innocent blood must be shed in order to win his favor or to divert the fictitious divine wrath.*

It was the Father's will for his Son to live life as a man of the realm and be subject to the same consequences as would befall anyone of us. Christ had the power to call upon legions of angels to avert the cruel destiny decreed upon him by evil men; but we mortals cannot. He lived among us as a mortal of the realm and chose to die as a mortal of the realm.

Rick gave us a tour of Sarasota. It is an upscale city with a prosperous pedestrian shopping district. John Ringling of Ringling Bros and Barnum & Bailey Circus built his mansion in Sarasota and, at his death bequeathed his fine-art collection to the people of Florida, now housed in the museum named for him and his wife. The city is a center for the arts: opera, theater, ballet, and the Sarasota Orchestra. Its beaches rivaled many Joe and I had seen. Our friend drove us over bridges to the Keys. Siesta Key had the most unusual white sand as fine as powder. It was velvety to walk on. We were impressed with the area, and Rick tried to talk us into staying, but we believed Walt Disney World was our destination.

The next week, we drove up to Orlando taking I-75 past the city of Tampa, and then headed inland to Central Florida. Walt Disney World is southwest of Orlando at Lake Buena Vista. Traveling around the area, we found ourselves in Kissimmee, a city just outside of Disney World. The main tourist road of Kissimmee is like the Las Vegas strip without the gambling.

With the Orlando Sentinel classifieds in hand, we began our search for a home. On the second day, we pulled into an apartment complex one block off the strip. We had found our place. It was on the third floor with a patio that looked out into a wooded area with Cardinals, Blue Jays, and Mourning Doves flitting about. It had a pool that we could see beyond the trees. We signed a lease. The apartment was unfurnished, so we went shopping for casual living and dining room furniture, plus bedroom ensembles for two rooms, keeping in mind it was going to be a vacation destination for family and friends. We moved in the day our king-size bed was delivered. The rest we accomplished in two weeks.

Before applying for a job, I made a trip back to California to stay with my eldest daughter and her family and catch up with friends. Visiting the Buena Vista Home Entertainment division, I went to see the executives I knew along with their secretaries. I received a warm welcome. In fact, the vice-president I knew so well said, "You're not back again?"

I explained I was living in Orlando and would like a recommendation to work at Disney World in the legal department. He had his secretary call personnel and find out whom I should contact there. With the woman's name in hand, I returned to Kissimmee.

Calling the manager of clerical personnel for the legal department, she made an appointment for me to come in and bring my resume. Joe drove me to Walt Disney Company's executive offices on the enormous Walt Disney World grounds. The building was across the street from Pleasure Island Downtown Disney. I rode the elevator to the fourth floor, introduced myself to the receptionist, and sat on a gray leather sofa to wait. The reception desk sat in front of a vast oval atrium running down the center of the building. Over the railing, you could see down to the first floor. On both sides of the atrium were gray cubicles as far as the eye could see, four or five deep even the carpeting was gray. I felt like crying. Never did I expect to be back sitting at a desk working as a secretary. I could not recreate my happy dream.

The personnel manager was a pleasant woman. She read my resume, gave me a short interview, then told me there were no openings at the moment, but she would keep me in mind if something came up. There were only twelve attorneys in the department. At the Walt Disney Studios in Burbank, there had to be two hundred attorneys and always an opening. At first, I was not dissuaded. Every week for three weeks, I called the manager and left messages with her assistant. Nothing!

Living unemployed for a year had taken a real toll on our finances. I was contemplating taking my resume to hotels and getting into the hospitality business. But Joe cautioned me to give it another week, "If you're going to work as a secretary, it makes sense it would be Disney."

On the next Friday, Rick and Vonnie came up to stay with us for the weekend. We went out to the Kennedy Space Center. Fascinating! Rocket ships, moon landings, mock-up space modules for the International Space Station, plus on the bus tour driving from building to building, in watery culverts by the road, lurking alligators lay in the sun like ominous clay figures.

Returning home, the answering machine was blinking, it was personnel from Disney asking me to call on Monday. A legal secretary had just given notice. After two more interviews, one with the attorney I would assist, I was hired. I got over my disappointment of returning to the clerical world when it turned out to be a 'happy' environment. The attorney I assisted was a nice guy, the other secretaries and paralegals were easy to work with, plus the job had many perks.

Of the twelve attorneys, only two dealt with talent contracts for entertainment acts that played at the different parks: Magic Kingdom, EPOCT, Animal Kingdom, and Disney's Hollywood Studios. It just so happened my boss was one of them. The best perk was the Silver Pass. I could take guests and get four people through the gate for free, among many other discounts. Joe and I would often go to EPCOT just to have dinner in a different country.

We had frequent visitors as we had hoped. My eldest daughter came out with her children. My son, who was now living in the states, brought his family; and later my youngest daughter came with a friend. My sister and brother-in-law and their son visited. Our Vieques friends managed trips, and the couple from Pittsburgh came often. Our beach of choice was Cocoa Beach.

When I started my job from a desk at the Walt Disney office, Joe was working from a desk at home. He purchased software and taught himself how to design websites. Within a month, he was in business creating his first website for a private company. It was an independent foreign car dealership. After seeing Joe's work, the owner hired him exclusively to buy and sell high-end autos over the Internet.

When we did not have visitors, we often went to Sarasota to spend the weekend with Rick. We rang in the New Year 2000 with him and Vonnie. And the world did not end with the fears of Y2K. That evening he told me the Foundation had filed a copyright infringement lawsuit against Harry McMullan and his Jesus book. Harry fought back with a new legal angle. This seemed like it would be the last gasp.

I continued my Spanish studies. I wanted to be able to read the Spanish translation of the book, El Libro de Urantia, published in 1993. During this period, Joe and I were living a normal life and experiencing freedom from serious cares. Things do not work that way for long on this planet. Mortals learn more through adversity than ease, but for the time being ease seemed fine with us.

In May, our good friend Rick suddenly passed away from a fatal heart attack in the night. We knew that he was experiencing health issues, but he was in such superior physical shape it took us all by surprise. Vonnie was in New York and had tried unsuccessfully to reach him that evening and into the night. She called the police to check. This was not an uncommon request in Sarasota, Florida, the home of many retirees. In the morning, they found him in his bed. It was quite a blow to her, but we all knew where he was headed, and we would see him again.

A couple of months before, Rick and I had reminisced about the Glen Ivy Conference. He told me that the theme "An Eternal Perspective" had changed his outlook on death. Although he had been studying the Urantia Papers for many years, he had never internalized the reality of his own eternity until then. He now saw death as it is: *Love of adventure, curiosity, and dread of monotony— these traits inherent in evolving human nature—were not put there just to aggravate and annoy you during your short sojourn on earth, but rather to suggest to you that death is only the beginning of an endless career of adventure, an everlasting life of anticipation, an eternal voyage of discovery.*

I look forward to consulting the Registry on the first mansion world and seeking Rick out to see what he has been up to.

Chapter 35

In January 2001, The Walt Disney Company announced austerity measures. It would be downsizing the white-collar workforce by ten percent in California and Florida. For our department, it meant two attorneys and twenty support personnel. The employees who voluntarily chose to leave would be given a severance package of three months' salary and earned vacation. The deadline to decide was March 15. If the quota was not met, then management would decide, and there would be no severance, just goodbye. My husband and I had some discussing to do. I was one of the last secretaries to be hired.

One day I was in the office of the other entertainment attorney, and she told me she was leaving to move to North Carolina to be closer to her family. She reminded me that her secretary had been with the company for many years. I took this to be a heads-up for me. It was logical that her secretary could easily work for my boss. Another consideration in my mind was that this secretary had a life in Orlando with a husband, children, parents, and a home. She should not be the one to lose her job because the attorney she worked for left. I could absorb the change, and change was what it was going to be.

The company Joe worked for was going through its own down period. We began to reassess our situation. One evening we were sitting on our balcony enjoying a glass of Chianti, when we decided it was prudent that I take the severance. Instead of looking for another secretarial job, I asked Joe, "What about moving back to your country? I'd like to experience living in Europe."

It has always surprised me how my husband and I are on the same page regarding our future as a couple. He answered, "I've been thinking about it. I believe I could get back into management there in the automotive industry. I still have friends in the business."

We discussed it for another week. Then it was settled; he called his brother in Germany and told him of our plans. His brother and sister-in-law could not have been happier. Within two weeks, Joe quit his job and went ahead to look for work. He flew from Orlando International Airport on Lufthansa Air to Zurich, final destination Rheinfelden, Germany, home of his brother.

The Rhine River divides the town of Rheinfelden between Switzerland and Germany. On the South bank is Rheinfelden, Switzerland and over the bridge on the North bank is Rheinfelden, Germany. The Swiss side is a charming old town with buildings dating back to the sixteenth century. The German side is modern with apartment buildings, a supermarket, and more recent pedestrian shopping areas. Zurich is the closest airport, a two-hour drive. After Joe arrived, he began looking for work.

I gave notice and worked until the end of March. Our apartment lease was up at the end of April. I wanted to see my children before going on to Europe. My son and his family had just moved into a larger home, and I asked him if he wanted our practically new furniture. He and his wife were happy to have it. It was decided that he would fly out to Orlando, and we would rent a U-Haul and drive to his home. Both my daughters came out to help me pack, and we had our last fling at Walt Disney World together with my Silver Pass.

When my daughters returned to California, my son arrived. We hired a couple of guys to help him load the rented truck, and then we were on the road.

Joe had not yet found work, which was a disappointment for both of us. I stayed with my son and his family, caring for my young grandchildren and saving daycare costs.

By the end of July, my husband still had not found work. It was becoming very stressful for both of us. One day I was sitting in the living room surrounded by my furniture, wondering if I would be packing it up and Joe would be returning. Perhaps we would move back to California. I was miserable. I could not bring myself to think that all the things I had just given my son and his family, I would take away. I did not think I could.

Joe and I were communicating mostly by email. He came up with an idea of how to get himself hired by a large, privately owned automotive group and wanted to write a business proposal with my help. We worked on it for two weeks. He took the proposal to a meeting with the president. His intention was to convince the gentleman and his board of directors that the firm needed him. It worked. He was hired in a management position. The company had dealerships in Germany, Austria, Croatia, and Hungary. We could relax and go back to sleeping at night. They were sending him to different dealerships for him to observe their company methods. He would be traveling for a while. His brother's apartment was his home base.

I stayed with my son and continued to be a live-in babysitter, enjoying my toddler grandson and granddaughter and cooking dinner to help my working daughter-in-law. After Joe's training, he became the manager of two dealerships in Rijeka, Croatia that were nearly insolvent. I made airline reservations to fly to Europe on September 12.

Needless to say, I did not fly out that day. The cruelest event hit the United States of America the day before. I was in the basement bedroom when my son knocked on the door, "Mom come upstairs. Something has happened in New York."

I entered the family room to see one of the Twin Towers billowing smoke on the television screen. As we were watching in horror, we saw a plane come around and head straight for the second tower. What a shocking sight!

My husband called later and said he had been in a board meeting when a worker suddenly burst in and told him to come to the television in the break room. The interruption was highly unusual, and he followed the man. There on CNN Italia were the towering infernos and then a rerun of the plane hitting the second tower. His first thought was, why was he being shown a Schwarzenegger movie? When he recognized that what he was seeing was real, he tried to contact me but was unable to get through. He could not help but wonder what was happening in other parts of the U.S., and if we were in danger. When he finally reached us, he was much relieved.

Ten days later, I was able to board a plane for Zurich. The airport was practically deserted. The whole historic episode was surreal. When I landed, Joe was in Frankfurt on business, and I knew that one of my in-laws would be picking me up. After clearing customs, my sister-in-law, who I had never met (or seen a picture of), was waiting for me. Fortunately, she had a better idea of what I looked like for I saw this tall, smiling, dark-haired woman tentatively waving at me. Approaching her, I asked, "Maria?"

"Yes, Yes," Maria spoke some English, and my German was okay, so we managed to communicate during the drive to Rheinfelden. My brother-in-law was at the apartment when we arrived, and we sat down to coffee and German pastries. Just before dinner, Joe arrived. It was wonderful to see him—he looked great! We were staying overnight and then bound for Rijeka, Croatia. I would get to know my in-laws better during future visits.

In the early morning, we packed the company car with our luggage and got on the highway for the eight-hour drive to Rijeka. We drove through the Alps, northeast Italy to Trieste, passed into Slovenia, through the border of Croatia, and finally, Rijeka.

Croatia is a beautiful country on the Mediterranean Sea, just opposite Italy. It is a coastline country with over one thousand islands off its shore. After checking into the Grand Hotel Bonavia in the center of Rijeka, we unpacked and went looking for a restaurant down the pedestrian-only city center. There were many people strolling about or sitting in outdoor cafes. When we decided upon a restaurant and sat down for dinner, I commented, "The Croatian men are good-looking."

He raised his eyebrows and smiled at me, "So are the women."

Perhaps it was true throughout the territory once called Yugoslavia.

The German auto firm wanted us settled as soon as possible. The next day we walked from our hotel and found a real-estate office. Joe was already speaking some Croatian. He had begun working two weeks before at the dealerships. The language was similar to Polish. Since he was fluent in Polish from his father's side of the family, and with his natural aptitude for languages, he was able to communicate adequately. He spoke with the real estate agent, explaining that we were looking for a furnished apartment or home to rent. The woman gave us the key to a house south of the city directly on the shoreline to check out. The home fronted the ocean but behind it was a busy road. It did not impress us.

Returning to her office, we found it locked. We waited downstairs at an outdoor café and ordered cappuccinos. The realtor walked down the broad avenue, saw us, and sat at the umbrella'd table. When we told her we would like to see something else, she said she had another apartment she thought we would like. An appointment was set up with the owners for that evening.

The apartment was in a ten-story nondescript cement block building on the main coast road. Surrounding the building on the ground floor was an annex that housed an Italian restaurant, a hair salon, a bakery, a convenience store, a children's clothing shop, and a local bar. There was an elevator in the small entryway. We got in and pushed the button for the ninth floor; there were four units per floor. The one we were looking for was #902. Knocking on the door, a distinguished, silver-haired gentleman answered and introduced himself, as his wife came up behind him. We entered and were pleasantly surprised. The spacious home was furnished in expensive, modern Italian decor with matching red leather sofa, loveseat, and overstuffed chair. A wall unit of Birchwood included bookshelves centered by a television and stereo speakers on either side. They showed us two bedrooms, a bath with a washing machine, and a modern European galley kitchen. Another striking feature was a large balcony overlooking the Mediterranean with a working shipyard just to the right on the coastline.

We sat with the couple and went through a friendly interview. They both spoke some English. He was a government official and was being transferred overseas as an ambassador. During the conversation, I thought that this couple would be superb representatives of Croatia to the country they were headed. The next day we signed a one-year lease at the office of the realtor. Within a week, we had moved into the turn-key home.

While we were still at the hotel, Joe and I walked the civic center to familiarize ourselves with the city. Whenever local merchants asked us what nationality we were, and Joe replied German, the people had no response. When I told them I was an American, I discovered the favorite English word of the young Croat was "Super!" People also expressed sincere condolences for the 9-11 terror attack. Many took it for granted I was from New York. My language skills did not enable me to correct them, and it did not matter. My country had been attacked, and almost three thousand people sitting at desks doing their jobs were killed.

Croatians were sympathetic to the USA being attacked by terrorists. It had not been so long ago that the Croats had been through a war with Serbia. After the fall of communism, the country of Yugoslavia broke up into ethnic states. Croatia declared its independence. Serbians fought to keep it in Serbia's hands. My husband and I could see evidence of battle in the presence of bullet holes in some of the buildings in the city.

After winning the war and gaining independence, there was a terrorist attack on the police station in Rijeka, using a suicide car bomber. Only the driver perished, but twenty-nine people were injured. The mastermind of the attack, Hassan al-Sharif Mahmud Saad was traced to Bosnia. Croatian forces hunted him down and killed him in a firefight.

Rijeka is a small city in European fashion with its wide pedestrian thoroughfare where butchers, bakers, greengrocers, bookstores, sophisticated boutiques, and a department store sell their products.

A bus stop was in front of our apartment building. I made use of the bus to travel to town to do my shopping. The movie theater showed new releases. Some of the films were in English with Croatian subtitles. One afternoon I went to see "Vanilla Sky." The critics did not give it a high rating, but I am a Tom Cruise fan, so it was a welcome piece of Americana for me. Afterward, I treated myself to a Big Mac and fries at McDonald's.

On weekends, Joe and I explored the countryside and often drove to Zagreb, the capital, on business. We visited islands that dot the Mediterranean, its ancient towns with narrow cobblestone streets

287

and Roman fortresses. The southern region, Dalmatia, is one of the most beautiful regions in the world.

While Joe was busy setting the two auto dealerships back on track, I wanted to study the Croatian language. People we met through business became friends, and while they spoke English well enough, I wanted to speak their language. A new friend introduced me to a tutor, and I began to study.

By now, my Spanish had developed well enough to tackle *El Libro de Urantia*. I soon discovered what an imperfect translation it was. The past policy of the Urantia Foundation was not to release a translation until it was as perfect as possible. This translation was terrible. A serious scholar would put the book down soon after reading only a few Papers. There was a disclaimer on the title page of the book explaining that only the Prologue and Part IV, *The Life and Teachings of Jesus,* were correct translations, and the other three parts were undergoing further revision.

One morning, sitting in the apartment reading Part IV, I found a glaring error. Checking the time in Chicago, it was 3:00 p.m., I called Bob, a friend and employee of the Foundation. After he got over his amazement that I was calling from Croatia, not Kissimmee, Florida, and I answered his question as to what I was doing there, I told him of an obvious mistake in Part IV. I explained to him that after the baptism of Jesus on page 1504, when John, Jesus, and his two brothers, James and Jude, are standing in the River Jordan and they heard, *"This is my beloved Son in whom I am well pleased."* It was translated as *"Éste es mi hijo amado en quien me siento muy complacido."* Yet only seven pages later, when the Father's identical statement is repeated on page 1511, the translation is "*Éste es mi Hijo amado en quien tengo.*"

Bob was surprised that no one had caught this error before. He told me a group in Spain was reworking the translation. I said, "Please be sure and contact them in case they assume Part IV did not need revision."

"I'll make certain."

Back in 1986, the Urantia Foundation had first undertaken the translation of *The Urantia Book* into Spanish. It has been the recommendation by the Revelatory Commission that a complete and perfect as possible translation of the book in foreign languages would take approximately 20 years. While the *El Libre De Urantia* translation was taking place, it was learned that the Uversa Press/Fellowship were planning to imminently release their own *El Libro De Urantia* and copyright it in various Spanish-speaking countries. Thus, the Urantia Foundation felt they had to act and release prematurely their first draft completed in 1993. It was a race between the two organizations, and the Foundation was able to beat the others to the punch. But unfortunately, not to an optimal outcome.

The inconsistency of the Spanish language used was colloquial to different regions. It was as if a different person from a different country translated every other Paper.

When I was in Puerto Rico, my girlfriend would take me into bookstores to pick out easy books for me to read and understand. For herself, she bought international bestsellers and explained to me that the Spanish of Puerto Rico was different from Mexico or Costa

Rica, or Spain, and bestselling authors used standard Spanish in which anyone who enjoyed good books would understand. But obviously, the Foundation had not had the time.

To complicate matters even further, after Mo Seigel and Gard Jameson took over the Foundation, they encouraged a group in Spain to create a further translation. Spain's translation of the "Edición European" was published in 2009 and called itself the 'civilized one,' which appears a bit arrogant. Plus, it is another imperfect translation. Not only are there idioms used only in Spain, but the translators took the liberty to dumb down concepts in the book. What a disservice to the entire Spanish-speaking world! Do they not trust the Spanish population to be able to read at the same level as the English-speaking world? Unfortunately, for over thirty years, our Spanish students have had these inferior translations.

In Central and South America, an unscrupulous element has become a huge problem—channeling. The Teaching Mission and another group of channelers, Hermandad YO SOY, have a disturbing foothold in numerous Urantia study groups in these countries. This problem is more widespread than in any other language the book has been translated. Perhaps it is not the result of terrible translations, but that seems a good place to start.

Chapter 36

At Christmas time, Joe and I made a trip to Rheinfelden to celebrate with his brother's family. It was a white Christmas, my first. Since Joe's two nephews were home from university, we stayed at a small cottage close by. The first night we checked in, I went outside to walk a short distance to a creek in the front yard. There was a full moon that glistened the packed snow. As I stepped on the pristine snow, it cracked under my boots. Upon reaching the dark blue rippling water, bordered by an evergreen tree laden with snow, the reflection of the light of the moon on the water was breathtaking—cold breathtaking—yet the entire scene was crisply serene.

Germany is famous for its Christkindlmarkt or Christmas Markets. I bought lovely crystal ornaments to send to my children and drank Glühwein, a hot red wine spiced with cinnamon, cloves, citrus, and sugar. It was a warm welcome on that cold shopping trip. Bratwurst on German rolls with München mustard completed the experience.

New Year's Eve 2002 was rung in at a party with business friends in Rijeka, and life proceeded apace.

In April, Rick Brinkman's lady friend, Vonnie, sent me an email, informing me of an IUA conference to be held in August in Dourdan, France. She asked if I would like to be her roommate. My husband was not too keen on the idea of my attending. He now had a less than favorable attitude about the movement. In fact, he pulled a male-dominating power trip on me and said we could not afford it. Now maybe he was telling the truth, but it did not seem that way to me. I wanted to see friends and talk shop, although I was not crazy about meeting the new Trustees. I decided not to argue about it and gave up on the idea. I emailed Vonnie that I would not be attending.

A couple of months later, I awoke from an early morning dream. In the dream, I was raising money by selling some Picasso artwork of my mother's in order to take a trip. I recognized the dream for its similar characteristic as my Disney dream on Vieques. I thought about it all morning. My mother never had any Picasso artwork. Then bing! Mom had left me two beautifully framed original watercolor paintings by the French artist Louis Icart. I had forgotten about them. They were left back in 1997 with my oldest daughter, who wrapped and stored them under her California-king bed. The two pieces were titled "Love Letters" and "Tosca."

I told my husband about the dream, and I was going to have my daughter sell them and use the money to go to the conference in France. (My husband liked those pieces.) I called her, and she agreed to help. She contacted art galleries. Many different potential buyers responded, but they were either enquiring if she had other works by Icart or were only interested in "Tosca." It was not worth selling only one, it would not cover the cost of the conference plus the travel. Time went by, and it did not look promising, no one was interested in "Love Letters." Then about a week before the conference, my daughter was contacted by a dealer whose client wanted both of them. The client was not interested in the frames. She met with the dealer, and after a little haggling, she got the amount I needed. Now I was able to attend the conference in France thanks to a French artist. My husband had nothing to say.

I contacted the Foundation and registered. It was too late to room with Vonnie, but I was able to fill in one of the last available conference slots. Researching the route I would have to take, it was doable on my own.

On August 2, Joe and I drove to his brother's in Rheinfelden and spent the night. The next morning, we drove to Basel, Switzerland, so I could board the train to Paris. I had a first-class ticket; the trip was pleasant. (I like traveling by train.) Arriving in Paris, the train station was cavernous. It took some time to get my bearings. I knew the next step was finding the metro located somewhere within the station. There would be one more metro transfer to Dourdan, the end of the line.

Carrying my bulky, leather garment bag folded in the center (a Christmas present from the time I was at The Jay Leno Show), I found the metro and purchased a ticket. Somewhere between the ticket window and the broad up and down stairways, I got confused and boarded the subway line going in the wrong direction. While I was sitting in the crowded car with my luggage squished in my lap, I noticed the colored metro lines on the map above the passenger seats where the different stops were indicated. Listening to the French announcement of the next station, it seemed I might be going the wrong way. When the next station was called, I was pretty certain. I felt panicky. I asked people around me in slow English if

I was headed to Dourdan. No one knew what I was saying until, one more stop later, a nice young woman across from me, figured out what I meant. Yes, I was going in the opposite direction. The people got a chuckle out of the lost American. I felt very insecure.

Getting off, I traversed more broad stairs going up, then again down, and boarded the subway going in the right direction. Changing onto another line was no fun either. I finally reached Dourdan just as the last shuttle to the conference location picked up a woman from New Zealand and myself.

The Villagium Le Normont, a resort outside the village of Dourdan, was a very suitable choice for the conference. The French and French Canadians had organized it. The first evening at the crowded garden bar, I was able to greet many friends including Marian and her husband, Tonia, Cathy Jones, and Seppo from Finland. I met a woman from Holland who had written a book about the varied and unique stories of how believers had originally been introduced to *The Urantia Book*. From Senegal arrived a spiritual leader along with his two eldest daughters wearing colorful traditional robes. To his people, he presented concepts of the book along with his teachings. There were many interesting personalities attending.

It was not until the next morning that I ran into Vonnie making our way to breakfast. We were happy to see each other. While we walked, she talked about the Harry McMullan lawsuit and how terrible it was that the Foundation had lost. I had not heard. The verdict had been delivered in June of 2001. Boy, was I out of the loop! The Trustees had filed an appeal and promised that they would pull out all the stops; there was no need to be concerned. Everyone believed that it would be reversed as it had been in the past.

The conference provided an interesting time with terrific plenaries and topical classes. We were in France, so the food and wine were superb. One dinner, Marian and her husband and I went into the village of Dourdan to a local restaurant.

On the second day, the conference offered a side trip to the Chateau de Vaux Le Vicomte, a magnificent castle built in the time of Louis XVI. After we got off the bus, my old friend Cathy Jones pulled me aside. Taking me by the arm, we walked a long expanse of lawn. She walked very slowly, actually taking baby steps, while everyone else passed us by. At first, I believed her tiny steps were because she was more elderly. As we talked and slowly advanced, I realized she had things to tell me and wanted the time. She filled me in on so much negative clamoring that had gone on, it made me frustratingly sad. I lamented, "How could this wonderful Revelation introduced to our world in 1955 have continued to evolve in the wrong direction and turn into an ugly power struggle?"

Cathy replied, "I think too many are blinded by their own egos and self-importance. *The Urantia Book* is an epochal revelation, and someday it will be seen as such. These leaders want to be recognized now. And they already are by some of us. You've witnessed the Trustees being looked upon as special people."

Nodding my head, "You're right. The woman who is my roommate was telling me last night what a deeply spiritual person

Gard Jameson is. I did not respond. What could I say? It's like celebrity worship."

"And they enjoy this roll."

I sighed, "In my heart, I had hoped things would normalize and the parties involved would redeem themselves to the good."

"That was my hope too."

"It's a miracle the book has as many sincere believers as it does, considering these self-seeking leaders."

Cathy looked at me and smiled, "They aren't the *real* leaders, are they?"

I smiled in agreement, just as we met up with our fellow conference participants to tour the Chateau that inspired Louis XVI Palace of Versailles.

On the last day of the conference, there was a meeting for the IUA Council of National Presidents and Vice Presidents. Friends insisted that I come along. Four Trustees presided: Mo Siegel, Gard Jameson, Georges Michelson-Dupont, and Rich Keeler. The meeting was casual, but it was nonetheless troubling when Rich Keeler broke down weeping at the head table, telling us his story of how the Internal Revenue Service was prosecuting him for a large amount of money. It was embarrassing. Georges had a disgusted look on his face; Mo Siegel and Gard Jameson ignored him. I thought, "What does your money woes have to do with this meeting? Man up!"

Here was not the place to be crying over how, according to Rich, besides his daughter, nothing was nearer or dearer to his heart than the Urantia Revelation. The way he was carrying on, it seemed that his money was far nearer and dearer.

So once again, I sat at a meeting more interested in the behavior of the participants than the content of what was being discussed. The Trustee, Dr. Kwan Choi, was not present. There had been so many people at the conference, this was the first time I noticed.

After the meeting as we were dispersing, I stopped a friend and asked, "How come Kwan isn't here?"

"You don't know? He's being removed."

"He doesn't want to be a Trustee anymore?" I asked.

"They don't want him...something to do with the legality of how the Foundation has managed its funds. He's an economics professor, remember?"

I shook my head, "Still a soap opera."

"You didn't hear it from me." And she walked away.

When the conference was over, I was so glad to be going back to live in another country. In my mind, this made it not my problem. How wrong I was!

Joe met the train in Basel, and we drove to Trieste, Italy staying overnight to do some shopping. The Italian boutiques were having summer-end sales. Even on sale, things were more expensive since the lira had changed to the euro, but I *really* needed a pair of Italian shoes. ☺

By September, business in Rijeka went through a change, a change my husband believed was best for the dealerships as well as the parent company. Since it was not long ago that Croatia had been communist, many of the wealthier and more powerful men had been

297

party members. After working for almost a year with a young salesman with a bad attitude that was affecting personnel in one dealership, Joe fired him. The fellow was the son of a VIP.

A few weeks later, my husband fired the manager of that dealership. The manager and his wife had gone out of their way to welcome us when we first arrived. I did not believe that letting him go would be good. But Joe was watching out for the company and knew that the man believed he had a job for life, as he would have in the past. Joe did not like the way he ordered the employees around with threats. Anyway, he fired the wrong guy. Not sure which one, maybe both.

One night coming home from work, my husband entered the foyer of the apartment building, and as he pushed the elevator button, two very tall men came up behind him and threw him into the wall of metal mailboxes. One man held him while the other put the cold steel of the barrel of a gun to his head. The man holding the gun said, "We know where you live. We know your wife. You have three days to leave the country."

The elevator door opened. The man holding Joe shoved him inside and with a long arm, reached in and pushed button number 9, our floor. He said, "We will be watching."

The doors closed, and Joe found himself alone in the elevator ascending to our apartment. When he came in, he wasn't wearing his usual smile and said, "I have to call Paul."

Paul was his supervisor in Germany. He went into the bedroom and made the call. They talked but a short time. Joe wanted to know if it was a certainty that the threat could be carried out. Paul told him it was dead certain. When he came back into the living room, he said, "We are leaving Croatia in three days."

At first, I thought we were going on a trip, but he made it clear I was to pack everything we owned. He told me it was a business decision. I did not want to leave.

The next evening Joe and I went to dinner with the son of the owner of our apartment and his girlfriend. The friendly couple had come to visit each month for the rent, and they always stayed a while to converse and practice their English. Joe took the young man away from the table to talk to him. When they returned, I could see the young man was perturbed. Joe later told me he expressed embarrassment for the behavior of his countrymen.

When Joe was at the dealership the next day, turning over responsibility to the assistant manager, he had the company logo removed from his car. When the car was parked outside the showroom without the logo, he got a call on his cell phone. "We see you are smart." Click.

Day three, once the car was packed and we were heading out, I wanted to stop and say goodbye to my tutor. Joe was reluctant, but I insisted. We drove the short distance, in the opposite direction out of town, to her apartment. I told her we were leaving Croatia, and I was sorry I could not keep up my studies. We said goodbye in Croatian and English.

Joe drove in silence the forty minutes to the border. At the border crossing, we were stopped. The officer walked around our car and noted our license plate. That had never happened before. He came to Joe's window, looked at him blandly, and motioned us on.

We crossed into Slovenia and slowed at their border kiosk. The officer just waved us through. Within fifty yards, we pulled into the parking lot of a duty-free shop and entered the establishment. I bought a sweater, and Joe bought a bottle of expensive Polish vodka.

Journeying on, it was getting close to sunset, and my husband said, "I'm tired. We should look for a place to stay."

Randomly, he turned left down a road we hoped would lead to the coast. (Slovenia, unlike Croatia, has very little coastline.) After a few miles, we arrived at a small bay and took a hotel room with a balcony overlooking fishing boats bobbing in the sea. There was no room service, so Joe left to find an ice machine. He returned and filled two glasses with ice cubes, pouring the warm vodka over. I was not sure what was happening. It all seemed so out of the norm.

While we sat on the balcony and sipped our drinks, my husband told me the truth. I had not seen it coming. He had not wanted to worry me.

In Rheinfelden, Joe's brother and sister-in-law were waiting for us. They knew what had happened. They welcomed us into their home. The firm Joe worked for did not have another position for him. They gave him a three-month severance and allowed him to keep the company car for that time. He immediately began looking for employment. He prepared his resume, sending it off and knocking on doors. But his brother was not encouraging. He told him you are never going to find work. You are forty-nine. You are too old. I could not quite believe that. In the U.S., it would not have been an issue with the impressive resume Joe had in sales and management in the auto industry.

Waiting, he kept busy between interviews by being my tour guide. We drove through the impressive Black Forest and stopped at a bakery in a small town. We each had a slice of Black Forest cake. Never had I eaten the authentic treat before or since. It was practically floating in cherry schnapps. It was the first time I got a buzz from a piece of cake.

On another day, we traveled to Strasbourg in Alsace, a beautiful city melded between German and French culture. Depending upon the century, the area changed hands between the two countries. After WWI, it was given to France in the Treaty of Versailles. During WWII Germany re-invaded, but at their loss of the war, it went back to France.

We visited castles and interesting Roman excavations. The most thought provoking was in Switzerland near Basel—the remains of a Roman colony founded in 44 B.C. The Augusta Raurica ruins offered an excavated open amphitheater, a temple, and public bath. The museum was a walk-through, lifelike replica of a Roman home, showcasing rooms and artifacts of personal items used in daily life. It made me think that Jesus would have visited such a home as a guest during his time spent in Rome as the language translator to the Indian businessman and tutor to his teenage son.

After three months in Rheinfelden, my German language skills were much improved, while Joe's patience was greatly stretched. Maybe his brother was right. Employment prospects were nowhere in sight. I thought to myself: "If Joe's brother and sister-in-law don't mind us being here, I don't think my sister and her husband with their empty-nest home would mind either."

I called Sis, and she was happy to have us. So once again, we packed up. We took a remarkable train ride along the Rhine River with another history lesson amid its ruined castles and ancient toll bridges.

Reaching the airport at Dusseldorf, our bags were searched by a friendly but thorough female airport official before being checked in. We boarded Lufthansa, settled into our seats, buckled up, and soon were racing down the runway. That small sensation of weightlessness when a plane lifts off always reminds me I am heading into the future. Looking out the window, I watched as the plane banked over Dusseldorf, the city lights twinkling farewell, and wondered what Providence had in store for us this time.

Chapter 37

At San Diego International Airport, my sister met two jet-lagged, blurry-eyed mortals at the exit of customs. We were soon on our way to her suburban home in her soccer-mom van. The car seemed huge, but she bragged she got good gas mileage. Joe said humorously, "You could never find a parking space in Europe for this thing."

My sister is the consummate hostess, always has been, and my brother-in-law is an easygoing guy. Joe and I had the entire second floor and were welcome to stay as long as we wished.

My husband's green card had expired, so we had to deal with that issue, using an attorney in Los Angeles we had hired before. That gave us the opportunity to drive to L.A. and stay with my eldest daughter and family. Once the paperwork was completed, INS had interviewed us and a green card approved, we were back in San Diego where Joe went looking for a job. He was hired within a week at a Mercedes dealership. I began volunteering for a charitable organization that operated a children's hospital just across the Mexican border.

Being the social butterfly that my sister is, we went to many parties with her and her husband during the Holiday Season. Ringing in the New Year 2003 in San Diego added yet another location where I had celebrated yet another new year. Joe and I were getting tired of change. We both agreed we'd had enough adventure in our lives and decided to make San Diego our home.

After a couple of months' search, we found a reasonably priced, small, two-bedroom condominium in La Jolla, a beautiful beach community just north of San Diego. We were able to take possession within six weeks. Having no furniture, IKEA became our home decorator.

The condo was a block from the beach, and I was back to my favorite activity, sitting upon a sandy shore, watching the sunset, and thanking my Mystery Monitor for *such a life on such a planet.*

In April, Urantia friends invited me to a study group at the home of Victoria, the woman with whom I had attended my first IUA Conference back in 1994. Fifteen women were present when I arrived, and I discovered the purpose was more than just a study group.

There was an important announcement: On March 11, the Appellate Court of Oklahoma upheld the previous verdict in Harry McMullan's copyright lawsuit. McMullan had won. The Trustees had lost. *The Urantia Book* copyright was ruled invalid. The book was back in the public domain, and this time for good.

The women sitting in Victoria's living room, at first, could not quite grasp the immensity of what we were hearing. It took some moments for the meaning to sink in. Then someone in the group demanded to know how the Foundation attorneys had managed to lose! And the answer was incredible! The Trustees did not send attorneys to argue the case.

They sent a legal brief—pieces of paper—to defend the copyright of celestial personalities authoring the Urantia Revelation to our world so in need. How strange and unimportant the judge must have thought was the case before him, certainly not important enough for the Plaintiff to bother with the expense of attorneys to argue their case in the courtroom.

Mouths dropped open. How could that be true? It had been difficult enough for the last thirty years of lawsuits to prevail. Unbelievable! To think, the Foundation had sent only a document to argue the last imaginable legal angle. The definitive lawsuit! This would have put an end to all future copyright infringement litigation by Harry McMullan or anyone else.

Someone else spoke up and said, "Why? Why only a brief?" The explanation: The Foundation did not have enough money to afford attorneys.

Silence once more befell the group. The Urantia Foundation out of money? Even if that was true, we all knew quite well that Mo Siegel, Gard Jameson, and Georges Michelson-Dupont were independently wealthy men. Mo was a millionaire many times over. Rich Keeler was still battling the IRS, yet seemed to be living in his normal, comfortable style.

As I sat there with my fellows, I thought to myself, "I would have sold my home, my car, given everything I have to save the copyright. What are these things but material possessions? Yet these wealthy men could not part with some of their own money. Pocket change to them. Astounding!"

So here we have four active Trustees who had taken an oath and failed in their duty. They lost the copyright of *The Urantia Book*. Time for some resignations? Would not honorable men do so?

Why does the Foundation still have Trustees? The oath they took in upholding the text of the book is no longer relevant. But as previously revealed, that oath was never taken seriously since Mo Siegel and Gard Jameson had already violated it in creating the book published by their Uversa Press and distributed by the Fellowship.

The Trustees promised they would take the decision to the U.S. Supreme Court. Everyone knew that was just an empty gesture. The Supreme Court rarely hears copyright cases and certainly not on such a highly unusual case as this would appear. Subsequently, the Supreme Court declined to hear it.

And the profane behavior continued… The official Urantia e-book published in 2010 by the Trustees is not what it purports to be. The original Urantia Book's publishing and copyright data (Copyright 1955, etc.) is followed by the book published by Uversa Press (1996), including the same added incorrect teaching and the Bible-like numbers in front of each and every paragraph of the 2,097 pages. It no longer represents what was originally approved by the Celestial Revelators and copyrighted by the original Trustees. Is that honorable, or even legal?

Now all the pieces have fallen into place. And there is but one conclusion. But of course!

The Prince of Darkness is inside the movement. This is the first place he would put his nefarious designs—the destruction of the

Fifth Epochal Revelation. Just as he participated in the downfall of the Material Son and Daughter, Adam and Eve.

And it all began a long time ago. The following facts to ponder:

A. Back in 1997, the Trustees did not stop the Uversa Press book's use of the title *The Urantia Book*. The Urantia Foundation owns the trademark—Urantia. That trademark infringement—alone—would have stopped the counterfeit book in its tracks.

B. After ultimately emerging victorious in the legal battles and holding onto the copyright, the Trustees declined to collect the close to $1,000,000 in legal costs from the Fellowship. Then, the Foundation sat back and watched as the Fellowship continued to sell its illegal book. (A good portion of the legal fees was from Rich Keeler, who had donated it to the Urantia Foundation as a charitable contribution and had subsequently been flagged by the IRS.)

C. The Uversa Publishers use of its dust jacket to portray its falsehoods of winged angels and, especially, the picture of the wimpy Jesus. *The Urantia Book* definitely states: *The paintings of the Christ have exerted a deleterious effect on youth...* But they didn't care.

D. The appointment to the Foundation as Trustees the very men, Mo Siegel and Gard Jameson, who had been fighting the Foundation and had caused its near bankruptcy with all the lawsuits from the book that they themselves were responsible for printing.

E. The removal of the *Banner of Michael* from the cover of the book. That banner must have really burned Daligastia. Like a crucifix thrust before Dracula.

F. When once again a lawsuit was filed—the one that would definitively end the copyright fight—all the Trustees, men of wealth, would not spring for the $$ to hire an attorney to plead our case and instead sent only a brief.

G. And…how and why did false language get into the Uversa Press book in Paper 119, "The Bestowals of Christ Michael?" Text: *These men of God visited the newborn child in the manger.*

NO! THEY DID NOT! *The child in the manger* is a nice earthly fable, but it isn't the truth. The original Urantia Book, page 1317, reads: *These men of God visited the newborn child.* Period. And that is because the Chaldean priests visited Jesus when he was three weeks old at the home of Joseph's cousin. So…who put that text in their book? And for what purpose?

H. Most recently, the latest strangest act, to say the least, is the creation and acceptance of a Mother Cult. Yes, a Mother Cult! Are they really going back to this ancient practice—Persephone would be fitting!

Please! There is no way anyone can read, let alone claim to study, the Urantia Papers and come up with a Mother Cult. It is just the product of hysterical women and cowardly men who do not possess the Spirit of Truth—the spirit of the Father and the Son. If they were guided by the Spirit of Truth, they would not waste their time on this nothingness. The appellation of the single word "Mother" is nowhere to be found in *The Urantia Book.* The very last sentence on the last page of the book: *When all is said and done, the Father idea is still the highest human concept of God.*

I. If I haven't yet convinced you, and you need more proof of the presence of Caligastia and Daligastia, how about the recent usage of **"the family of the children of Michael and mother."** Really?!

The only family in the Urantia Book is *The Family of God*. But **"the family of the children of Michael and mother"** would exactly fit the teachings of Lucifer's manifesto. All the rebellious personalities are atheists. The do not believe in the existence of the Father—God. All of them know Michael, their Creator Son; and they assert that the Universal Father is a myth, and that the Michaels are its propogandists. The Creator Sons supposedly teach us these lies in order to keep control of the grand universe. So of course, **"the family of the children of Michael and mother"** is right up their nefarious alley!

Welcome to the Lucifer Rebellion and the Caligastia Betrayal!

ADDEMDUM

January 10, 1997 UNITED STATES COURT OF APPEALS FOR THE NINTH CIRCUIT No. 95-17093: URANTIA FOUNDATION, a non-profit foundation, Plaintiff-Appellant KRISTEN MAAHERRA, Defendant-Appellee Argued and Submitted Jan. 14, 1997

June 10, 1997 UNITED STATES COURT OF APPEALS FOR THE NINTH CIRCUIT No. 95-17093: URANTIA FOUNDATION, a non-profit foundation, Plaintiff-Appellant KRISTEN MAAHERRA, Defendant-Appellee / D.C. No. CY-91-00325-SMM OPINION

January 29, 1999 UNITED STATES DISTRICT COURT FOR THE DISTRICT OF ARIZONA CIV 91-0325 PHX WKU: URANTIA FOUNDATION, a non-profit foundation, Plaintiff vs KRISTEN MAAHERRA, Defendant. MEMORANDUM AND ORDER ON PLAINTIFF URANTIA FOUNDATION'S MOTION FOR DECLARATORY JUDGEMENT

May 8, 2000 IN THE UNITED STATES DISTRICT COURT FOR THE DISTRICT OF ARIZONA CIV 99-2062-PHX-RGS: URANTIA FOUNDATION, Plaintiff vs. MICHAEL FOUNDATION, Defendants Harry McMullan

May 16, 2000 IN THE UNITED STATES DISTRICT COURT FOR THE WESTERN DISTRICT OF OKLAHOMA Case No. 00-885-W: MICHAEL FOUNDATION, INC, a Foreign Corporation, Plaintiff v. URANTIA FOUNDATION, an Illinois Charitable Trust, COMPLAINT FOR DECLARATORY JUDGEMENT.

March 04, 2001 IN THE UNITED STATES DISTRICT COURT FOR THE WESTERN DISTRICT OF OKLAHOMA: MICHAEL FOUNDATION, INC., a Foreign Corporation, Plaintiff and Defendant-in-Counterclaim v. Case No. CIV-00-885-W, URANTIA FOUNDATION, an Illinois Charitable Trust, Defendant and Counterclaimant, RESPONSE TO MOTION IN LIMINE.

March 10, 2001 IN THE UNITED STATES DISTRICT COURT FOR THE WESTERN DISTRICT OF OKLAHOMA, AFFIDAVIT OF HARRY MCMULLAN III, MICHAEL FOUNDATION, INC., a Not For Profit corporation, Plaintiff and Defendant-in-Counterclaim v. Case No. CIV-00-885-W, URANTIA FOUNDATION, an Illinois Charitable Trust, Defendant and Counterclaimant.

March 14, 2001 MARCH 04, 2001 IN THE UNITED STATES DISTRICT COURT FOR THE WESTERN DISTRICT OF OKLAHOMA: MICHAEL FOUNDATION, INC., a Foreign Corporation, Plaintiff and Defendant-in-Counterclaim v. Case No. CIV-00-885-W, URANTIA FOUNDATION, Counterclaimant and Third Party Plaintiff vs. HARRY MCMULLAN vs. HARRY MCMULLLAN III, a citizen of Oklahoma Third Party Defendant and MICHAEL FOUNDATION INC.

September 7, 2001 IN THE CIRCUIT COURT OF COOK COUNTY, ILLINOIS, COUNTY DEPARTMENT, CHANCERY DIVISION: E. KWAN CHOI, individually and on behalf of URANTIA FOUNDATION, URANTIA CORPORATION, URANTIA BROTHERHOOD ASSOCIATION, and ANDITE CORPORATION, Plaintiff v. K RICHARD KEELER, GEORGES MICHELSON-DUPONT, MO SIEGEL, GARD JAMESON, AND JAMES RYAN, not individually, Defendants.

311

April 22, 2002 IN THE CIRCUIT COURT OF COOK COUNTY, ILLINOIS COUNTY DEPARTMENT, CHANCERY DIVISION No. 02 CH 4053: E KWAN CHOI *individually, and on behalf of* Urantia Foundation, et al., Plaintiff v. K. RICHARD KEELER, et al., defendants. VERIFIED MOTION FOR A TEMPORARY RESTRAINING ORDER.

March 11, 2003 UNITED STATES COURT OF APPEALS 10TH DISTRICT, Case No. 02CH 0453: MICHAEL FOUNDATION, a Foreign Corporation, Plaintiff-Appellee, v. Urantia Foundation, an Illinois Charitable Trust, Defendant – Third Party Plaintiff – Appellant v HARRY MCMULLAN, III. Third-Party-Defendant-Appellee. Case No. CIV-885-W ORDER AND JUDGEMENT.

Also by Carole Jett

A BOOK OF ANSWERS